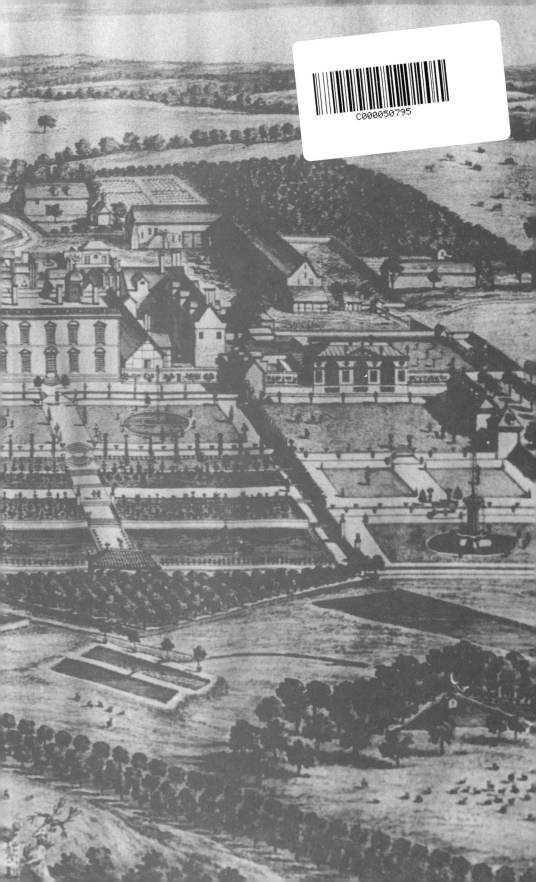

THE KIRKLAND PAPERS
1753–1869

THE KIRKLAND PAPERS

1753-1869

The Ferrers Murder and the Lives
and Times of a Medical Family in
Ashby-de-la Zouch

ARTHUR CRANE

CRANE PRESS

THE KIRKLAND PAPERS

First published 1990 by the Crane Press
30 South Street, Ashby-de-la Zouch, Leicestershire, LE6 5BT

ISBN 0-9517074-0-X

A catalogue record for this book is available from the British Library

Photoset in Garamond by
Chippendale Type Ltd.,
Otley, West Yorkshire.

Printed and bound in Great Britain by
Mackays of Chatham, plc, Chatham, Kent

For Joan

Contents

Illustrations

Acknowledgements

When Thomas Kirkland MD dedicated his 'Enquiry into the present state of Medical Surgery' to the Earl of Huntingdon in 1783, he compared himself with a navigator who after failing in the quest of knowledge returns to communicate his discoveries. These he presented to his patron out of gratitude to him. I have never sought any quest of knowledge but if I have succeeded in any measure in revealing the lives and times of the Kirklands – father, son, and grandson – this has only been achieved as a result of the help, encouragement and professional assistance of many people, all of whom I now regard as my friends. My thanks are firstly due to the Right Honourable Earl Ferrers for the wealth of detail he has placed at my disposal and for permitting me to reproduce the hitherto little-known portraits of the 4th Earl Ferrers and his Countess. I am also most indebted to him for writing the Foreword to this book. I am also deeply grateful to Miss Kate Thompson, the Leicestershire County Archivist, and Mrs Heather Broughton, the keeper of the Leicestershire County Records and their staff for their unfailing help and courtesy. Next Mr John Bowker for having re-produced with consummate skill many of the illustrations including the colour engraving of Dr Kirkland. He is a fine professional photographer with a deep sense of history.

I have necessarily imposed myself greatly on a number of my medical and legal friends and am obliged to them for ensuring accuracy in professional details – among these I must mention my sister Dr Catharine Smith, Mr R. T. Austin of the Leicester Royal Infirmary, Dr E. C. Cawte, Dr Richard A. Davis, Dr M. C. S. Kennedy, Dr Ruth Vincent-Kemp, Dr C. A. H. Watts and Sister

Angela Wilson. US Federal Judge Bruce Evans, Mrs Elizabeth Arnold, and my son John Crane have perused my legal work. On the historical aspects Mr Kenneth Hillier, that distinguished local historian and writer, has given generously of his time by reading the proofs, and I have received valuable assistance from other local historians notably Mr David Jackson, Mr J. Gillies Shields, Mr John G. G. Shields, Mr Robert O. Jones, and from Mr Hugh Dixon. Others have helped me greatly by looking up records in inaccessible places and of these I would like to thank Mrs Joanna Wallace, for visiting the National Maritime Museum and Madame Henriette Gillet, the Ministère de la Défence (Marine), in Paris.

My friends Mr L. H. Matthews, Mrs Heather Tellis, Mrs Doreen Bullen, and Mr James Tyldesley, have also checked the proofs for grammar and punctuation and supplied me with useful details and information.

Typing and copying my often illegible proofs has been carried out by Mrs Gill Gibbons and Mrs Clarissa Laker with accuracy and forbearance, whilst the secretarial labours have been efficiently discharged by Miss Amy Rice and Mrs Barbara Wallis. I must also acknowledge the practical help provided by my former partners at Messrs Crane & Walton, Solicitors Ashby-de-la Zouch, Coalville, and Leicester, by the use of the word processor and other office equipment.

I must also acknowledge with thanks the permission given to me to publish in whole or in part, documents made available to me by Leicestershire County Record Office, Derbyshire County Record Office, Staffordshire County Record Office, the William Salt Library at Stafford, the Public Record Office, the House of Lords Record Office, the Ashby-de-la Zouch Museum, the Trustees of the Wedgwood Museum at Barlaston, the National Maritime Museum at Greenwich, the Ministry of Defence in Paris, the Cambridge University Library, the Leicestershire County Library, the Wellcome Institute, the Repton School Library, the Greater London Record Office, and the Librarian at the Leicestershire and Rutland Masonic Library. Among publishers and others who have kindly given me consent I would include Hodder & Stoughton Ltd., David & Charles Publishers plc, the Clarendon Press, S. Straker & Sons Ltd., the British Broadcasting Corporation, Phillimore & Co. Ltd., William Collins, Sons & Co. Ltd., The Lodge of Research No 2029, Dr Marylyn Palmer, *The Dictionary of National Biography*, Oxford University Press, Edinburgh University Press, Theobald Books Ltd., Elizabeth Lane, George Weidenfeld & Nicolson Ltd.,

Mr Levi Fox, the *Daily Telegraph*, the Honourable Society of the Middle Temple, the University of St Andrews, the *British Medical Journal*, Mr P Pollak, archivist, The Kings School, Canterbury and Parker & Sons, Burton upon Trent.

Finally, I would like to thank Mr Anthony Mott, Mr Andrew McClelland and my son David Crane, all professional publishers, for their vision and practical encouragement, without which the book would never have been published, and my wife Joan and all the family for their constructive criticism and down-to-earth comments.

As I first became interested in Dr Kirkland forty years ago, my wife has perforce had to live, not only with me, but also with the good Doctor as well. A perpetual lodger puts a strain on the happiest household and in the Doctor's words should have 'closed the scene in a very short time'. Such was not the case however. On the contrary, whenever I came to the conclusion that the Kirkland Papers were too intractable, she was there to exhort and cajole me to press on. If I have had to omit, by reason of space, my thanks to other helpers, I trust that they will forgive me.

Ashby-de-la Zouch   Arthur Crane
19th November 1990

Foreword
By The Right Honourable Earl Ferrers PC DL

This book is a remarkable chronicle of the family of Kirkland, who lived in Ashby-de-la Zouch. The compilation of the history of this family has not only been carried out with great assiduity but it has been presented in a most readable and captivating fashion.

The Kirkland family has always contributed to the society in which it lived, notably in the field of medicine and in soldiering. In the days when surgery was something of a novelty, and a distinct hazard, Thomas Kirkland was a pioneer and a man of profound knowledge. Despite that, like all great people, he remained humble.

The account of the murder by the 4th Earl Ferrers of his Steward, Johnson, is given in astonishing detail as seen through the eyes of Dr Kirkland. He was called to provide medical attention to the injured Johnson and, at the same time, he had to placate the mercurial temperament of Lord Ferrers.

The somewhat gruesome story, told with such vivid clarity in this book, has gained the doubtful reputation of being a 'classic'. Part of this is due to the fact, as the book makes clear, that the trial and execution of Lord Ferrers in 1760 may have been a factor in ensuring that there was no equivalent of the French Revolution in England – on the basis that, if a Peer can be hanged like any other common felon, there cannot be much wrong with the law.

November 1990

Ferrers
Ditchingham Hall

Preface

Miss Alethea Bangham lived the whole of her long life in the attractive and historic market town of Ashby-de-la Zouch in Leicestershire. She was a doctor's daughter, and she was the last direct descendant of her grandfather Dr Thomas Smith Kirkland. She was thought to be slightly eccentric because of her interest in spiritualism which caused my irreverent family to maintain, after her death, that the creaking corner cupboard in my parents' drawing room was none other than Alethea seeking to join in the conversation. 'That is Alley again' they would say. Shortly before the Second World War, presumably because I was interested in local history, she invited me to see a portrait of her great great grandfather Dr Thomas Kirkland MD. My knowledge of Dr Kirkland was limited to what I had read of him in *The Story of Ashby-de-la Zouch* by the Reverend W Scott. Miss Bangham died in May 1950 at the age of ninety-four and her effects were disposed of by Messrs John German & Son of Ashby-de-la Zouch, who discovered an eighteenth century notebook which seemed to them to be unusual. The late Mr C. G. Waite, of that firm, allowed me to study it. The book contained a list of deaths in alphabetical order including in most cases the date of death and occasionally other details; e.g. 'Eaton, Mr Thos murder'd in London 16 May 1793.' These entries commenced in 1788 and continued until 1930. There follows details of marriages commencing in 1792 and lastly entries commencing in 1789 which constitute a selective diary of events, mostly local, which were of interest to the diarist. The different handwritings can be identified as those of members of the family and the work as a whole presents a valuable picture of eighteenth and nineteenth century life in Ashby-de-la-Zouch.

The selective nature of the notes renders almost unnecessary any editing. Each individual record is of engaging historical detail and uniformly accurate. Dr Thomas Kirkland himself wrote nothing in the book although his death is recorded. Nevertheless, the Doctor is always present in the notes even over a hundred years after his death. His reputation as a physician and surgeon, as a medical writer, and above all as the brave and upright Christian gentleman who, as a man of honour, refused to be tempted by the bribes or deflected by the threats of the most powerful local member of the aristocracy, remained a source of family pride which grew deeper as the years passed by. For nearly forty years I have researched the individual entries and have grown to know, almost as old friends, the principal characters concerned. There was Thomas John, a son of Dr Kirkland, a careful and orderly surgeon who succeeded to the practice. There was Nicholas Smith, Thomas John's younger son, the *Vanity Fair* type of officer in Wellington's Army, who was generally in financial difficulty. There was Thomas John's son-in-law, a Lieutenant in the French Navy, prisoner of war at Ashby, who arrested his Commanding Officer for cowardice. Lastly there was Thomas Smith, who followed his father and grandfather in their service to the community. The lesser characters who pass across the stage are also of absorbing interest.

My labours were ultimately rewarded in 1987 when I was informed by the Public Record Office that among the Treasury Solicitor's papers of the trial of Earl Ferrers in 1760, was a contemporary narrative written by Dr Kirkland which was so damaged by age as to be illegible. By skilled endeavours it was restored and I was able to read it in 1988. This document discloses many facts concerning the murder of John Johnson hitherto unknown, and I am now persuaded that the people of Ashby-de-la Zouch and district, and possibly a wider public, should be permitted to share with me a true story that needs to be told. All these documents, together with Thomas Kirkland's medical writings, comprehend the Kirkland Papers. I was still faced with how to edit the notes without disrupting them by excessive commentary. I trust that this objective has been achieved by prefacing the notes with biographical details of the principal characters and thus reducing the commentary to a minimum. The lists of deaths and marriages should prove interesting to the ever-increasing number of family genealogists.

Thomas Kirkland 1722–1798

Surgeon and Witness for the Crown

On the main road between Ashby-de-la Zouch and Castle Donington in the north-west corner of Leicestershire lies the village of Breedon-on-the-Hill, nestling at the foot of a huge and rugged but picturesque limestone rock about 250 feet high and half a mile long. The ancient Saxon and Norman Church of SS Mary and Hardulph stands on the top of the rock and can be seen from a great distance. In the churchyard, just to the south of the eastern footpath leading to the Church, is a slate gravestone inscribed as follows:

> *Released from the evils of this frail world*
> *in pious expectation of the reward of his virtues*
> *John Johnson*
> *departed this life Jan XIX MDCCLX aged L*
> *He was many years*
> *the esteem'd and faithful servant*
> *of*
> *the Honble Laurence Shirley Esquire*
> *with unshaken integrity*
> *he continued in the office of Steward*
> *to*
> *his son the late Right Honble Laurence Earl Ferrers*
> *till near the fatal period of his life*

1

uncorrupted by any view of self interest
no hopes no fears
could divert him from the steady pursuit of that path
his duty to God and man pointed out
he was a worthy example of
the tender father the affectionate husband
the firm and valuable friend
the sincere and humble Christian
his many excellent qualities
rendered him highly respected
and his untimely death
much lamented

At the western end of the same churchyard is another stone erected to the memory of, 'Margaret daughter of Richard Clifford by Margaret his wife of Staunton Harrold who departed this life the 3rd August 1785 in the 64th year of her age'. These inscriptions are typical of eighteenth century England and similar examples can be found in any churchyard in the land. One finds the effusive eulogy in the one and the simple English in the other. In fact these gravestones unintentionally commemorate an event which shocked Leicestershire, intrigued Georgian England and brought fame and fortune to a prudent local surgeon. That surgeon was Thomas Kirkland.

Thomas Kirkland was born at Ashbourne, Derbyshire, and baptized at the parish Church there on 14 October 1722. He was the eldest child of Thomas Kirkland and Mary Allsop, his second wife. Thomas Senior was a solicitor in the town, as was his younger son John. One of his daughters, Anne, married Thomas Dalby, a solicitor of Loughborough. Kirkland attended grammar schools at Ashbourne and later at Tamworth. His father intended him to enter one of the learned professions, and early in life he developed an abiding interest in medicine and surgery. On leaving school he was apprenticed to Mr Holbrooke, a surgeon in Loughborough, where he made very good progress. Many years later he recollected his work at Loughborough, when he had attended a contused wound in the leg of a man who had been a hard drinker. The wound was not larger than a sixpence upon his skin attended with inflammation; and the man, 'lying in a poor little cottage upon a squab with his leg against a wretched door. Spreading Gangrene soon appeared and

2

finished his life.'[1] On leaving Loughborough he went to London, attending the lectures of Dr Thomas Lawrence[2] and other eminent medical men and getting acquainted with the London Hospitals.

Kirkland set up practice in Ashby-de-la Zouch as a surgeon prior to 1747. His father was buried at Ashby on 27 March 1751. He had married Dorothy Palmer, daughter of a Barrister-at-Law at Packington Church on 3 August 1747, and by her he had twelve children between 1748 and 1768, six of whom died young or in infancy. Dorothy's mother was Elizabeth Bate, so Kirkland was connected to a family much respected in Ashby. Her grandfather Thomas Bate (1675–1727) founded the Bate Library in St Helen's Church. John Throsby (1740–1803), the Leicester antiquarian, visited Ashby in 1790 and recorded that it was, 'a market town in this County, but of less note as a market town than Loughborough, Hinckley, Melton or Harborough. It stands . . . on sandy soil and is tolerably well built.' On the business of the town he commented, 'the manufactury here is chiefly in inferior hats . . . This place has long been famous for conviviality. Dr Kirkland has been many years at the head of the renouned [sic] musical meetings: and the late facetious Mr Springthorpe was foremost at the Bacchanalian Rounds.'[3]

Influential Patients

Thomas Kirkland was a man of his time and in eighteenth century England success in one's profession depended much on who one knew. There were perhaps no more than four hundred great landlords forming the aristocracy. The source of wealth was land and between them these families owned one fifth of the cultivable land.[4] The Earl of Huntingdon and Earl Ferrers were two of these privileged noblemen and both were patients of Kirkland. Kirkland's patron was Francis, 10th Earl of Huntingdon (1729–1789) who resided at Donington Hall. He was the eldest son of Theophilus, 9th Earl of Huntingdon and Selina Shirley, the second daughter and one of the co-heirs of Washington, 2nd Earl Ferrers. Huntingdon's father died 'of a fit of apoplexy' when Huntingdon was only seventeen. His mother was a very devout lady and an early supporter of John and Charles Wesley and of George Whitfield, the founders of Methodism. She devoted her long life to righteous works, founding Lady Huntingdon's Connexion with chapels throughout the land, and fearlessly spread the gospel to the aristocracy. The Establishment and the Nobility generally

3

regarded her as an 'enthusiast' and her enthusiasm as rather bad form. However to such an extent did she impress King George III that he declared that he wished he had a Lady Huntingdon in every diocese of his kingdom. She courageously nursed her ailing sister who had to suffer the amputation of both of her breasts with no anaesthetic other than fervent prayer.[5]

She bore her husband seven children between 1729 and 1737. Huntingdon became a deist under the influence of Philip Dormer KG, 4th Earl of Chesterfield (1694–1773), 'the celebrated Lord Chesterfield', Ambassador, Cabinet Minister, and Lord Lieutenant of Ireland: and Frederick, 3rd Viscount Bolingbroke who died in 1787. Deism is the belief that God is not known otherwise than by the works of nature. As such Huntingdon acknowledged only natural religion and rejected the revelation of God by Christ as propounded in the Bible. His dislike of religion was 'an affliction' to his mother.[6] Lady Huntingdon's younger sons George and Ferdinando both died of smallpox while at Westminster School, aged fourteen and seventeen respectively, and at George's funeral at Westminster Abbey she received some comfort from John and Charles Wesley.[7] Her daughter Selina died an infant and of the remainder Henry died in 1758, aged nineteen, and she outlived all the others except her daughter Elizabeth, later Countess of Moira. Although Huntingdon was a disappointment to his mother he left her his best enamelled gold snuff box in his Will 'as a token of his gratitude and affection.'[8]

In August 1747 he departed on a grand tour of Europe after having attended Westminster School and Oxford University but without taking a degree. In Paris he met and had an affair with Louise Madeleine Lany (1733–1777), the French ballerina of whom Noverre wrote 'Mlle Lany has effaced all those who shone by the beauty, the precision and strength of their technique. She is the first dancer of the universe . . . '[9] Indeed she was thought to have been the first *danseuse* to achieve the *entrechat six et huit*.[10] Lany's brother Jean (1718–1786) was the ballet master at the Paris Opera. He was barely five feet in height, having very thick legs, and excelled in comic roles. Lany was a pupil of her brother Jean, and made her first appearance at the Paris Opera after dancing in Berlin. Her début on 25 June 1746, in *Les Fêtes d'Hébé*, by Rameau, was a triumph. According to Noverre, 'She had a superb figure, a beautiful *ballon*, and executed her dancing to perfection. She displayed strength and elevation and brilliance in all her leaps.[11] But this dancer, having undergone the harshest training, and being continually ill-treated by her brother, had developed a nervousness which was undoubtedly the result of her apprenticeship. This sense of fear never left her, and deprived her features of the power of expression, which she might have been able to add to the charms of the most correct execution.'[12] The Earl of Chesterfield, who regarded Huntingdon as his adopted son, was an enthusiastic admirer of Lany, and when she was already six weeks pregnant, as a result of her association with Huntingdon, was writing to him from London on 11 July 1751, 'Neither the sly insinuations of envy nor the open attacks of malice shall ever make me entertain an opinion injurious to the many virtues and particularly the chastity of Mlle Lany. Her profession of dancer at the Opera and her rank as first dancer are to me more than sufficient pledge of her innocence and purity.' The child was born in Paris on 11 March 1752, but Huntingdon moved on to Madrid six months later, and seems initially to have been callously indifferent to his mistress' condition, despite humanitarian appeals from his friend Viscount Stormont, who wrote to him on 20 November 1752 from Paris, 'I have been to pay court to a fair lady who longs much to hear from you. The young Ascanius I have not yet seen'. And again on 18 December 1752, 'The Lanilla is extremely uneasy at not hearing from you, and I own my dear Lord, that I am almost tempted to wish that you would write to her at least once. Her present situation seems to entitle her to some measure of this favour.'[13] However, by December 1752, it seems that Huntingdon's sister, the Countess of Moira, in Ireland, had taken upon herself the care and upbringing of the child,[14] and Huntingdon always acknowledged Charles as his natural son, and became very proud of him. Lany meanwhile continued her successful professional career until 1767. She married the singer, Nicholas Gelin, in 1764, and was granted a royal pension of 1,500 livres on her retirement.

On his return to England, Huntingdon took his seat in the House of Lords, and was appointed Master of Horse to the Prince of Wales, (later George III) in 1756. He continued in that office when George III succeeded to the throne in 1760. He was then appointed a privy Counsellor, and carried the sword of state at George III's coronation. He was, 'groom of the stole', for the next ten years. During this period, Huntingdon was much involved in public life, and was Lord Lieutenant and *Custos Rutulorum* for the West Riding of Yorkshire, and of the City and County of York. He was an able man, with excellent natural abilities. Huntingdon brought great efficiency to the office of Master of the Horse during his period in office. His organization of the bookkeeping records and journals are still the basis of the office today.[15]

In 1765 he took offence when his claim to the Dukedom of Clarence was rejected and he then withdrew from public life. He continued however to exercise himself on behalf of his family and friends. He approached Lieutenant General Clinton[16] to obtain an ensigncy in the 12th Regiment for his natural son Charles. On Kirkland's recommendation he concerned himself in supporting The Reverend John Prior, cartographer, musician, classical scholar and man of letters, whom he had appointed Headmaster of Ashby-de-la Zouch Grammar School in 1763 and who he intended to present to the living of St Helen's Church, Ashby-de-la Zouch when it should become vacant. He also wrote to Lord Romney of the Society of Arts on 20 January 1778 strongly recommending Prior's map of the County of Leicester.[17] Huntingdon presented Prior as the Vicar of Ashby and was reputed to have met Kirkland sometime later and to have commented, 'Well Doctor, your friend the Vicar seems to be a poor preacher' to which Kirkland replied, 'But my Lord you should hear him fiddle.'[18]

On 8 June 1780 Fanny Burney records that she met Huntingdon at Bath with other company and describes him as 'a very deaf old Lord.'[19] At all events Huntingdon died as became an epicurian, when sitting at dinner with his nephew Lord Rawdon telling a good story; and earned for himself the epilogue that 'the late Earl was a man whose virtues would reflect honour on his ancestors had they been if possible more honourable than they were.'[20] He never married. The Duchess of Hamilton said of him when Master of the Horse, 'I can never believe that Lord Huntingdon will ever marry. He holds women in such a contemptible light that to be sure he will never trust one of us with his honour!'[21]

An Urgent Call*

On Friday 18 January, 1760, Kirkland had travelled during the afternoon, to Coleorton, a village about three miles from Ashby-de-la Zouch, to set a child's arm. At about 5 p.m. Earl Ferrers' lad, one Henry Wales, arrived at Kirkland's house in Ashby with news that John Johnson, Ferrers' Land Steward, was ill and would soon be dead and that Ferrers desired him to attend at Staunton

---

* The description of the murder of Johnson and the arrest of Earl Ferrers which follows is based on the *Kirkland Narrative*. All unattributed quotations are taken from that narrative. See note 25.

6

Harold Hall immediately. As no horses were available Kirkland's servant rode over to Coleorton on the lad's horse and delivered the message. Laurence, 4th Earl Ferrers, was then thirty-nine years of age, and had succeeded to the title in August 1745. He matriculated from Christ Church, Oxford, but left the university without taking a degree. Ferrers, as a peer of the realm and owner of large landed estates in Leicestershire, Derbyshire and Northamptonshire, was a man accustomed to having his own way in everything. His behaviour was notoriously eccentric but he was quite capable of managing his affairs. He was 'of an ungovernable temper, at times almost amounting to insanity'[22] and this caused him to be ostracized by his fellow members of the nobility, who preferred not to have to meet him. Kirkland was well acquainted with Ferrers and no doubt aware of his unpredictable temperament. He had kept as his mistress since about 1743, Margaret, the reputedly good-looking daughter of his agent Richard Clifford, and by her he had four daughters: Margaret, born 13 August 1744, Anna Maria, born 16 March 1745, Elizabeth, born 4 April 1748 and Mary, born 8 September 1749.[23] She was known as 'Mrs Clifford'. However, he married Mary, the teenage youngest daughter of Amos Meredith of Henbury, Cheshire, on 7 September 1752 and the marriage proved to be a disaster. Ferrers was credited with saying that the young Countess trepanned him into marrying her by ensuring that he was drunk at the betrothal and the wedding and for the whole of the intervening period. 'As he was seldom sober before or afterwards, it is hardly fair to impute his excesses to this pretty, and, unless it was a crime to wish to be a Countess, very blameless person.' All this must have been public knowledge because Ferrers' behaviour had been the chief topic of conversation in London for the preceding twelve months. He had been excommunicated from the Church of England and this disqualified him from giving evidence against Page, the notorious highwayman, at Hertford Assizes and resulted in the prisoner being acquitted. He was fond of both his mistress and his wife 'and used both ill: Lady Ferrers so ill – always carrying pistols to bed and threatening to kill her before morning, beating her, and being jealous without provocation – that she obtained a separation from him by Act of Parliament.'[24] The Act provided that the Ferrers estate be vested in Trustees and that Johnson, who had been steward to Ferrers and his father for many years, be appointed receiver of the rents; that particular appointment was at Ferrers' express desire. However, the necessary association between the Trustees and Johnson made Ferrers jealous and he convinced himself that

Johnson was more concerned with the interests of the Trustees than he was with those of himself. Ferrers had told Margaret Clifford that he would make Johnson repent having had anything to do with the Trustees and that he would shoot him. At this time Ferrers had resumed his association with Margaret Clifford, who was living at Staunton Harold with her four daughters and acting as housekeeper. Kirkland was well aware that Ferrers had served a notice on Johnson to quit his farm at Lount by 25 March 1759 and that Johnson, with the support of the Trustees of the estate, had not complied with the notice but had remained in possession of the farm. Ferrers was not the kind of man to accept such a situation, as he had planned to grant a lease of the farm to Margaret's father. However he changed his tactics and for some time afterwards treated Johnson with civility.

An unenviable situation

Kirkland must have suspected something unusual because, instead of proceeding directly to Staunton Harold, which was about a mile and a half from Coleorton, he and his servant called at Johnson's farm at Lount, to enquire what had occurred. It was there that he heard for the first time that Johnson, who was also one of his patients, had been shot by Ferrers and that the news was spreading fast. Kirkland proceeded from there on foot, accompanied by several colliers, because he thought it essential to arrest Ferrers. However, before he got to the Hall, he met Elizabeth Saxon, one of the servant girls.[25] It was dark and the terrified girl gave him the alarming news that Ferrers had been charging and loading guns and pistols and that he was threatening to shoot anyone who tried to arrest him. Persuaded by the girl, Kirkland ordered the men to stay behind and went on with her alone. The story was evolving that Johnson had negotiated coal contracts with two local landowners named Burslem and Curzon, which Ferrers regarded as detrimental to his interest. He therefore planned to get rid of Johnson, and devised a harebrained scheme to effect his purpose. He called at Johnson's house on 13 January 1760, and stayed with him for an hour and a half. Ferrers seemed to be in a very good humour, and gave Johnson some foreign coins. He then asked him to come to the Hall to settle some outstanding accounts, before he went to London at the end of the week. He suggested Thursday for the appointment, but as that did not suit Johnson, it was agreed that he should call on Friday at 3 p.m. Ferrers arranged for everyone to be out of the house at that time, except for three servant girls. He also had the horses shod, and ready for the journey to London as soon as possible. At the appointed time, Johnson arrived at the Hall, and knocked on the door of a room which was at the upper end of a long passage. Ferrers directed him to the still room, telling him that he would call for him. Some time later he called him in and locked the door. The maids in the kitchen could hear them talking and laughing, but after about an hour they heard Ferrers shouting and say, 'Sir, down on your other knee, and declare what you have against Earl Ferrers.' They then heard a pistol shot.

'Crime of the most horrid nature'

Johnson immediately got up and told Ferrers that he was shot. Ferrers asked him where he was shot and Johnson replied, he could not tell but he believed in his hip. Ferrers said that he could not have been shot, and that he was only frightened. Johnson sat down in a chair and Ferrers summoned Elizabeth Doleman, another of the servant girls, to go upstairs and attend to Johnson. Johnson made his way upstairs, and Elizabeth brought a bed out of the garret into 'the striped room'[26], where Johnson was. Johnson lay down on the bed. Ferrers then came into the room and took hold of Johnson by the wig exclaiming, 'I'll send a bullet through your head.' Johnson replied, 'No matter how soon.' Ferrers also sent a message to Margaret Clifford at her father's house, and she came back immediately. When Ferrers told her that he had shot Johnson she said, 'I am sorry for that.' He then told her to go to Johnson and give him such assistance as she could. As she went she heard Ferrers say, that as Johnson would not confess to what he thought he was guilty of, he thought to do what he did. Ferrers, in the meantime, having seen the maid and Johnson walk upstairs together, was not yet thoroughly satisfied that he had been shot. Margaret, however, examined Johnson and showed Ferrers the wound. He was then convinced about it and ordered Margaret to wash it with arquebusade – presumably a cleansing lotion. Ferrers also sent for Johnson's family, and his daughter Sarah now arrived. Sarah met Ferrers in the kitchen and asked him why he had sent for her. Ferrers, who may well have been drunk, asked her what her name was. When she had told him he said that he would like her to go upstairs to see her father and ordered a maid to accompany her. When she had seen her father, Ferrers sent for her downstairs and told her that if

9

her father died, he would be responsible for the family, provided they did not prosecute him. After this Ferrers went upstairs and abused Johnson, who expressed a wish that a surgeon should be sent for, and that that surgeon should be Kirkland. Ferrers then sent his lad to Ashby on his 'little stone horse called Cupid'. Ferrers at this time was anxious lest Kirkland, having heard what had happened, might refuse to come down to Staunton Harold. Kirkland was not at all keen to go there, but he thought it cruel to leave Johnson there without medical assistance, although he appreciated that any such visit to attend the patient might have serious consequences.

Kirkland met Ferrers and Margaret Clifford in the yard. Ferrers immediately called out, 'Who's there?' thinking perhaps that someone was coming to arrest him. When he had satisfied himself that it was Kirkland, he said, 'Come along,' and Kirkland and Ferrers went into the house arm-in-arm. Kirkland immediately noted that Ferrers had had too much to drink, and as they walked along Ferrers told him that he had shot Johnson, and that he did it on purpose, but that he desired, as Johnson was not dead, that Kirkland should do what he could for him. He said, 'If he dies I will go and surrender myself to the House of Lords and if anybody attempts to seize me, I will shoot them.' Kirkland assured Ferrers that nobody should meddle with him.

The Patient comes first

They then went upstairs, where Kirkland examined Johnson and found him complaining of pain in his bowels from, 'a wound made in his left side by a bullet in the Illiac [sic] region.' The wound was immediately under the lowest rib and was large enough to permit Kirkland to insert the end of his little finger into it. Kirkland took out his detector, in order to determine the direction of the bullet, when he was interrupted by Ferrers who said, 'Pass your instrument downwards and rather slaunting, for I held the pistol in this manner.' Kirkland found that the bullet had penetrated into the cavity of the abdomen and, as it had not passed out of the body, he thought that all further search for it was unnecessary. Kirkland's objective was to keep the inflammation within proper bounds and, as Johnson had not lost much blood, Kirkland bled him and dressed the wound superficially. There followed an unseemly exchange of question and answer between Ferrers and Kirkland, in the presence of the patient and his distraught daughter, as to the nature of the wound, and the location of the pistol ball. Kirkland had already, as a careful and correct medical man, taken the view that his prime duty was to his patient, and his next duty was to ensure that Ferrers did not leave Staunton Harold, and that all other considerations, including the truth if necessary, were secondary. He therefore decided he would have to go along with Ferrers and noted all he said concerning the angle of the shot. However, Ferrers grew concerned when Kirkland indicated that he could not extract the bullet. Kirkland answered him that as the bullet was lost in the cavity of the abdomen, it would be best for the ball to remain where it was, because he had known of instances of bullets remaining in the body for many years without any effect. He said that any attempt to extract the ball would aggravate the inflammation and would be impracticable. It would irritate the wound, increase the inflammation, and might allow air to enter the abdomen, and result in putrefaction of the extravasated blood. This seemed to satisfy Ferrers, although he remained querulous about the performance of his pistol. He rambled on, that he had tried out the pistol by shooting at a board of wood, which had been penetrated, and damaged some brickwork behind it. How therefore could such a bullet not pass through the body of a man? Ferrers left the room and Johnson in his pain muttered, 'What a villain this is!'

Kirkland then applied a fomentation, which seemed to ease Johnson's pain somewhat; however he was in great discomfort, through being unable to pass urine. He was constantly trying to vomit, his pulse was very weak and his hands cold. Ferrers came into the room again, and hearing Kirkland ask for a flannel, desired Margaret Clifford to fetch one of his flannel waistcoats. Then observing that Johnson could not pass water, he imagined that the bladder was injured, and asked Kirkland what would happen if the kidneys or bladder were damaged. Kirkland replied, that he had lately cured a patient with a wound in the kidney, and added that wounds in the bladder were very frequently cured, and he mentioned some instances of recoveries after such injury had been caused by a ball. He added that he could not conclude from the strangury that the bladder was harmed, as it might be caused by the nerve which served that part being injured. Kirkland had noticed that Ferrers now hoped that Johnson would recover, and he thought it wise to make it appear that it was very likely that Johnson would recover. He thought that if Ferrers knew the true situation, he would become desperate and try to escape.

Ferrers insisted that Kirkland should stay with Johnson all night, and should be provided with whatever he needed. He then said,

11

'Kirkland, I believe Johnson is more frightened than hurt; my intent was to have shot him dead, and finding he did not fall at the first shot, I intended to have shot him again, but his complaining of pain made me forbear. There I confess nature did take place in opposition to the resolution I have formed, and I have spared his life. I desire you would take great care of him, for it would be cruel not to have him relieved of his pain; if he dies I shall be glad, and therefore, Kirkland, when you speak of this affair, do not say I repent. I am not sorry for it. I had some time before charged the pistol for the purpose, being determined to kill him, for he is a villain and deserves death, but as he is not dead, I desire I may not be seized for I will not run away. I will stay here until he is either better or dead. If he dies I will go and surrender myself to the House of Lords. I have enough to justify the action; maybe they will not excuse me, but it will satisfy myself.' Here he placed his hand on his breast, and added, 'Do not go in the morning without letting me see you, that I may know whether he is likely to recover or not. I will be here at dawn or at any time you call, and you will let me know if you think him in any danger.' Kirkland told Ferrers that he was not an early riser, and that he would sit up with Johnson; Ferrers was most likely to be up first, but if that did happen, he would come to Ferrers' chamber and inform him what he thought about the matter, and when he went home would effectively prevent anyone from trying to meddle with Ferrers. Ferrers asked Kirkland what he would say if questioned on the matter; Kirkland replied that he would say that Johnson had been shot, but that there was every probability of him making a full recovery. At this stage Margaret Clifford came into the still room, announcing that Johnson had made water. She brought a sample and, as there was no blood in it, Kirkland concluded that the bladder was not injured. He then wrote out a prescription, and sent it by his servant to Ashby to be made up.

'A Bad Supper'

Supper was then served in the room where Johnson had been shot. Kirkland was not very hungry, and reported, 'I made a very bad supper out of a very fine cold turkey and brawn.' Ferrers also ate very little, but he drank a great deal, and appeared to Kirkland to have been drinking uninterruptedly since he had shot Johnson. He was not incapable however. On the table Kirkland saw several pistols and, amongst them, a horse pistol that had been fired.

12

Ferrers next told Kirkland that Curzon had written to him, informing him that he was about to start proceedings against him in the Court of King's Bench. Ferrers then repeated that Johnson had been a villain to him, and had assisted Lady Ferrers and his enemies in obtaining the Act of Parliament that had deprived him of his estate. Johnson had also been acting in the interest of Burslem and Curzon, and he had insisted on Johnson drawing up and signing a paper, confessing the circumstances and whatever else he knew of what had been transacted against him. Johnson had refused to do this, confirming that he had never done anything to Ferrers, contrary to Ferrers' best interests, in his life. Upon this happening, Ferrers said that he ordered Johnson to kneel down and ask his pardon, and said, 'Johnson, if you have anything to say, speak quickly, for you must die,' and immediately fired. 'I know he did not think I would have shot him,' says he, 'I was determined and I made sure of hitting him, for I took aim; I always aim in this manner,' pointing with his hand, 'when I shoot with a pistol, and I was quite cool when I did it.'

Deranged Justification

Time and again Ferrers returned to the question of why the ball did not pass through Johnson's body. 'I wonder the ball did not go through him, for he was not above three yards from me, and at last had it, for this pistol carrying a ball through an inch and half board at a considerable distance – I have long wanted to drive him out of the farm, and I fancy, Kirkland, that if he recovers he will go into Cheshire, from whence he came, and give me no further trouble.' Kirkland replied, 'It will certainly drive him off the premises.'

Ferrers went on then to complain of Johnson having £100 a year for attending to the Receivership. He said that Johnson was very much indebted to the Shirley family, and owed everything he possessed to them.

Ferrers and Kirkland drank another glass or two after supper, and then went up to Johnson's room again. This time Kirkland found Johnson somewhat easier, though his, 'Stranguary and reaching to vomit still continued' [sic]. Ferrers again grew anxious about this, but once more Kirkland said, 'these symptoms were to be expected and they would probably go off after a while as the inflammation abated.' On this occasion they did not stay long in Johnson's room, and little happened apart from Ferrers inquiring as to what Kirkland thought would happen to Johnson if his bowels were injured. Once again Kirkland told him that Johnson was more free from pain than he thought he would be, and there was every reason to expect his recovery. He added, 'People frequently get well after having the bowel shot thro.' Ferrers, thus reassured, called for a bottle of port, which Margaret Clifford brought to them. He then said, 'I own I did not shoot Johnson hastily: the shooting of him was . . . premeditated [*sic*] – he deserved death. I can justify the action in my own conscience.' They then sat down and began the bottle of port, and Ferrers said, 'I've long intended to shoot the villain, but I will tell you, Kirkland, the reason I did it this time was Curzon and Burslem's affair, for he assisted and advised them about the coal and slack. As you say, Kirkland, this I imagine will prove a slight affair – however, if he recovers, I will make him confess his being a rogue to me, or I will shoot him through the head or heart. Be sure Kirkland, you don't tell me any lies, for by God, I shall break your head if you do.'

Margaret Clifford came into the room after this, and sat down with them. She asked Kirkland if Johnson could not be taken home. Ferrers replied that he should not be removed until he was out of danger. He then added, 'I'm glad I have him under these circumstances in my own house, for I can plague the rascal.' He then added, 'You shall see, Kirkland, in the morning I shall make him confess his being a villain, or I will whip him to death.'

After this Ferrers' conversation became maudlin, as he was now extremely drunk. He started quoting Shakespeare's plays, and then said in a joking manner, 'If Johnson died, and they take off my head, I will turn up this lock of hair, its only one chop, and there is an end – will you be present Kirkland?' Kirkland replied that this was a very disagreeable subject. He hoped that Johnson would recover and nothing of that kind should happen. Ferrers persisted however, and said, 'but if my head is cut off, I insist on you being present.' Kirkland promised he would be present. Ferrers said that Johnson had begun his villainy in 1753, and asked Kirkland if he thought that in view of all that had happened, Johnson did not deserve shooting. Kirkland replied that Ferrers had very high provocation indeed.

Ferrers than started talking about his, 'exploits and amours with women, upon which subject we were very merry,' and the bottle being finished about 12 o'clock, he said, 'Come Kirkland pull off your boots, we will go and see Johnson, and then to bed, but be sure you do not go in the morning before I see you – I owe you a bill, and if you will set this affair in a favourable light, so that I may not

14

be seized, or if Johnson dies – then I may go and surrender myself to the House of Lords without being molested, you may have some money now, and the remainder when you want it.' He then assured Kirkland that he would not leave the house until Johnson was either better or dead. He added that he could easily have gone if he had wanted to, but that he had not attempted such a thing. Kirkland told Ferrers that he hoped there was no danger, and that Johnson would recover. Any question of arrest was therefore unnecessary. As to his bill, 'I did not desire it but when it was most convenient for his Lordship.'

They then went up to see Johnson again, but this time Ferrers went to the foot of the bed, and shouted at Johnson, that he had been a villain to him. Johnson did not answer, but indicated that Ferrers ought to leave him alone. Sarah Johnson and Margaret Clifford also pleaded with Ferrers to leave Johnson alone, but he still insisted on Johnson confessing his being 'a rogue,' and mocked him when he complained of pain in his bowels. Ferrers worked himself into an even greater rage, and began to pull the bedclothes off the bed. This was prevented by Kirkland and the women, and Johnson then said, 'I believe I have done wrong as well as other people.' This made Ferrers even more angry, and he made as if to strike him. Sarah Johnson accordingly lay across her father to defend him. Ferrers then shrieked out, 'What did you say? Have you not been a villain to me?' Kirkland then went up to the bedside and winked at Johnson, who then said, 'I may have been a villain to your Lordship.' Kirkland then said, 'I beg your Lordship will come away. This treatment will do him harm, and I have heard him confess he's a villain.' Upon this Ferrers went and stood at the fireside.

Despite this behaviour to Johnson, Ferrers was full of consideration for Sarah Johnson who was crying. He said, 'Miss Johnson, I'm sorry for you, but you know your father always talked and acted against me.' Sarah replied between her tears 'He never did.' Ferrers continued, 'But do not you make yourself uneasy, for if your father dies and you do not prosecute, I again promise you, before Kirkland, who I desire will be witness, that I will take care of your family, you shall never want.'

After this, Ferrers left the room and Kirkland wished him goodnight. The medicines had come from Ashby, and Kirkland administered these. Once again however, Ferrers sent for Kirkland downstairs, and he then said, 'I'm afraid I've made Miss Johnson uneasy by talking to her father, but tell her I will certainly be a friend to her.' They then came up to the landing together, and, 'though his Lordship was so full of liquor that he could hardly stand,' he said, 'Do you think, Kirkland, Johnson will recover and I may go lie with P—y* tonight in safety?' Kirkland assured him that he could.

The Escape

Kirkland then acted quickly and returned to Johnson, who implored him to get him away from the Hall. He heard Ferrers open the bedroom door and call up his pointer. This caused Johnson further alarm lest Ferrers should return. However, Ferrers shut the door again and once more Johnson entreated Kirkland to remove him. Kirkland thought it prudent to move him for a number of reasons. He believed that Johnson was dying and he feared that if Ferrers found that this was so, he would become resentful of him for having deceived him. Secondly, Johnson was anxious lest he be shot again and Kirkland was afraid that, as he was a man of weak constitution, he might die of fear. Kirkland accordingly told him that he would go to Lount and bring 'a posse of men . . . and carry him away upon a couch.' Kirkland then arranged for Sarah Johnson to give signals by placing a candle in the window. They also agreed that, if Ferrers came before Kirkland returned, he was to be told that Kirkland had been called away upon 'emergent business and would be there again early in the morning.' Johnson added, 'I think you had better bring arms with you, I have a gun, and you may borrow another, and if my Lord should get up while you are gone and your scheme be defeated, bring a proper number of armed men, to take me away by force.' Kirkland promised he would do this.

Kirkland and his servant then went off to Lount and they gathered together seven or eight colliers. Armed with two guns, they went back to Staunton without disturbing anybody. Johnson was ready, and with Sarah's assistance he was dressed and walked to the bottom of the back stairs, leaning on Kirkland's servant's shoulder, 'where he was received into a great chaise lined with pillows, blankets and the like. When he came into the great flats I asked him how he did. He said, 'I am faint but I feel easier, thank God, I am got out of my Lord's reach.' We marched very slowly: being carried upon poles,

---

* Ferrers would seem to be referring to Peggy – presumably Margaret Clifford.

16

he bore going home very well, the blankets kept him very warm, though it was a frosty night.' When Johnson got home, he walked into the parlour where he usually slept and was put to bed.

Kirkland then enquired closely of Johnson whether Ferrers had been drunk when he shot him. Johnson was sure that he was not. He believed however that he got drunk afterwards. 'I did not think he would have shot me, I thought he only wanted to frighten me and make me sign a paper.' Kirkland then said, 'Pray, were you down on your knees when my Lord shot you?' Johnson replied, 'My Lord bid me kneel down, but I think – though I cannot be sure, being hurried – that he fired at me just as I was arising.' Johnson said, 'I shall die, he has killed me, and it will rid the country of a villain.' Johnson said that although he was shot it did not affect his movement. He was able to stand up, and he was only conscious of a soreness in his thigh and knee. Kirkland then asked him whether he had set his affairs in order. Johnson said he had not, and asked Kirkland to make a Will for him. However, Kirkland quickly realized that Johnson was no longer in a condition to make a Will. When he got home, Johnson asked to be moved to another room, lest Ferrers should shoot him through the window. Kirkland stayed with Johnson until about 7 a.m. when he was 'weak and low and cold in the extremities.' Realizing that nothing more could be done to save Johnson's life, Kirkland hastened to seek advice from Mr Piddocke and Mr Pestell as to what he should do.* Kirkland was advised that Ferrers be 'seised' immediately. Johnson died at 9 a.m., and shortly afterwards his friend Springthorpe, (presumably the 'facetious' gentleman of the 'Bacchanalian rounds') who lived at Park Farm, called to see him, and found that he was dead.

The Arrest

Public indignation was immediately aroused, and Springthorpe was asked by the self same Mr Burslem of the coal contract to assist in

---

* The Pestells and the Piddockes were respected legal families in Ashby in the eighteenth century. 'Mr Piddocke' is likely to have been Leonard Piddocke who presented the brass candelabrum to St Helen's Church in 1733. 'Mr Pestell' would seem to be Charles Pestell who was practising in the town in 1749 and was amerced the sum of three shillings and four pence by the Court Leet 'for muck in the street' at Michaelmas 1774.[27] They almost certainly advised Kirkland to write a detailed account of all that had happened. This formed 'Mr Kirkland's Narrative' which was deposited with the Crown Counsel's papers and not rediscovered until 1988.

securing the arrest of Ferrers, and bringing him to justice. Arming himself with a pistol from Burslem, he went to Staunton Harold with an ever increasing crowd of local people. Margaret Clifford, the family and the servants, were all let out of the house, and Ferrers found himself all alone. In the Hall yard Burslem saw Ferrers going towards the stable, strangely attired, with his stockings down and his garters in his hands. Ferrers turned towards Springthorpe and asked him what he wanted. Springthorpe said it was him he wanted and he would have him, and pointed his pistol at him. Several fire arms were discharged at Ferrers, but all missed the target. Ferrers then ran into the house, and Springthorpe saw nothing of him for two hours until he came to the garrett window. Springthorpe stood under the window and asked Ferrers what he wanted. Ferrers enquired after Johnson, and Springthorpe said that he was dead. Ferrers replied, 'You are a lying scoundrel, God damn you.' When Springthorpe repeated that Johnson was dead, Ferrers said, 'I will not believe it till Kirkland tells me so.' Springthorpe again repeated that he was dead and this time Ferrers asked him to disperse the people and he would go and surrender. 'Let the people in and let them have some victuals and drink.' Springthorpe said that he had not come for victuals but for him, and he would have him. Ferrers went away from the window, swearing that he would not be taken. Another two hours passed, and reports came in that Ferrers was on the bowling green. Springthorpe ran round there to find Ferrers being held by two colliers. The *Gentlemen's Magazine*[28] recounts that a collier named Curtis, forbear of Joe Curtis, for many years verger at St Helens Church, Ashby-de-la Zouch, during the earlier part of the twentieth century, had boldly seized Ferrers, although he was armed with a loaded pistol. Kirkland who was not present, names the collier as Henry Cutler. Springthorpe fired the pistol, 'and it made a great impression against the stone.' Ferrers said that he had shot a villain and a scoundrel and, clapping his hand upon his bosom he said, 'I glory in his death.' Ferrers was taken to Ashby-de-la Zouch, and lodged at the White Hart, a public house kept by Mr Kinsey and was there confined until the inquest had been held. Here the Reverend Hall, a Justice of the Peace, visited Ferrers and entered into a long discourse with him. The clergyman was overheard intimating, 'to his Lordship, as a clergyman, that his Lordship seemed to be pretty much in liquor at that time, and desired he would not make use of these expressions.' Ferrers told the Reverend gentleman, he was extremely obliged to him for his good advice, but, he knew his duty perhaps as well as a Justice of the Peace. Kinsey told the House of Lords that, 'his Lordship behaved very well with me, and decently, from the Saturday to the Monday at 10 o'clock.'

Custody

Kirkland was not concerned with the arrest of Ferrers, but he examined the body prior to the Coroner's Inquest, which was held in Johnson's house, at Lount, on 20 January, before William Tilly junior, one of the Leicestershire Coroners. Depositions were taken from the three servant girls, none of whom could sign her name, Margaret Clifford, Sarah Johnson, Kirkland, and William Tomlinson, an ironmonger from Newbold, who had been present at the death. Kirkland's autopsy report reads as follows:

> January the 20th 1760. Upon this day, examining the body of John Johnson deceased, I found a wound made by a leaden bullet immediately under the lowest rib on his left side, which bullet passing obliquely downward had made another wound thro' the Gut called Colon and going under the Psoas Muscle and thro' the Os Inominatum at its junction with the spine rested in the Os Sacrum, from which place I extracted it.
>
> There was a considerable quantity of extravasated blood in the abdomen, the viscera in consequence of the violent injury done to the parts were greatly inflamed; and I am therefore of opinion that the wound above described was the cause of his death. TK.[29]

The Coroner's Jury consisting of twelve jurors from Ashby, Breedon-on-the-Hill, Worthington, and Coleorton, having returned a verdict of wilful murder, Ferrers was committed to the County Gaol, at Leicester, on 21 January. Leicester was full of excitement in the early February, because Brigadier General the Duke of Grafton, and the Suffolk militia, were quartered in the town and, at a Common Hall, held on 8 February, it was ordered, 'that Mr Mayor give such a feast to the Duke of Grafton and the Suffolk Militia Officers now in the town as he shall think proper.' The feast was the costliest ever given up to that date by the body corporate, 'and', says Throsby, 'one of the most inebriating. Mr Mayor at night was assisted by the Duke downstairs; and the

Duke soon after by the town servants; there not being a soul left in the room capable of affording help to enfeebled limbs; Field Officers and Aldermen, Captains and Common Council, were perfectly at rest – all were levelled with the mighty power of wine.'[30] Whilst all this was going on, Ferrers was in the close custody of James Lambert, the gaoler, who was the father of the 57 stone 11 lb giant, Daniel Lambert (1770–1809), who succeeded to the office. In this dire situation, Ferrers began to consider what would happen to Margaret Clifford and his four daughters in the event of his conviction, so he persuaded Lambert to act as trustee for a deed poll, which he then intended to make in favour of his daughters. Despite the verdict of the Inquest Jury, Ferrers was committed for trial before Leicester Assizes by a true bill presented by the Grand Jury. As a nobleman, Ferrers could not be tried at the assizes, so a writ of *habeas corpus* was issued out of the Court of Kings Bench and a writ of *certiorari* was moved for the trial to be transferred to the House of Lords. He remained in Leicester Gaol until 11 February, when he was removed to the Tower of London, travelling in his own Landau and six, with a strong military guard to await his trial before the House of Lords. He arrived in London on 14 February at about noon, dressed like a jockey in a close riding frock, jockey's boots and cap and a plain shirt. He was taken before the House of Lords, and committed to the custody of Black Rod and ordered to the Tower where he arrived at about 6 p.m. He was confined in the Round Tower, near the drawbridge, with two warders constantly in the room with him. There was another warder at the door and two sentries placed, one at the bottom of the stairs, and another on the drawbridge, both with fixed bayonets.[31] These momentous events so shocked the neighbourhood, that the Leicester Journal shrank from even naming the prisoner, whose family had been identified for centuries with the county. On 16 February Ferrers executed a Deed Poll, appointing James Lambert as Trustee, and settling his silver and plate, horses and cattle, carriages and carts, together with £500 owing to him by John Stevenson, and £3,500 in East India Bonds, on his four children on attaining twenty-one years or earlier marriage.[32]*

---

* Whilst awaiting his trial at the Tower, Ferrers executed two deeds on 12 March. The first was an indenture assigning his interest in assets to provide £1,200 for Johnson's children, discharge certain of his debts and to make some provision for his brother Walter Shirley. The second was a Deed Poll under which a further £2,000 was to be paid to his natural children.[33]

Tried by his Peers

The trial opened before the House of Peers in Westminster Hall on Wednesday 16 April 1760. Robert Henley, 1st Earl of Northington (1708?–1772), Keeper of the Great Seal, having been created Lord Steward upon the occasion. Henley had been an MP for Bath, Attorney General, and Speaker of the House of Lords, Lord Chancellor, and Lord Lieutenant of Hampshire. Eldon described him as 'a great lawyer, and very firm in the delivering of his opinion.'[34] Kirkland found himself to be the principal witness for the Crown. Not only was he a witness as to the facts, but he was also the only expert witness as to the cause of death called by the Crown. Ferrers had been persuaded by members of his family and by his Counsel to plead not guilty and to base his defence on partial insanity. It is necessary to remember that in 1760, and for many years thereafter, a prisoner charged with a capital offence was not permitted to be represented at the hearing by Counsel, but had to conduct his own defence. Counsel could only address the Court on points of law. This strange rule, so at variance with the jury system and the long established principles of English Criminal Law, was justified by the assumption that the judge would care adequately for the interests of the accused and Counsel was accordingly unnecessary. Contemporary jurists were however severely critical of the rule which denied Counsel to a prisoner whose life was at stake, but permitted representation in petty misdemeanours and trifling civil claims. Furthermore, until the passing of the Criminal Evidence Act in 1898, a defendant in criminal proceedings was not at Common Law generally permitted to give evidence on oath in his own defence. This was because of the rule of law, that 'held as inadmissible the evidence of any witness who was interested in the outcome of the case.'[35] A prisoner facing a capital charge, certainly had an interest in the verdict. However, prisoners were permitted to make an unsworn statement in their own defence, but could not be cross-examined and naturally this did not carry as much weight as the sworn testimony of other witnesses. These rules of evidence and procedure placed Ferrers in an impossible situation and well might he complain, 'I have been driven to the miserable necessity of proving my own want of understanding and am told the Law will not allow me the assistance of Council in this case, in which, of all others, I should think it most wanted.'

The trial was indeed a *cause célèbre*. No-one could remember a noble Earl being tried by his Peers for murder. All the solemnity

21

and pageantry were in evidence. Ferrers was treated with the greatest courtesy and good manners. When opening the case for the Crown Sir Charles Pratt, the Attorney General (1714–1794), declared that he would 'neither aggravate nor observe'. If Ferrers had, 'any defence God forbid that he should not have a fair opportunity of making it. Let him be heard with patience. The prosecutors will be as glad as your Lordships to find him innocent.'

The evidence for the Crown was extracted from the witnesses under the professional skill of the Attorney General, the Solicitor General, Sir Charles Yorke (1690–1764), Mr Perrott, Mr Gould, and Mr Norton of Counsel. The three servant girls with their local sounding names, Elizabeth Burgeland, Elizabeth Saxon, and Elizabeth Doleman, used Leicestershire expressions, and no doubt spoke in Leicestershire dialect. So Burgeland when asked what Ferrers said, replied, 'he hooped and hollood. Where are you all?' and Saxon's reply to the question as to what had become of Ferrers' family was, 'I don't know. Mrs Clifford and the Misses were gone out – my Lord came into the still house and said they might go and fetch a walk.' Later, when Burgeland was recalled, and asked if Ferrers was drunk or sober she replied, 'I did not observe he was much in liquor then: but soon after he was quite fuddled.' Sarah Johnson was still shocked and confused. Margaret Clifford, no doubt for reasons of delicacy, was not called to give evidence. Kirkland's evidence was prudent, exact and without embellishment. When Ferrers came to cross examine him, he reproved him for talking with him as a friend over a bottle of wine and intending to betray him. Kirkland replied, 'I do own, my Lord, that I intended to deceive you and I thought it absolutely necessary.'

The Case for the Defence

When the time came for Ferrers to open his defence, he applied for an adjournment of one day. Lord Henley reminded him that he, 'hath had a great deal of time. You have had Counsel assigned to you, and all the defence witnesses had been summoned', and his application was refused. Ferrers then asked for an adjournment for the remainder of the day, so that he could confer with Counsel. On this, Lord Mansfield, with the full authority of the law, argued that if Ferrers declined to give some reason why he was not prepared to open his defence, it would create a dangerous precedent, establishing that a trial might be adjourned merely because the case for the prosecution had closed. However, if Ferrers could give a reason for seeking an adjournment, the Lords could consider it on its merits. Ferrers did not press the point, and after Elizabeth Burgeland had been briefly recalled, he entered uncertainly and reluctantly on the defence, 'what my family have considered for me.' Ferrers' family had assembled all the evidence, but he had no idea what the witnesses were going to say. The defence was, 'occasional insanity of mind', and he was convinced, 'from recollecting from within myself that at the time of this action I could not know what I was about.' The strategy of the defence planned for Ferrers by his family, consisted of evidence given by persons who had known him for a number of years, and who would give instances of symptoms which indicated lunacy. The defence would be concluded by calling an expert medical witness, who would give his opinion on the conduct described. The case is the first recorded instance of a medical man being called to give evidence in a psychiatric role.[36] The conduct to be established included jealousy and suspicion without cause, carrying firearms, quarrelling with friends without cause, going armed when there was no danger, spitting in the looking glass, talking to himself, making odd gestures, and drinking coffee out of the spout! A further indication was thought to be heredity and examples of lunacy within the family were to be proved. From about 1756 Ferrers' mental condition had deteriorated, and it was thought that this was a result of his dispute with Lady Ferrers, which led to the Act of Separation. There had been an outburst following dinner, when the ladies had left the table, leaving Ferrers and his brother the Reverend Walter Shirley to take their time, as was customary, over the brandy. The Reverend Walter seems to have disapproved of the quantity being drunk by his brother, and rejoined the ladies on his own. Ferrers followed him and stood silent for some time with his back to the fire. He then worked himself up into a violent temper, and insulted and provoked his brother at great length, using foul language and obscenities. Understandably, Walter did not visit his brother again. In 1758 he quarrelled with Sir Thomas Stapleton, at Lord Westmoreland's house, and proposed to his lawyer, Thomas Goostrey, that he should issue a challenge to Stapleton, publicly imputing cowardice to him, should he fail to give him satisfaction. Goostrey formed the opinion that Ferrers was too insane to give him instructions, and declined to act for him further. Ferrers then commenced the examination-in-chief of the various witnesses assembled. There was John Bennefold, the peruke maker, clerk to St James's Parish in the City of London. He had known that the late Henry Lord Ferrers was a lunatic, and had heard that Lady Barbara Shirley was disordered. He said that Ferrers had 'always behaved in a very strange manner, very flighty, very much like a man out of his mind, more particularly so within these two years past, such as being in liquor, and swearing and cursing and the like, and talking to himself very much like a man disordered in his senses; and then he has behaved himself as any other gentleman at times.' Cross-examined by the Attorney General, Bennefold could not recollect Ferrers giving him insensible answers, and he positively refused to confirm that Ferrers could not distinguish right from wrong. Very improperly, the Attorney General pressed the peruke maker to give the House of Lords his opinion as to Ferrers's sanity. This again Bennefold declined to give. The witness was finally demolished, by being unable to give a single instance of any act that denoted a disordered mind, and by agreeing that Ferrers was, if anything, more intelligent than other men. There followed Ferrers's Attorney, Thomas Goostrey, who gave evidence of receiving erratic instructions from him, and he could only account for this, 'otherwise than by apprehending that he had been at times out of his mind.' Furthermore he persisted in disregarding his Lawyer's advice! Goostrey was obliged to agree, under cross-examination, that Clients did not always accept their Lawyer's advice, and finally had to admit that he had witnessed Ferrers's execution of a Deed. Ferrers's brothers, The Reverend Walter Shirley and the Honourable Robert Shirley, spoke of his unfraternal behaviour towards them, and the embarrassment of themselves and everyone else, so that the Attorney General only questioned them very briefly and 'very tenderly with as much propriety as I can.' It emerged, however, that Robert Shirley had written to his brother, Captain Washington Shirley, suggesting that they should take out a commission of lunacy against him, but nothing was ever done. Then there was his uncle, Gold Clarges, who had known Ferrers since his birth. The examination of this witness proceeded thus:

EARL FERRERS: Did you look upon me to be afflicted with any and what distemper?
CLARGES: Indeed, I have looked upon your Lordship as a lunatic for many years.

Generally reputed a lunatic

However, professional witnesses and witnesses of quality for the defence, found difficulty in being positive about Ferrers's madness. All too often he had behaved towards them as if he was sane. Witnesses from the lower orders had no such reservations, and Roger Griffiths, who had known him at Muswell Hill, bluntly affirmed that he was, 'generally reputed a lunatic: some said crak'd in his head.' Another witness, by name Peter Williams, who had been minding a mare for Ferrers from January to April 1759, had heard that Ferrers was not in his right senses. In support of this, he testified that on 1 April 1759 Ferrers came to his house with two servants, all armed, knocked the padlock off the stable door and when his wife came to enquire what he wanted, Ferrers felled her with his fist, and ran a rapier into Williams' body, causing a serious wound that required a surgeon's attention. The Solicitor General commented that anger and action of this kind, against a negligent servant, was an everyday occurrence and entirely justified, and if that was a symptom of madness, few people would be sane. Again, the comment was improper, because no evidence of any negligence or neglect had been adduced against Williams. Doctor John Munro MD (1715–1791), physician to the Bethlem Hospital, London, the second of four: father, son, grandson and great grandson to hold that office, was the expert medical witness for the defence and he had attended Ferrers when, 'he was under the unhappy influence of lunacy.' He gave it as his opinion that all the strange actions attributed to Ferrers, were 'symptoms of lunacy'. He was not cross-examined by the Crown, who took the view that his evidence was of a general nature, and not particular to the noble prisoner.

Wild Delusion

By far the strongest evidence of Ferrers's delusion was never mentioned directly at the trial, although Ferrers referred to it obliquely on more than one occasion. There is a popular tradition in the district that the real reason why Ferrers shot Johnson, who had been a widower since 1757, was that he had either received a report that Johnson was involved in an illicit relationship with Lady Ferrers, or had deluded himself into believing such an allegation. It is surmised that when Johnson arrived at Staunton Harold on 18 January, Ferrers confronted him with the story, and demanded that he should confess to it. This Johnson refused to do and, in a fit of ungovernable temper, he shot the unfortunate man. Later on in the evening, Ferrers again tried to make Johnson confess in Kirkland's presence. It seems strange that Ferrers did not tell Kirkland of his suspicions concerning Johnson and Lady Ferrers, but according to Kirkland he only maintained that Johnson had been a villain to him and that he gloried in his death. He did however tell Kirkland that his action was justified, presumably as a *crime passionnel*, and that even if the House of Lords did not excuse him, his action would satisfy his own conscience. It may be that Kirkland regarded the allegation as so defamatory of the deceased, and Lady Ferrers, that he feared to repeat such scandal as hearsay evidence. Ferrers was no doubt advised by his Lawyers that, even if he could establish the truth of his assertion, it would not excuse the crime at law, whilst the raising of such an unmentionable accusation against the character of an already much-injured lady might well influence the King in not re-granting, to the succeeding Earl, the estates that would be forfeited by the conviction. Perhaps the most unsatisfactory omission from an unsatisfactory trial, was the inadequate cross-examination of Kirkland. Ferrers, as a layman, cannot be blamed for this, and the fault rests with the harsh rules of procedure governing capital trials at the time. Ferrers regarded Kirkland as being cautious to the point of dishonesty as he, 'drank and conversed with me in order to betray me.' It clearly emerges that Kirkland deliberately and falsely told Ferrers that the wound was not fatal, because he was fearful of the Earl's resentment both against his patient and himself if he had told the truth. Later on, he winked at Johnson, to prompt him to make some kind of confession, in order to calm Ferrers down. These events happening so soon after the fatal shot was fired, would have provided the best evidence, that he was temporarily deranged, and indeed in Ferrers's words, 'the most irrational of all madmen at the time of my doing the deed.'

Ferrers addresses his Peers

Ferrers's unsworn statement, read out to the House of Lords by the Clerk, was a model of reasoned brevity and may well have been drafted by his lawyers. In a modern study, Mr Nigel Walker, Reader in Criminology at Oxford University has written, 'In effect [Ferrers] was attempting a defence of what later came to be known as 'irresistable impulse'. Two hundred years later it would have

been listened to seriously, if not actually accepted in his case.'[37]
It reads as follows:

It is my misfortune to be accused of a crime of the most
horrid nature. My defence is, in general, that I am not
guilty: the fact of homicide is proved against me by
witnesses who, for ought I can say to the contrary, speak
truly. I know myself at this time, I can truly affirm, I
was ever incapable of it, knowingly; if I have done and
said what has been alleg'd, I must have been depriv'd of
my senses. I have been driven to the miserable necessity
of proving my own want of understanding; and am told
the Law will not allow me the assistance of Council in
this case in which, of all others, I should think it most
wanted. The more I stand in need of assistance, the
greater reason I have to hope for it from your Lordships.
Witnesses have been call'd to prove my insanity – to
prove an unhappy disorder of mind, and which I am
griev'd to be under the necessity of exposing. If they
have not directly prov'd me so insane as not to know
the difference between a moral and immoral action, they
have at least prov'd that I was liable to be driven and
hurried into that unhappy condition upon very slight
occasions. Your Lordships will consider whether my
passion, rage, madness (or whatever it may be called)
was the effect of a weak or distemper'd mind, whether
it arose from my own wickedness, or inattention to
my duty. If I could have controul'd my rage, I am
answerable for all the consequences of it – but if I could
not, and if it was the mere effect of a distempered brain,
I am not answerable for the consequences. My lords,
I mention these things as hints – I need not, indeed I
cannot, enlarge upon this subject: your Lordships will
consider all circumstances, and I am sure you will do me
justice. If it be but a matter of doubt, your Lordships
will run the hazard of doing me injustice if you find me
guilty. My Lords, if my insanity had been of my own
seeking, as the sudden effect of drunkenness, I should
be without excuse. But it is proved, by the witnesses
for the Crown, that I was not in liquor. Mr Kirkland,
who drank and conversed with me, in order to betray
me (Mr Attorney may commend his caution, but not

27

his honesty), represents me as the most irrational of all madmen, at the time of my doing a deed, which I reflect upon with the utmost abhorrence. The Council for the Crown will put your Lordships in mind of every circumstance against me. I must require of your Lordships' Justice to recollect every circumstance on the other side. My life is in your hands, and I have every thing to hope, as my conscience does not condemn me of the crime I stand accused of; for I had no preconceived malice; and was hurried in the perpetration of this fatal deed by the fury of a disordered imagination. To think of this, my Lords, is an affliction, which can be aggravated only by the necessity of making it my defence. May God almighty direct your judgments, and correct my own.

Ferrers could have added that he had made no plans for disposing of Johnson's body, or for making good his own escape.

The Solicitor General Sums up

The case for the Crown was summed up by the Solicitor General with damning logic. Ferrers had weighed the motives, he had proceeded with deliberation, and he understood the consequences. These facts were not compatible with temporary insanity. He told Sarah Johnson that he would maintain her and her family, if she did not prosecute. He tried to tempt Kirkland with promises in order to prevent the neighbours from arresting him. Despite all the evidence of Ferrers's behaviour in the past, he was clearly conscious of everything he was doing at the time that the offence was committed. Added to all that, Ferrers had convinced the peers of his sanity by the sense and sagacity with which he had conducted his defence. Lastly, he argued that in a sense every crime is committed in a moment of insanity. That maxim, though true in philosophy, was dangerous in judicature, as finding extenuation for crime and excuse for punishment. If the defence of partial insanity was not founded on truth, 'I am persuaded that no other consideration respecting the rank and quality of the noble prisoner, and his relation to your Lordships, will turn your attention from the evidence, nor make the least impression upon the firmness of your justice.' The Solicitor General spoke strongly in Kirkland's defence. He argued that Kirkland's caution proceeded from his

28

honesty. He knew that it was his duty to prevent Ferrers from escaping. To achieve this object and to prevent Ferrers from being alarmed and attempting to escape, he told him that he thought Johnson would recover. Kirkland had served the needs of civil government, justice and humanity. Despite the Solicitor General's emphasis on the necessity for truth in establishing the defence of partial insanity, it was a verdict regularly found by inquest juries of the time, often on no evidence at all, other than the fact that self-inflicted death had occurred. Suicide was a felony and, where so found, resulted in forfeiture of the suicide's property and effects, and the infliction of mutilation on the mortal remains, and burial near the public highway. Essentially however, it was a spiritual crime, and in eighteenth century England, rationalism was replacing clericalism, and juries were prepared to give the suicide the benefit of the doubt, where there was a possibility of temporary derangement.

The Verdict and Sentence

The Lieutenant of the Tower was then required to remove Ferrers and the Lords adjourned to the Chamber of Parliament. Sometime later, they adjourned back to Westminster Hall, and each was asked for his verdict individually by the Lord High Steward, starting with the youngest peer, who was George Lord Lyttelton. All of them, including the Lord High Steward who gave his verdict last, replied 'Guilty upon my honour,' each laying his hand on his breast.*

Ferrers was then recalled and informed of the verdict, and the House was adjourned until the next day. On Friday, 18 April, when the Court reassembled, Ferrers was asked what he had to say, before sentence of death was passed upon him. Ferrers then spoke as follows, and the Clerk repeated what he had said:

> My Lords, I must acknowledge myself infinitely
> obliged for the fair and candid trial your Lordships
> have indulged me with. I am extremely sorry that
> I have troubled your Lordships with a defence that
> I was always much averse to, and has given me the
> greatest uneasiness; but was prevailed on by my family

---

* According to Horace Walpole many peers were absent. Lord Foley and Lord Jersey attended the first day only. Lord Huntingdon and Lord Oxford withdrew without voting, because of their family connections.

to attempt it, as it was what they themselves were persuaded of the truth of; and had proposed to prove me under the unhappy circumstances that had been ineffectually represented to your Lordships.

This defence has put me off what I proposed, and what perhaps might have taken off the malignity of the accusation; but as there has been no proof made to your Lordships, can only be deemed at this time my own assertion; but that I must leave to your Lordships.

My Lords, I have been informed that this intention of the family before; and your Lordships, I hope, will be so good to consider the agony of mind a man must be under, when his liberty and property are both attacked; my Lords under these unhappy circumstances, though the plea I have attempted was not sufficient to acquit me to your Lordships, according to the Laws of this country: yet I hope your Lordships will think that malice, represented by the Council for the Crown, could not subsist; as I was so unhappy as to have no person present at the time of the fatal accident, it was impossible for me to show your Lordships that I was not at that instant possessed of my reason. As the circumstances of my case are fresh in your Lordships' memories, I hope your Lordships will, in compassion to my infirmities, be kind enough to recommend me to his Majesty's clemency.

My Lords, as I am uncertain whether my unhappy case is within the late Act of Parliament, if your Lordships should be of opinion that it is, I humbly hope that the power of respiting the execution will be extended in my favour, that I may have an opportunity of preparing myself for the great event, and that my friends may be permitted to have access to me.

If anything I have offered should be thought improper, I hope your Lordships will impute it to the great distress I am under at this juncture.

The Lord High Steward then addressed Ferrers thus:

Laurence Earl Ferrers, His Majesty from his Royal and equal regard to justice, and his steady attention to our constitution, (which hath endeared him in a wonderful manner to the universal duty and affection of his subjects) hath commanded this enquiry to be made, upon the blood of a very ordinary subject, against your Lordship, a peer of this realm; your Lordship hath been arraigned; hath pleaded, and put yourself on your Peers; and they (whose judicature is founded and subsists in wisdom, honour, and justice) hath found your Lordship unanimously guilty of the felony and murder charged in the indictment. It is usual, my Lord, for Courts of Justice before they pronounce the dreadful sentence ordained by the Law, to open to the prisoner the nature of the crime of which he is convicted, not in order to aggravate or afflict, but to awaken the mind to due attention to, and consideration of, the unhappy situation into which he hath brought himself.

My Lord, the crime of which your Lordship is found guilty, murder, is incapable of aggravation; it is impossible, but that, during your Lordship's long confinement, you must have reflected upon it, represented to your mind in its deepest shades, and with all its train of dismal and detestable consequences.

As your Lordship hath received no benefit, so you can derive no consolation from that refuge you seemed almost ashamed to take, under a pretended insanity; since it hath appeared to us all, from your cross-examination of the King's witnesses, that you recollected the minutest circumstances of facts and conversations, to which you and the witnesses only could be privy, with the exactness of a memory more than ordinary found; it is therefore as unnecessary as it would be painful to me, to dwell longer on a subject so black and dreadful.

It is with much more satisfaction, that I can remind your lordship, that though, from the present tribunal before which you now stand, you can receive nothing but strict and equal justice, yet you are soon to appear before an Almighty Judge, whose unfathomable wisdom is able, by means incomprehensible to our narrow capacities, to reconcile Justice with Mercy; but your Lordship's education must have informed you, and you are now to remember such beneficence is only to be obtained by deep contrition, sound, unfeigned, and substantial repentence.

Confined strictly as your Lordship must be, for the very short remainder of your life; according to the provision of the late Act; yet, from the wisdom of the legislature, which to prevent as much as possible this horrid Offence of Murder, hath added Infamy to Death: you will still, if you please, be entitled to converse and communicate with the ablest divines of the Protestant Church, to whose care and consolation, in fervent prayer and devotion I most cordially recommend your Lordship. Nothing remains for me, but to pronounce the dreadful sentence of the Law; and the judgment of the Law is, and this High Court doth award; that you, Laurence Earl Ferrers, return to the prison of the Tower from whence you came; from thence you must be led to the place of execution on Monday next, being the 21st day of this instant April; when you come there, you must be hanged by the neck till you are dead, and your body must be dissected and anatomised; and may God Almighty be merciful to your soul.

Ferrers cried out, 'God forbid.' However he almost immediately resumed his composure and added the words, 'God's will be done.'[38]

Last Days

Because of his rank, Ferrers's execution was respited until 5 May. Many versions exist of Ferrers's conduct and behaviour during the period that elapsed between the trial and execution and some of these must be treated with reserve. The story of the wicked earl must have been recounted to many children, to illustrate the inevitable reckoning in store for the wilful and the bully, and as a moral story it was usual to emphasize the badness of Ferrers, and to dismiss his madness as an unworthy and fanciful excuse. He was not 'mad', merely 'bad'. One such account maintains that Ferrers showed no signs of remorse for what he had done and that on the very night of his sentence he played piquet with his warders, insisting on playing for money, and would have renewed the gamble every evening, but that they refused and that the thing which seemed to occupy most of his thoughts was the desire that his allowance of wine should be increased 'for' he said 'what I have is not a draught.' Furthermore, at one time, he actually proposed to take his leave of his four illegitimate daughters on the scaffold, and to read to them a denunciation of his wife for obtaining from the House of Lords the Act of Separation: however to the advantage of common decency he was persuaded to give up this idea.[39] It is, however, a fact, that he was visited at the Tower by his cousin, the Dowager Countess of Huntingdon, who was much concerned for his eternal soul. She it was who brought his four children to him on the day before his execution when 'he took a cool farewell of them.'[40] He also purported to make a Will, leaving £1,300 to Sarah Johnson, £1,000 to each of his four daughters and an annuity of £60 to Margaret Clifford. However, as the Will was executed after his conviction, it was invalid.

'Sir Ferrers Executed'

At the same time work commenced on the erection of the scaffold under the gallows at Tyburn (now Marble Arch). The method of hanging had not changed since medieval times and involved the barbarous use of a cart, ladder, and three-cornered gibbet.[41] At a given signal, the horse and cart were driven away, leaving the victim suspended. Death ensued not by breaking the neck, but by slow and painful strangulation, although the executioner generally hastened the process, and shortened the agony by jerking down the body. Part of the new scaffold, about one yard square, was raised 18 inches above the floor, with a device which caused it to drop down when a rope was pulled. One nineteenth century source maintained that Ferrers's family, not wishing that he should be swung into eternity like a plebeian felon, instructed George Cole, the family undertaker, to design and construct the contrivance which was referred to as 'the new drop', and thereafter it was taken into general use.[42] Ferrers had written to King George II, begging that he might suffer beheading like his ancestor the Earl of Essex, on Tower Hill. He had hoped to the last that his petition would be granted, and felt confident because he had the honour of quartering part of the same arms as the King and of being related to his Majesty. Nothing came of it of course, and to the end he thought it hard, 'that he must die at the place appointed for the execution of felons.'

Margaret Clifford and the four children, had taken lodgings in Tower Street and daily messages had been passed between them. Perhaps because she was a potential witness for the Crown, but more likely because of her situation as his mistress, Margaret Clifford was never permitted to see Ferrers. However, he was allowed to receive visits from the children. On 5 May, the journey from the Tower to Tyburn took two and three quarter hours because of the enormous crowds. Ferrers was permitted to travel in his own coach and six, with his coachman weeping openly. Mr Sheriff Vallaint joined Ferrers in the Landau, as did the Reverend Humphries, the Chaplain to the Tower. Ferrers was dressed in his light-coloured wedding suit, explaining to the Sheriff, 'You may perhaps, Sir, think it strange to see me in this dress, but I have my particular reasons for it.' He was, no doubt, making the point that his marriage had been the cause of his death. All he said during that trying journey, and perhaps some things he never said, were avidly recorded, and his remarks seemingly throw some light on his mental condition. One account records that on seeing the enormous crowds he quipped, 'They have never seen a Lord hanged and perhaps will never see another.' He also observed that the apparatus of death, and the passing through such crowds of people, were ten times worse than death itself.[43] As to the crime of which he had been convicted he declared, 'that he was under particular circumstances, that he had met with so many crosses and vexations, he scarce knew what he did.'[44] He protested most solemnly that he bore no ill will against Johnson. Perhaps, in these two short sentences, he gave the most succinct description of his illness.

'This Horrid Lunatic'

Ferrers was regarded by his fellow peers with detestation. Certainly the military presence at the execution was unnecessary, because nobody had any inclination to rescue him. Horace Walpole (1717–1797) sums up the scene with cynical wit. 'This extraordinary history of Lord Ferrers is closed. He was executed yesterday. Madness, that in other countries is disorder, is here a systematic character; it does not hinder people from forming a plan of conduct, and from even dying agreeably to it. You remember how the last Ratcliffe died with the upmost propriety; so did this horrid lunatic, cooly and sensibly. His own and his wife's relations had assented that he would tremble at last. No such thing; he shamed heroes. With all his madness he was not mad enough to be struck with Lady Huntingdon's sermons. The Methodists have nothing to brag of his conversion, though Whitfield prayed for him and preached about him. I have not heard that Lady Fanny dabbled with his soul.'[45]

Ferrers, however, was completely sane on the day of his execution. Even when allowance is made for the cheapness of life in the eighteenth century, Ferrers's conduct and composure showed personal courage of outstanding quality. It was traditional for peers of the realm to face death with dignity on such occasions, and Ferrers would have remembered the executions of Lords Kilmarnock, and Balmarino, following the 1745 rebellion and Lord Lovat in 1757. Not only did he show no fear, but he remained courteous, affable, humorous, and cooperative with the Sheriff, and engaged in discourse with the Chaplain, without in any way retracting his long-held personal religious beliefs. So that when Mr Humphries, in an endeavour to extract some confession or acknowledgement of contrition for the crime, sought him to say what he could in the short time remaining, because the world would be inquisitive concerning the religion he professed, Ferrers replied with some impatience: 'Sir, what have I to do with the world, I am going to pay a forfeit life, which my country has thought proper to take from me? What do I care now, what the world thinks of me?' He had made arrangements to bid farewell to Margaret Clifford, who was waiting for him in a coach near to Tyburn. When he requested the Sheriff to halt the procession for this purpose, he was easily dissuaded and the Sheriff promised to deliver a notebook and some guineas to her. Towards the end of the long journey he expressed the wish to the Sheriff that his body might be buried at Breedon or Staunton Harold. On arrival at Tyburn he mounted the scaffold, which had been draped with two hundred and fifty five and three quarter feet of black baize, at a cost of £21.6s.3d (around £2,000 in present values), which was included in the funeral account.[46] The hangman was Thomas Turlis, who with his assistant, asked Ferrers's forgiveness. He granted this, and at the same time handed five guineas mistakenly to the assistant hangman. This resulted in a disgraceful dispute between Turlis and his assistant, which had to be terminated by the Sheriff. Ferrers eventually repeated the Lord's prayer, and was heard to pray for forgiveness. He stepped on to the raised part of the scaffold, where the noose was placed around his neck and a cap drawn over his eyes. He said, 'Am I right?' and on the Sheriff giving the signal, (Ferrers himself had refused to give one), 'that part upon which he stood instantly sank down from beneath his feet, and left him entirely suspended. For a few seconds his Lordship made some struggles against the attacks of death, but was soon eased of all pain by the pressure of the executioner. From the time of

35

his Lordship's ascending upon the scaffold, until his execution, was about eight minutes during which time his countenance did not change, nor did his tongue falter.'[47] There appears to be no foundation for the oft repeated statement that Ferrers was hanged with a silken cord, although he wished that such a halter could have been used.[48] 'There was', says Horace Walpole, 'a new contrivance for sinking the stage under him, which did not play well; and he suffered a little by the delay, but was dead in four minutes.'[49]

Symbolic dissection

After hanging for an hour as was customary, 'the coffin was raised up with the greatest decency to receive the body' which was taken away in the hearse to Surgeons' Hall, where it was dissected and anatomized, 'according to the sentence', and 'a large incision was made from the neck to the bottom of the breast and another across the throat, the bottom part of the belly was opened up, and the entrails removed. They were examined by the surgeons and found to be remarkably sound. In fact, in the whole course of their practice, they had never seen such obvious signs of longevity in any subject they had anatomised.'[50] The body was then exhibited to the public in an upstairs room, in the coffin, which was stood upright for the purpose. An armed soldier was posted at the top of the stairs and two of the undertaker's men, 'in black' watched over the body day and night from Monday to Thursday. On Thursday evening six men called, 'to put the body in order for soldering'; but the surgeons prohibited it until the Friday.

Private Burial – a promise fulfilled

Eventually the body was released and the coffin was soldered down by the undertaker's men in the library. Thence the cortège proceeded to St Pancras Church, (old St Pancras Church, Pancras Road, N1) where the body was interred below the belfry at 2 a.m. on the Saturday.[51] The Burial Register briefly recalls, 'Burials An Dom. 1760. May 10 Earl Ferrers. Hang'd for Murder.'[52] The funeral service was conducted by 'Mr Ford', who was not the vicar of the parish. According to the funeral account, after the burial, six men went to St Pancras on two occasions to remove the body. The Honourable Robert Shirley, Ferrers's younger brother, had promised Ferrers that his body would be interred in the vault at Staunton Harold. Robert succeeded to the Earldom in 1778 and on 3 June 1782 his promise was honoured.[53] The following verse (in imitation of the Duke of Buckingham's epitaph, *'Dubius sed non improbus vixi'*) was found in Ferrers's chamber at the Tower of London:

> *In doubt I lived, in doubt I die,*
> *Yet stand prepared the vast abyss to try,*
> *and undismayed expect eternity.*[54]

Was Kirkland present at the execution? There is no direct evidence that he was. However, he was a man of his word and he had promised Ferrers that he would be there. He also retained a print of the execution entitled 'A correct view of the Scaffold, gibbet and manner of execution of Lawrence Shirley, late Earl Ferrers at Tyburn for the barbarous murder of Mr Johnson, his Lordship's steward. Drawn from the spot at the time of his execution.' This was signed by Kirkland. Kirkland built up, during his life, a museum which he passed onto his son Thomas John, which may have contained the rope used. The undertakers could have removed the halter from the coffin before soldering it down. Kirkland's copy of the trial before the House of Lords, which he signed on the first page and initialled at the end, was acquired by the late Mr John Thomas Hood, of Ashby-de-la Zouch, who presented it to the author.

National effect

Mary Grose, of The Priory, St Helen's, Isle of Wight kept a diary from 1760 and her contemporary account illustrates the profound effect Ferrers's trial and execution had upon Georgian England:

> Sir Ferrers executed, Monday 5 May 1760, for shooting his steward was hanged in his wedding clothes which were white cloth embroidered with silver, and white silk stockings.
> Hanged at Tyburn. He went in his own landau of six attended by the sheriffs, one was with him, he was guarded by a party of Horse and Foot and Constables of Middlesex. A black coach of six, a hearse and six followed.

When he mounted the stage he knelt for about three minutes with the clergyman, whom it was said to be his brother, then was executed where he hanged a full hour, was then put in a shell not undressed and carried to Surgeon Hall'[55]

It could indeed be germane to suggest that the trial and execution may have been a factor in ensuring that no French Revolution occurred in England subsequent to 1789. If a Lord could be hanged at Tyburn, like any other felon, there was not much wrong with the law. Certainly, the Counsel appearing for the Crown at the trial all attained great distinction in their profession. Sir Charles Pratt became Chief Justice of the Common Pleas, and was created Baron Camden in 1765. He was appointed Lord Chancellor in the following year, and Lord President of the Council in 1784, when he was created Viscount Bayham and Earl Camden. Sir Charles Yorke also became Lord Chancellor, but died before the patent confirming to him the title of Baron Morden had been completed. George Perrott (1710–1780) was made a Judge in 1763, and later became a Baron of the Exchequer. He was never knighted and was not considered to be a profound lawyer. Horace Walpole maintained that while on circuit he 'was so servile as to recommend' from the bench a congratulatory address to the King on the Peace of 1763. He is chiefly remembered for his curious power of discrimination, which is illustrated by the conclusion of his summing up in a trial at Exeter as to the right of a certain stream of water: 'Gentlemen, there are fifteen witnesses who swear that the watercourse used to flow in a ditch on the north side of the hedge. On the other hand, Gentlemen, there are nine witnesses who swear that the watercourse used to flow on the south side of the hedge. Now, Gentlemen, if you subtract nine from fifteen there remain six witnesses wholly uncontradicted; and I recommend that you give your verdict for the party who called those six witnesses.'[56]

Fletcher Norton (1716–1789), was a famous advocate who prosecuted Eugene Aram for murder. Some regarded him as a hectoring lawyer, and he was nicknamed, 'Sir Bull-face double fee', in satires and caricatures. He was attacked by Junius in letter 39. He was MP for Appleby and for Wigan, Solicitor General (1761), Attorney General (1763), and Speaker of the House of Commons (1769–1782). He was created Lord Grantley, Baron of Markenfield (1782).[57] Henry Gould (1710–1794), was a Bencher of the Middle Temple by 3 May 1754, and became a Sergeant-at-Law and a Baron of the

Exchequer Court in 1761, and a Judge of the Court of Common Pleas in 1763.[58]

'A Providential Circumstance'

In *The Story of Ashby-de-la Zouch* Scott quotes from *Links with the past* by Mrs Charles Bagot.[59] The story had been told to her by William, Second Lord Bagot, when he was a very old man, and had been related to him by Kirkland himself. She recounted how, on 18 January 1760, Kirkland went with a friend to a meeting of gentlemen at a neighbouring village. After dinner, Kirkland and his friends returned to Ashby on horseback. During the journey Kirkland stopped to allow his horse to drink whilst his companions continued their journey. Kirkland felt himself in a trance, and was roused by a magnificent funeral procession, with the hearse bearing the Ferrers Coat of Arms. He hastened after his companions, asking them if they had seen the procession. No one had. When he returned to Ashby he received a message to proceed immediately to Staunton Harold. This story is completely at variance with Kirkland's narrative and his evidence at the trial, where he stated that he received the message at Coleorton at about 5 p.m. and proceeded to Staunton Harold from there via Lount. What really happened is recorded in the *Gentlemen's Magazine*, from a contribution by Richard George Robinson, dated 17 February 1798 which reads as follows:

> An ingenious correspondent has sent me the following
> remarkable anecdote: 'The death of my late worthy
> and ingenious friend Dr Kirkland leaves me at liberty
> to relate a remarkable circumstance that happened to
> him on 18 January 1760, the day on which a noble
> Earl shot his steward and probably about the time the
> murder was committed. The Doctor had promised to
> visit a friend that afternoon at Coleorton, and while
> he was riding over Coleorton Moor, he suddenly had
> the idea of being before the House of Lords giving
> evidence in a case of murder. He continued about five
> minutes, and he thought no more of it until one of the
> servants came to tell him at the house of his friend, that
> Lord— had sent to him to go to S— H— immediately
> when, the recollection of it rushing into his mind, he
> instantly declared it to be his opinion that his Lordship

had shot Mr—. Instead therefore of going directly to S— H—, he went to a place called the Lount, about half a mile beyond it, where Mr— resided and where his opinion was confirmed.' He has frequently told me he considered the circumstance a providential one as it put him upon his guard, the condition and temper of the unhappy Earl rendering it necessary for him to act with the greatest caution. Some years ago I asked his permission to publish it in your valuable miscellany, which he granted, but desired me to defer it till after his death.

Richard George Robinson, Lichfield, 17 February.[60]

Epilogue

Johnson's house at Lount is a fine example of late seventeenth century domestic architecture. It was tenanted by Johnson's family and descendents for over two hundred years, when it was purchased from the Ferrers' estate by a member of the family who still retains it.

Margaret Clifford's father, Richard Clifford, made a Will on 1 July 1762, appointing his 'loving wife Margaret' and his son Richard, executors and, 'plese God my loving wife dies the stock to be valued and disposed of at my Executors' discretion'. The witnesses were John Knowles, William Paget and Daniel Hatton. The Will was sworn on 6 July 1770, on probate being granted.[61]

Ferrers's younger brother, the Honourable Washington Shirley, who had entered the navy at an early age and was a Captain in the Royal Navy, took his seat in the House of Lords on 19 May 1760, as 5th Earl Ferrers. The attainder of his brother being for felony did not forfeit the titles which were protected by the statute *De Donis,* though it would have been otherwise if he had been attainted of treason, or if it had been a case of a barony in fee simple.[62] He was elected a fellow of the Royal Society on 14 December 1761 for his observations on the transit of Venus and 'other useful discoveries tending to the improvement of mathematical knowledge.'[63]

An Inquisition into the 4th Earl's Estate took place at Towcester on 19 October 1761. The liabilities amounted to £7,000, of which £1,548 was due to Countess Ferrers under the Act of Separation. In response to a petition by the 5th Earl whose 'income being very scanty and not sufficient to support the dignity devolved upon him',[64] King George III by letters patent dated 6 December 1763, 'in consideration of the many eminent and faithful services to us and our royal predecessors', restored to the 5th Earl the estates of the 4th Earl, which had been forfeited on his conviction for murder. These letters patent contained a proviso that the estate should remain subject to all liabilities incurred by the 4th Earl, and also to the terms of the Deed Poll dated 16 February 1760 in favour of his natural children, and also the deed of gift dated 12 March 1760 in favour of Johnson's children.[65] The 4th Earl's four daughters each subsequently acknowledged receipt of £500, so it would seem that the Deed Poll of 12 March 1760 was also honoured by the 5th Earl. No payment from the estate was made to Margaret Clifford, but she was, no doubt, provided for by her children. Her tombstone in Breedon churchyard would indicate that her family held her in affection and regard, although the mores of the time prevented them from identifying themselves or even acknowledging their own existence. Of the 4th Earl's daughters, Margaret married Philip Godkin, gent, of Melbourne, Derbyshire, where there is a memorial in the Parish Church to their thirteen-year-old daughter Mary, who died on 6 February 1783; Anna Maria married John Louis Pasteur, who is also remembered in the same church. Pasteur died on 2 August 1782 aged twenty-eight, whilst Anna Maria survived until 26 January 1819; their grandson, John Lewis Pasteur, died on 22 May aged seventeen and a memorial in the churchyard was erected to him by his three surviving sisters Ann, Sarah, and Elizabeth; Elizabeth married Samuel Leech, a linen draper of Bread Street, Cheapside, London; Mary remained a spinster, living at Melbourne until her death in August 1823. Margaret Clifford, their mother, also resided at Melbourne until her death.[66]

Lady Ferrers married Lord Frederick Campbell, Lord Clerk Register of Scotland, on 28 March 1769 and was accidentally burnt to death while reading in bed, at Coombe Bank, Sundridge, Kent on 26 July 1807 aged 71. The 5th Earl attained the rank of Vice-Admiral of the White, and died at Chartley on 2 October 1778. He sold the family estates at Ashwell, Brailsford and Shirley and out of the proceeds rebuilt the house at Staunton Harold in its present Palladian style.[67]

The 5th Earl left no issue nor did his brother Robert. The present Earl is descended from the 4th Earl's youngest brother the Revd Walter Shirley.

The Bloody Hand

One last popular misconception can be disposed of by the following quotation from the late Mr H. J. Wain's *The Story of Staunton Harold*:

> There is an absurd legend that as a consequence of this crime a 'bloody hand' was painted on the family coat of arms, and it was believed that this could only be removed if someone could be found willing to renounce the world and live as a hermit or anchorite for a specified period of years. According to another version, one finger of the 'hand' was wiped out on the accession of each successive holder of the title.
>
> These stories found widespread belief in local circles, and it was useless to explain that the 'bloody hand' was in reality the 'red hand' of Ulster which was added to the coats of arms of all baronets after the Order had been created by James I in 1611.
>
> The number of baronets was limited by the King to 200, and Sir George Shirley, ancestor of Earl Ferrers, was fourth on the list to receive this honour. Each applicant for this hereditary title had to provide 30 foot soldiers for three years at eightpence per day for the settling of Ulster (hence the 'red hand'). Most of the applicants however compounded for a single payment of £1,095.[68]

Thomas Kirkland MD –
The Respectable Leech

The medical writer

Kirkland's first medical work was entitled *A Treatise on Gangrenes*, and was published in 1754. In the seventeenth century the use of Cinchona was introduced from the New World. The bark of the Cinchona tree was taken as remedy by the aborigines. It was introduced into Europe by Jesuit missionaries and became known as Jesuit's Bark, which had been popularized by Thomas Sydenham.[1] Cinchona is the plant from which quinine is derived, and it became the standard practice in Kirkland's time to divide fevers into those which responded to Cinchona and those which did not. Kirkland had doubts as to the efficacy of Cinchona in the treatment of gangrene, and seems to have adopted a scientific approach to the use of the bark. Quinine was not isolated from Cinchona until early in the nineteenth century. Accordingly Cinchona was administered in powder form or it was burned in the sick room. When, in the Walcheren Expedition (1809), the British troops succumbed to Walcheren fever (now known to be Malaria), the powdered bark was so unpalatable that an issue of gin or brandy accompanied the medicine. 'Against relapses of fever was no security unless the patient continued to take an ounce of the powder every ten or twelve days throughout the autumn. The most effectual way to make a soldier continue taking it in order to prevent a relapse is to infuse it in gin or brandy.'[2]

The Respected Physician and Surgeon

Following the trial and execution of the 4th Earl Ferrers, Kirkland

44

had become a nationally known figure, but he had only published one medical work. He continued writing on a wide range of medical subjects from 1763 until his death. He was a hard worker, and a prolific writer, and throughout his published works he laments the lack of formal teaching for surgeons, and the separation of the profession into physicians and surgeons. The surgeons carried out surgery and, despite considerable advances made in the eighteenth century, operations were often a question of last resort because of the limitations imposed by the absence of anaesthetics. Obstetrics and the treatment of venereal disease were also dealt with by the surgeons. Surgery was cursed by the constant fear of sepsis, which led to many cases of death and suffering, and surgeons were for this reason reluctant to perform many operations that would be regarded as trivial today.[3] The great surgeons were speedy, dextrous and cautious. Kirkland, who sought to calm his patients by making use of a red tourniquet and a very small knife when operating, wrote 'Surely suffering the medical practice of surgery to degenerate is disgraceful to the science and highly injurious to society. For he who omits to inform himself in the methods of preventing operations will perform more than are necessary, and many a limb which might, I am persuaded, have been saved, has been taken off, because the operator had never attended properly to the art of healing. Every blockhead can amputate a leg: but how much more praiseworthy is he, whose skill enables him to effect a cure, and preserve a limb', and 'the chief mistake committed by medical surgeons is leaving off their studies just when they have qualified themselves for pursuing them.'[4]

Surgeons in Kirkland's time, except those who held appointments at major hospitals or were members of the Royal College, had no formal training. Physicians, on the other hand, had some tuition in anatomy and the opportunity to study through dissection of the human body. Treatment of illness by drugs must have relied on remedies used by repute or custom and without the knowledge to purify or assay. In his writings, Kirkland advocated a combined training for physicians and surgeons, and recommended a period of practical application before commencing in general practice. This method of training was eventually introduced by the Medical Act of 1858. Kirkland had a good knowledge of anatomy, and seems to have taken every opportunity available to him to perfect the art. He was very observant, and appears to have adopted a generally conservative approach to treatment, because he advocated light dressings for ulcers and ulcerated wounds, rather than the corrosive ointments of the local untrained surgeons. To him is attributed the invention and preparation of 'Kirkland's neutral cerate' as a healing ointment. All his life, Kirkland worked among the colliers of Coleorton, Measham, and Oakthorpe, and gained much experience in the treatment of fractures and dislocations. In 1763 he published, *An Essay on the methods of suppressing haemorrhages and divided arteries*, and in 1767 another, *Towards the improvement in the cure of diseases which are the cause of fevers*, in which he discussed the application of cold air and cold water in the treatment of fevers.

Two years later, he became an MD of St Andrews University, his testimonials having been signed by Erasmus Darwin[5] (1731–1802), a physician from Lichfield, and by John Davison, a physician from Nottingham. These physicians reported that, 'his long experience in pharmacy, his extensive and successful practice in surgery, the immediate connection between these branches of the profession with what is called medicine, his great industry and attention to every article, will abundantly justify you and recommend him to the public.' Kirkland did not submit a thesis to the University. Darwin is remembered for having declined an invitation to be physician-in-ordinary to King George III, and for being the grandfather of Charles Robert Darwin (1809–1882), the great naturalist and author of *The Origin of Species*.

In 1769 Kirkland wrote a reply to *Mr Maxwell's Answer to his Essay on Fevers, wherein the utility of the practice of compressing them is further exemplified*. In the following year, he wrote, *Observations on Mr Pott's general remarks on fractures etc. with a postscript concerning the cure of compound fractures*. Percivall Pott (1714–1788) was a surgeon at St Bartholomew's Hospital, London. He was a brilliant operator and a prolific writer and has given his name to Pott's Fracture and Pott's Disease. Pott took the view that if amputation was unavoidable, it should be carried out as soon as possible to reduce the incidence of infection. Kirkland preferred a wait and see policy, arguing that it was better to wait for the limb to 'slough off' and to amputate when the limb was dead and painless. In 1774 he wrote a *Treatise on child bed fevers* with 'two dissertations, the one on the brain and nerves and the other on the sympathy of the nerves etc.' Kirkland never accepted that puerperal fever was a separate disease, and his reasoning was entirely logical at a time when bacteriology was unknown.

The author is much indebted to Mr R. T. Austin, FRCS Ed, of the Leicester Royal Infirmary, for the following study of Kirkland's medical career.[6]

A writer of depth

Kirkland's daily professional life was busy, and his services were often in demand in the surrounding towns. Allowing for the pressure of work, his writings were notable for the variety of the subjects and the depth in which they were considered. His clinical descriptions were lucid, accurate, and usually diagnostic. The management that he describes, reveals him as being self-confident and optimistic.

A man between 20 and 30 years of age, being near
the lime-kiln at Ticknall, was knocked down with
lime-stone, from a blast, and one of the parietal bones
was so violently broken that when all the loose pieces
were removed an opening was made into the cranium
more than 7 inches in circumference. The quantity of the
cineritious part of the brain taken up from the ground
at the time of the accident filled a large pill box, which
the people had at the house, and a rough stone more
than half an ounce weight, which had penetrated the
substance, was removed at the first dressing.
　The man being unexpectedly alive, I went next
morning with my son to see him, and had I not have
known that lacerated wounds of the substance described
would, under particular circumstances, heal like wounds
in other parts of the body, I should have given up all
hope of recovery, so dreadful was the aspect; a bare
possibility of success encouraged us to pursue proper
treatment. We removed all the lacerated brain which
lay in the wound, and upon minute enquiry discovered
a still larger piece of stone forced lower down, which
was extracted by a pair of forceps. Much more of the
cineritious substance was discharged in the matter
the ulcer afforded at each dressing for some time, but
at last the ulcer became clean, and healed, leaving a
hemiplegia on the contrary side to that on which the
accident happened. Insensibility, stupor, and sleepiness
immediately followed the accident, but gradually went
off in a few days without one true apoplectic happening;
whereas if instead of being extravasated and discharged,
the fluids had been obstructed and accumulated within
the vessels belonging to the brain a coma and death
would probably have been the consequence.

On the lethal effect of raised intercranial pressure arising from a closed head injury:

A keeper in the forest of Needwood was set upon by some deer stealers, who beat him violently on the head with their weapons and he instantly became insensible, and hemiplegia seized his right side; he was delirious and slept without either snoring or sonorous respiration. Several days passed before I saw him, and as no surgical treatment had been pursued, I laid the skull bare but neither fracture nor fissure could be found. Suspecting the contents of the cranium to be injured, a trephine was applied on each side of the sagittal suture; the dura mater was found black from blood stagnating in its vessels and fibres, and distended by fluid underneath. Upon dividing this membrane with a lancet a considerable quantity of coagulated blood and bloody serum was discharged; nor did this kind of evacuation cease over a week or ten days, but at last gradually decreased, the patient got perfectly well, and was able to shoot his deer as usual, which I think would not have happened if pressure from extravasating blood had been capable of producing an apoplexy [sic]. In the present instance I look upon the insensibility and hemiplegia to be owing to concussion, because they immediately took place, and the discharge from the opening probably unloaded the vessels etc; and prevented putrefaction of the membranes and brains. Indeed I have opened the heads of several who died of fractured skull, in which the veins were turgid and more or less coagulated blood was found; and yet I do not remember having seen one of them die of the apoplectic symptoms described.

On an industrial disease:

We have in this neighbourhood pot kilns in which much lead is used. The workmen who powder the scoria of this mineral, are subject to the bellon and to paralysis of the limbs from swallowing the dust that arises in this operation, till it is almost impossible to conceive the quantity of lymph, which it secreted into, and became ropy in the stomach etc. and being coloured by the lead, is called by these artificers, sludge. I have several times seen both the colic, and the paralysis, cured by repeated vomiting and smart purchase; for a stronger purchase is required in this instance than in any I know of.

On serious bacterial infections:

But the most dangerous of all abscesses that belong to the abdomen, is the lumbar abscess, that forms in the ciliary membrane about the psoas muscle, and points in the thigh, groin, back, or sometimes at the anus. Of these patients, few, I believe, recover, nor indeed is it to be expected; as the source of the disease can seldom delay it drying, and the caries of the backbone is sometimes added to the malady. Some, however, I have seen survive these collections of matter, either tumour being suffered to break of itself and its contents to drain gently off through a very small aperture, which prevents the free ingress of air, and violent spasms; for when a large tumour of this sort forms on the inside of the thigh and breaks in a large opening in such a manner that the air has ready passage, we frequently see a violent colliquative fever succeed, but closes the scene in a very short time ... the greatest hope of recovery is when the matter is mild and good, owing to it perhaps being a common purulent abscess; whereas when it is seropurulent, it seems to indicate a scrofulous origin.

Notwithstanding Kirkland's mistaken view on the origin of the infection the summary that he produced is remarkably sound. Roughly ten years before, the surgeon Charles White (1728–1813) of Manchester had removed, by sawing, part of the upper shaft of the humerus of a sixteen-year-old boy with scrofula, and subsequently a further section of the shaft sloughed off spontaneously. Kirkland was familiar with this type of problem:

The shoulder is seldom affected with abscess of the joint, compared with their frequency in the hip; yet there are not wanting instances of abscesses in this part, either from foul bone or diseased ligaments; and of the head of the bone, either re-separating spontaneously,

49

or being removed by operation. There is now in the neighbourhood of Burton-on-Trent a man from whom the head of this bone and several injuries adjoining to it, came away by itself, when a boy. He was also cured by a common apothecary; the man has a useful arm, and the cicatrix shows the greatness and extent of the disease.

Kirkland had removed bone in cases of fracture:

The lower end of the radius and ulna, and the upper and lower end of the tibia and fibula, have been removed by myself and others, in compound dislocation with very little defect in the motion of the joint.

Richard Wiseman, surgeon to Charles II, first distinguished tuberculous disease of the joints as a 'white swelling' of the joints. Kirkland had his own views on the morbid anatomy of the disorder.

From dissections in these instances, it appears that the ligaments became much more swellen, thickened, and even pulpy. The cellular membrane is loaded with a viscid glairy lymph. Abscesses are formed in the neighbourhood of the joint and the joint itself is often full of seropurulent matter. The cartilages are eroded, and the ends of the bone carious. In the beginning, provided the disease is local, it comes on slowly without pain, and the parts within the capsular ligament are unaffected; the patient undergoes no great inconvenience, except from being incapable of using the limb. In length of time the joint becomes contracted, in consequence of the weakness of the extensor muscles, and the ascendancy of those who bend the limb.

Concern with obstetrics

Kirkland also wrote on obstetrics. Thus to Charles White of Manchester, a pioneer of antiseptic midwifery:

I must confess, Sir, I cannot approve of the modern doctoring, which asserts that the puerperal fever is a disease *sui generis*, and that it always arises from the same cause; this opinion I apprehend is liable to many objections and may be productive in consequence which we shall hereafter have occasion to mention.

I saw another woman lately, where part of the afterbirth had been brought away by force, and the part left behind; but from the account given me it does not appear that her attendant, or those about her, were apprehensive of anything being amiss till four or five days after when they were disappointed in the coming of her milk, though a quick pulse and fever were discovered, yet she was able to get up and notice her child, danger was not thought of till nearly a week after, when my assistance was desired. I found her dying, with flaccid breasts, a sore tender belly after having been troubled by what they called after-pain: and all the symptoms, except a looseness, which usually attended puerperal fevers.

And on the technical management of delivery:

The immediate extraction of the placenta, a practice in fashion when I was a pupil to Dr Smellie: I think I have seen again fatally, even in the hands of those, who frequently perform this operation . . . I was called to give my assistance in bringing away the afterbirth; but upon arrival, I found the woman dead and the uterus inverted, and I believe without any violence being used . . . I was desired to examine the vagina, where so firmly united, but it was impossible to separate them without the utmost deliberation, without lacerating the placenta, leaving part of it still joined to the womb.

A Musical Physician

A charming character study of Kirkland has been left to us by William Gardiner:

About the year 1788 I went to Dr Kirkland of Ashby-de-la Zouch with a friend who wished to consult him on a surgical case. He received us at breakfast in

51

a morning gown and crimson velvet cap; his whole figure put me in mind of the picture of Franklin. Dr Kirkland's skill in surgery was pre-eminent, but like many others he seemed not at all to estimate the talent which made him great, but attempted to distinguish himself in a science for which nature had not fitted him. Like Gainsborough, he would become a musician, and followed it with similar ardour. Such was his love of the art that by his support oratorios were commenced about the year 1770 at Ashby-de-la Zouch and regularly held in the autumn for a series of years at which my father frequently assisted. The Revd Mr Prior and his son were co-adjutators of the Doctor in these festivals, The Revd Mr Pixcel, Mr Tilley and the Valentines of Leicester, Hogg the basoon player and Foster, the obo, Masters of Rudgeley the celebrated Mr Savil and the choristers of Litchfield Cathedral formed the principal part of the orchestra. The music was entirely Handel's and the church performance was not made up of a selection of pieces, but each day an entire oratorio, the *Messiah*, *Joshua*, or *Saul* was performed and in the evening in the concert room, *Acis and Galatea*, *Alexander's Feast* and Boyce's *Solomon*.

In his conversation the Doctor was fond of using the vulgar accent of his neighbours, the colliers upon the Coleorton Moor, as his talents and genius gave him the licence to be singular. He was a prominent performer in the orchestra and maintained his part stoutly. When asked what his favourite instrument was, he used to reply, 'I am the first Hoboy player in Ashby, and the worst in all England, e-god, lad!' At these festivals the Doctor's house was filled for a couple of days with the principal families of the neighbourhood. Music in this way was a fashionable amusement.[7]

Kirkland made a similar impression on The Revd William Bagshaw Stevens (1756–1800), the disillusioned Headmaster of Repton School, domestic chaplain to Sir Robert Burdett, scholar, wit and minor poet, who by idleness and neglect of his duties was reputed to have reduced the school to one boy at the time of his death, and to have died of a fit of apoplexy, following immoderate laughter at the antics of a monkey attending an Italian organ-grinder on Repton High Street.[8] Kirkland's niece Ann Dalby, daughter of John Dalby of Castle Donington, solicitor to the school governors, was a favourite guest at the house of the headmaster and his sister W B Stevens.[9] Stevens met Kirkland when he was preaching at Stanton-by-Bridge in 1793, and commented, 'a stranger would take that respectable leech to be a mere charlatan. His tongue drops manna. I do not mean that he is an eloquent man.' Again, Stevens was stuck by Kirkland's 'blunt style', as when he addressed a patient, a Miss Biddulph, who had returned from Sussex unwell, 'Zoons, madam, your blood is as bad as the Devil'. Later that year Stevens records, 'Preached at Foremark – ditto in the evening at Stanton. Dr Kirkland there – G G no better.* His wife's prudence cannot impose on his abstinence from the bottle. Kirkland says his disorder will terminate in the gout. A happy issue!'[10]

'Many Sick Folk . . . had recourse to him'

Certainly by 1770, Kirkland was regarded as a consultant. The accounts for the overseers of the poor for the parish of Nailstone record that the local surgeon John Power who practised at Market Bosworth and who inoculated the poor of the parish before Jenner[11] introduced vaccination, sent to Ashby-de-la Zouch to consult Kirkland who received a fee of one guinea. Some years later the parish paid Power £8 for a whole year's work and his regular charge was 3s 6d per visit (double at night!)[12]

In 1774 Kirkland published *Animadversions on a late Treatise of the Kink-Cough* to which is annexed an essay on that disorder. Kink-Cough was whooping cough and the organism that causes the disease was not discovered until 1906 when Bordet and Gengou isolated *haemophilus pertussis*[13].

In May 1777 Kirkland joined the Medical Society of Edinburgh and later that of London. Subsequently he wrote *Thoughts on amputation* and *An essay on the inseparability of the different branches of medicine*. These were followed by his great work *An inquiry into the present state of medical surgery* (1783) in two volumes. An appendix to this work was published posthumously in 1813 by his son James Bate Kirkland then surgeon apothecary

---

* Rev George Greaves BA (1747-1828) Rector of Stanton-by-Bridge, Derbyshire, 1770-1828. Vicar of Alstonfield, Staffs, 1775-1801, Rector of Swarkestone, Derbyshire, 1795-1828.

to the Tower of London. His interests were so wide that in 1792 at the age of seventy he wrote *A commentary on the apoplectic and paralitic affections and the diseases connected with the subject.*

The Humble Student

Despite all he achieved in his long and distinguished career Kirkland remained humble and always a student. Thus in the dedication to his *Inquiry into the present state of medical surgery* addressed to the Earl of Huntingdon he wrote 'Thirty-six years have now elapsed since I was first honoured with the patronage and friendship of your noble family; and now like the Navigator who after failing in quest of knowledge returns to communicate his discoveries I from gratitude dedicate to your Lordship the result of my observation and experience.'[14] His aim was to recommend the surgery branch of the profession. His object was to assist nature without harming the patient and to lessen the necessity of manual operation. In 1783 he was asked by Sir Henry Harpur of Calke Abbey, Derbyshire to investigate a serious and fatal disease in his cattle, probably contagious bovine pleuropneumonia. In his observations he stressed that the aim of medicine was not to cure disease – some diseases being incurable – but 'the chief hope is in preventing its happening. This indeed is the most desirable part of medicine, and in the present instance it seems capable of being accomplished'.[15]*

The Public Spirited Citizen

In addition to his love of music Kirkland had wide local interests. He was one of the subscribers to the formation of an agricultural society for the County under the presidency of Lord Rawdon on 2 April 1788. Other members included Colonel (later Sir Charles) Hastings and such important local gentry as Messrs Abney of Measham, Bakewell of Dishley, Cave Brown of Stretton-en-le-Field and The Revd Gresley of Drakelow.[16] He also delighted himself and his close friends, by maintaining a large and beautifully maintained garden at the back of his house with a waterfall fed from the Hollywell Brook and 'adorned with numerous statues of heathen deities' at which

---

* Kirkland recorded that 'one hundred and nineteen (cows and heifers) were bled in all, ten of which died of swelled necks'.

during spring and summer he frequently acted as a generous host. He was a man of literary attainment and of benevolent disposition: a typical eighteenth century country gentleman.[17]

Nicholls the Leicestershire historian who was a contemporary of Kirkland wrote of him as follows:

> His memory will be for ever held in estimation by a numerous set of relations and friends, who can never forget his general hospitality, disinterestedness and benevolence . . . His different publications on many of the most material branches of this science, of the most melancholy and dangerous tendency to the patient and the unrivalled success of his doctrines in every part of the country have immortalised his fame and render every attempt at eulogium unnecessary and vain.[18]

The Kindly Master

Kirkland's kindly nature is illustrated by his attitude towards servants and animals. He employed one Joseph Hollingsworth for many years and he may well have been his companion during the dramatic events of 18 January 1760. He died on 1 January 1803 and was still in Kirkland's employment when the Doctor died in 1798. Hollingsworth drove Kirkland's Spanish gander, which lived to be over thirty , to pasture every day for over twenty-five years. There is something charming about the character of a man who employs a servant for fifty years and keeps a gander for twenty-five![19]

'Few Equals none Superior'

In 1794 John Raphael Smith, the portrait and miniature painter and mezzotint engraver[20], sketched Kirkland whilst he was writing out a prescription.* At the age of seventy-seven, while still engaged in

---

* Kirkland's prescription consisting of sea salt, water, and angustura bitters would seem at first sight to be a placebo. However, Epsom Salts were derived from sea water and when administered in small quantities was used as a mild aperient. Bitters were thought to act beneficially upon the system by imparting tone to the stomach, thus improving the appetite. Kirkland would seem to have been administering a general tonic.

active practice and working on his almost completed *Inquiry into the present state of medical surgery*, Kirkland himself was taken ill. Following about two months 'during which there appeared at times flattering hopes of his recovery' he died, 'being worn out he expired having endured his last sufferings with the patience and fortitude of a Christian and a philosopher'. His obituary notice in the *Gentlemen's Magazine* recorded that 'his whole life had been employed in the most unremitting attention to the study and practice of the duties of his profession and his genius shone most conspicuously in the science and practice of the various parts of medical surgery wherein he had few equals none superior.'[21] His funeral took place at St Helen's Church; three elder clergymen proceeded the coffin and six robed clergymen acted as pallbearers supported by his old friends Thomas Fisher and James Richards with other gentlemen and tradesmen of Ashby. There followed his sole surviving sister, his sons, daughters, grandchildren and other relations and 'a great concourse of people.' He was buried just to the west of the chancel but no monument was erected to his memory in the church for nearly sixty years. Kirkland survived his wife Dorothy by thirteen years.

The following poetic tribute was published in the *Gentlemen's Magazine*:

Lines sacred to the memory of the late Dr Kirkland

Mors sua quemque manet
Accept respected and lamented shade
These artless lines yet fraught with love for thee
Whose mem'ry holds her seat in this frail frame
What tho' thy healing pow'r (which oft has snatched
A father, mother, or relation dear,
From dreaded dissolution; – and which oft
The fever raging with increasing heat
Timely assuag'd) is now no more; yet still
Thy work, dear man, remains fresh in the breast
Of every feeling and afflicted soul;
But far more in the minds of those to whom
Thy bounteous care extended, they indeed
Inspir'd by gratitude, and pleasing thought
Of thy good deeds, will gladly speak thy praise.

Long didst thou shine midst thy contemporaries
With just and envy'd glory; till at last,
Stern death, sure end of all the human race,
Remov'd thee hence, and sent thee to receive
The blessings of a Merciful Redeemer![22]

Thomas John Kirkland 1760–1824 –
Tom the Second

A Diligent and successful practice

Thomas John Kirkland was born on 25 June 1760 at Ashby-de-la Zouch. He was the ninth child of Thomas and Dorothy Kirkland. Like his two elder surviving brothers Francis Bate Kirkland and James Bate Kirkland he was apprenticed to his father as a surgeon but unlike them he worked with his father visiting patients in his company and succeeding to the practice on his father's death in 1798. 'Tom' as he was generally known, was a sociable individual who clearly realized that his father was a difficult man to follow. He set about his profession by careful and meticulous study. He it was who commenced to write the *Kirkland Notes* in 1788. The notes are written in a hide-bound book in which are recorded the names and dates of death of local persons in alphabetical order under the heading of 'Deaths' but clearly not intended to be a record of the doctor's less successful achievements. There follows a similar but less extensive record of marriages and then singular matters of local and national interest. The records appear under the hand writings of Thomas John Kirkland from 1789 to 1799, his son Thomas Smith Kirkland from 1799 to 1864, his daughter-in-law, Hannah Kirkland, his granddaughter Lucy Bangham and his great granddaughter Alethea Bangham from 1865 onwards. Thomas John was never a physician and does not seem to have written any medical works. At the time of his father's death England was under threat of invasion by France. The British Army was under-manned and ill-equipped. The militia was increased from 45,000 to 100,000 and the volunteers went about their duties with great enthusiasm.

Active preparations were made for the struggle to come and a royal pavilion was built at Weedon in Northamptonshire to act as a headquarters for King George III in the event of London having to be evacuated in face of enemy attack. So Thomas John records that the Ashby infantry marched to church in their uniforms for the first time on 29 July 1798 and when Captain Needham gave an entertainment to the Infantry at the Lamb on 10 July 1799 the food cost £3.10s whilst the bill for ale amounted to £4.10s! When James Richards of the Mansion House died on 30 August of that year he was, as Captain of the Ashby Cavalry, buried with full military honours. John Simmonds of Butt House, Blackfordby, the farmer son-in-law of Joseph Wilkes, (1732–1805) inventor and pioneer in communications, spent £8.8s on cavalry business and 10s 6d for his militia subscription.[1] Thomas John had many and wide interests and was actively concerned in local affairs. He continued to reside and practise at his father's house in Market Street, Ashby-de-la Zouch and add to the museum there in which were to be found such objects as 'Sir Edward Verney's skull slain at Edge Hill, being the King's standard', 'twenty-seven halters that have hung several noted characters' and 'reptiles in spirits'. His assets included 'genteel household furniture, china, glass, books, gig harness, capital hunter, valuable museum and other effects'.[2]

Prize Fighting

Thomas John retained throughout his life a keen interest in sport. He entertained Daniel Mendoza, the celebrated pugilist, who dined with him on 11 December 1798. John Simmonds, was present on this occasion and watched Mendoza spar 'and spent the night with him at the White Hart.' Simmonds commented, 'I think him a very clever man.' Thomas John supped with Mendoza at the Tripe Club on 14 December and watched him spar at Ashby 'with a man by the name of Peter from Normanton on 2 January 1799.' It must indeed have been an occasion to have seen Mendoza. He was then thirty-five years of age and had been boxing for twelve years. He was of Jewish parentage, 5 feet 7 inches in height, had a well-formed chest, strong arms, great courage and good wind. He developed the style of boxing known as the 'School of Mendoza' and always contrived that his fights should be well-contested. He also promoted his image by making sparring tours around the country. Although old for a boxer when he visited Ashby, Mendoza continued to take part in prize fights for a further twenty-one years, not retiring until 1820. Boxing was a bare-fisted sport and fights were of unlimited duration. On 21 March 1806 Mendoza defeated Henry Lee at Grinstead Green in fifty-six rounds.[3]

The notes also refer to the famous fight between Tom Cribb (1771–1848) and Tom Molineaux at Crown Point, Thistleton Gap, near the Leicestershire, Rutland, Lincolnshire and Nottinghamshire border on 28 September 1811. Tom Cribb was a champion pugilist, originally fighting under the name of 'Black Diamond', winning his title on 7 January 1805 over seventy-six rounds. Tom Molineaux, an athletic American negro, challenged Cribb and they fought on 18 December 1810, when Cribb won after eighty-six rounds. Molineaux was not satisfied, so the re-match took place at Thistleton Gap. The fight was watched by 20,000 spectators, but in the ninth round Molineaux sustained a fractured jaw and was unable to stand in the eleventh round. Like Mendoza, Cribb was a fine sportsman and an ornament to pugilism.

Family and the French Connection

Thomas John married Mary, daughter of Nicholas Smith, an Atherstone surgeon. She bore him four children: the eldest Thomas Smith Kirkland also known as 'Tom' was also a surgeon and followed his father in the practice. Nicholas Smith Kirkland, the second child, known as 'Smith' was educated at Repton School and purchased a commission in the 27th regiment of foot, The Royal Inniskilling Fusiliers, and attained the rank of Captain.[4] He served with his regiment in the Peninsular War and his services were publicly acknowledged in the town following a 'patriotic feast'[5] held in the Market Place on 1 December 1813 'to celebrate the glorious victories obtained by the British and Allied Armies'. Despite his moment of glory, Nicholas Kirkland seems to have fallen on hard times after the war and was heavily in debt by 1831.[6] He married Mary Beavington, the daughter of a local wine and spirit purveyor, and they were certainly more successful in bringing up eleven children, none of whom died in infancy or childhood. Thomas John's third child, William Henry, became a surgeon and practised in Warrington. The fourth child Mary Ann married Louis François le Normant de Kergrist, a Lieutenant in the French Navy, who was a prisoner of war on parole at Ashby from 1806 to 1814. Marriage between English women and French prisoners of war was strongly discouraged by the Transport Board (the Government Department responsible for prisoners of war) who instructed agents that such 'pretended marriages' were 'nothing but concubinage' and informed all clergy that the marriages of French prisoners of war were not recognized by the French government. However, the Revd William McDouall, Vicar of Ashby, was an independent man and either paid little attention to these pronouncements or regarded them as erroneous – in which even he was proved to be correct, because in 1814 he furnished a certificate of this marriage to the French civil authorities, which was accepted without question. It seems strange that this marriage should have taken place at all, let alone that it proved to have been so happy and well suited. The ceremony took place at St Helen's Church, Ashby, on 4 June 1812 when Mary Ann was 23 and Kergrist 10 years her senior. One of the witnesses was Maria Chapman, a cousin of Mary Ann, and another was Louis Ulliac, an Ensign de Vaisseau who had been taken prisoner of war from a brig of war in 1804.[7] In 1811 Ulliac asked to be allowed to exceed the limits of Ashby-de-la Zouch to teach drawing, but the authorities refused despite support from the local gentry saying 'if complied with generally the prisoners would become dispersed over all parts of the country without any regular control over their conduct'.[8] Thomas John had been appointed surgeon to the French prisoners of war at the new Ashby Depot, which had been set up by the Transport Board in 1804. He was paid fees for attending individual prisoners by the Transport Board, receiving £20.2s.0 for the period of January to June 1806 and £11.17s. 6d for the period July to December of that year. For the year 1807 he was paid £40.6s. 6d.[9] Surgeons employed by the Transport Board at depots were required to sign each week the Board's Agent's list of sick prisoners before this was sent off to London. To this the surgeon had to attach his own account, setting out details of each prisoner, his complaint, period of nursing and date of attendance. All this had to be supported by an Affidavit.

The arrival of the first French prisoners of war is recorded in the notes under the date of 21 November 1804. The Ashby depot, like others in the country districts, was set up because the traditional system of parole and exchange of officers had broken down during the Napoleonic Wars. Previously depots were located near to London or the principal ports so that exchange could be effected speedily. When the war broke out again in 1803, following the short-lived peace of Amiens, which had been celebrated with an illumination in Ashby on 9 October

61

1801, the French invaded Hanover taking 17,319 officers and men of the Hanoverian army prisoners of war. The French government argued that these prisoners, who had all been released, were to be taken into account for the purpose of exchange. The British did not agree, maintaining that as the Hanoverians had not been under British command, Britain was under no obligation on their account merely because of the coincidence that the King of Great Britain also ruled in Hanover.[10] Consequently the government found itself faced with a situation in which hundreds of French officers were being lodged unguarded within a short distance of important military and naval installations and were in a position to support any invading force that might land. Furthermore, many of the French officers did not conform to the traditional pattern of 'officer and gentleman' which in earlier wars had been the norm. No longer was the breaking of parole regarded as a disgrace meriting disciplinary action by the officer's superior, and Napoleon on occasion even encouraged officers to break their parole, as when he supported Madame Lefrebre-Desnouettes when she travelled to England in disguise to aid the escape of her husband General Charles Lefrebre-Desnouettes in 1812. 'Let her go' he said, 'Let her go.' By 1811 there were about 100 officers and civilians on parole at Ashby[11] and another source maintains that there were 200 officers in the town at times.[12] The officers were billeted with the local people and at inns and were under the control of a civilian government agent and local grocer named Joseph Farnell, who was described by the painter, Colonel (later General) Louis François Baron Lejeune (1775–1848) as 'certainly the tallest, thinnest, and most cadaverous seller of dry goods in the world.' Le Jeune continues 'This worthy man, who seemed to move by clockwork, bowed politely, and proceeded to explain to me the routine to be followed by the prisoners. He gave me leave to lodge where I liked, and I was free to walk out of the town for one mile in any direction, but no further. Amongst the prisoners I found several distinguished naval officers, including Captain Hulliac, brother of a friend of mine, Captain Kergrise, with M. Boulan and Colonel Stoffel ... with many others. I determined to lose no time in mastering English, and I was working very hard at it when I received an invitation to form one of a party of guests at the residence of General Hastings, about a mile from Ashby. General Hastings was the brother of Lord Moira, the intimate friend of the Prince of Wales. General and Lady Hastings had given a home to Miss Moore, daughter of the celebrated General Sir John Moore, who was killed in Spain at the battle of Corunna. The young orphan who was a very bright, interesting and charming girl, was quite the life of the circle which her host and hostess gathered about them. The courtesy and kindness with which I was received did much to cheer my spirits, prisoner though I was.'

Shortly after he had settled in at Ashby, Le Jeune received a messenger from France who informed him that his escape could be effected. Le Jeune did not believe the offer to be genuine, but after clearing the details with Stoffel, he decided to accept it. 'I went to a merchant (negotiant) named Baudins, who had been very civil to me and whose frank ingenuous countenance had inspired me with confidence. I said to him straight out, "I have come to show you how I trust you." ' Le Jeune, in effect, asked him for a loan of 5,000 francs to facilitate his escape and the wine merchant arranged for it to be paid to him the next day in gold, free of interest! Le Jeune recounts: 'There was a ball that same evening at which my friend Mr Baudins and his daughter were present ... I did not go to speak to him all evening. But I danced with his daughter. Mr Farnell, the grocer, was there too, and never did I see anything more comic than the appearance this provincial dancer presented, with the air of proud reserve suitable to a man who had charge of the French prisoners. It was really quite worth a journey to England only to watch him.'

Le Jeune's memoirs are inaccurate in a number of details. General Sir Charles Hastings was not the brother to the Earl of Moira nor was there anyone in Ashby by the name of Baudins. However, Thomas Smith records that the Reverend William McDouall married Miss Gaudin on 7 February 1815. She would have been the daughter with whom Le Jeune danced. Her father, John Gaudin, was a Swiss Huguenot from the Canton of Vaud and had married a Scottish lady by name of Emma Euphemia McKenzie, and had set up business as a wine merchant in Wood Street, Ashby.[13] He had been initiated into the Tyrian Lodge of Freemasons, at Derby, on 28 July 1801, but never attended a meeting after 1803 and took no further masonic degrees in the Tyrian Lodge. Gaudin's wife died in 1805 and he died in 1817, having buried four of his children. The family misfortune continued because Gaudin's daughter, Euphemia, died in 1826, having borne the Vicar nine children in ten years. The Gaudin memorial in St

Helen's Churchyard, Ashby, contains the following tribute to Euphemia Gaudin:

> *Here lies in early years of life*
> *The best of mothers and the kindest wife*
> *Who neither knew or practised any art*
> *Her love for him still prevalent in death*
> *Prayd Heaven to bless him with her latest breath.*

It does seem extraordinary however, that such a prominent Ashby citizen should have been prepared to compromise his liberty and fortune by actively assisting a prisoner of war to escape. Perhaps his masonic principles outweighed his patriotic duty. However, Le Jeune took his leave from a grand dinner party given by Sir Charles and Lady Hastings at Willesley Hall to some of the French Officers but, instead of returning to his lodgings, he made his way with difficulty across the park on a very dark night to the place where he was to meet Stoffel and the French Emissary. No-one was there and he felt certain that he had mistaken the route. He waited there for an hour in dreadful suspense and at last heard rustling among the leaves near to him. He hid behind a bush until he could recognize Stoffel and the guide. They were then led to the first posting stage and two minutes later were comfortably seated in a stage coach. They passed rapidly through Northamptonshire and thence through London to Reigate and on to Hythe, arriving there the following night. The coast was strongly guarded and Le Jeune and Stoffel were advised to pretend that they were aged invalids there to take the waters. In the event more than two weeks passed before they were able to get a passage to Boulogne on a fishing smack, disguised as fishermen, an earlier attempt having nearly ended in disaster when they paid over all their money to a surly, ferocious looking smuggler named Brick, and were warned at the last moment by the woman at the house they were staying that Brick made a practice of murdering his passengers in the channel and dropping their weighted bodies over the side. Eventually Le Jeune landed in France and had an audience of Napolean and repaid Gaudin's loan. Gaudin's complicity in the escape was never revealed![14] This strange story was concluded by Gaudin being admitted, most unusually, to his remaining Masonic degrees in the French Prisoner of War Lodge – Les Vrai Amis de L'Ordre – at Ashby in 1814, being described in his Masonic certificate as possessing 'In a high degree all the qualities of a true and worthy Mason'.[15]

French Prisoners

The officers were required to assemble every day for roll call carried out by the agent and they were paid 1s. 6d a day if of superior substantive rank in the French Service. Inferior officers received one shilling a day and this caused resentment amongst those officers who held acting rank or were unable to produce evidence of their commissions. Farnell took up one of these complaints with the Transport Board, but was tartly informed that if the officer was not satisfied he could elect to be taken into close confinement. Farnell retained his office until the end of the War despite rebukes from the Transport Board for permitting prisoners to retain their arms, and for allowing 14s for a hatband for the funeral of one of the officers! These payments were the subject of acrimonious representations between Great Britain and France over many years, because no payment of any kind was made by the French Government to British prisoners of war. The prisoners were permitted to walk one mile from Ashby in any direction, but the permission of the agent was required for any journey in excess of that distance. The land between Upper Packington Road and Leicester Road on which Priorfields Estate is now built was popularly known as Frenchman's Fields. It seems likely that this restriction of movement was not always strictly enforced at Ashby because in 1811, as we have heard, General Sir Charles Hastings invited some French officers to dine with him at Willesley Hall and on other occasions they visited the Earl of Moira at Donington Hall on masonic business, and attended English masonic lodges at Leicester and elsewhere. As they were unable to communicate with the Grand Orient of France, these French freemasons applied to the Earl of Moira for warrants to form prisoner of war lodges in Ashby, and these Moira was pleased to grant despite official discouragement of freemasonry among prisoners of war. On 5 May, 1813, Kergrist and his brother-in-law Thomas Smith attended the St John's Lodge at the White Swan Inn, at the Market Place, Leicester, and Kergrist was recorded as a member of the French 'Justice and Unity' Lodge (Loge de la Justice et de l'Union) at Ashby-de-la Zouch. The first prisoners had mostly been taken at St Domingo. These officers did not regard themselves as prisoners of war, having placed themselves under British protection to avoid likely massacre by the revolutionary islanders who had taken over control of the French colony. They believed that British officers had given their word that the French would be landed at a French port. The British Admiralty thought otherwise however and many of them in consequence remained prisoners for as long as ten years.[15]

Service in the Indian Ocean

Mary Ann's husband was very much a professional sailor. His father was the 'noble homme Louis Jacques Le Normant de Kergrist' and his mother the 'Dame Marie Thérèse Hyacinthe Couppe de Lestimber' and he had been baptized at the Church of St Magloire, Chatelaudren, in Brittany on 3 December 1779. He served in the French Navy for forty-six years attaining the rank of Capitaine de Vaisseau.[16] Although he enlisted as a common sailor in 1794 he was from the old officer class and not the kind of man to break his parole. He saw active service with the fleet in the English Channel from 1794 to 1799 and distinguished himself at Belle Isle, where he was commissioned at sea on 29 April 1799. He fought at St Domingo, where he was wounded and lost the use of his right arm. He may well have consulted Thomas John about this difficult wound and met Mary Ann at her father's house. In April, 1800, Kergrist was appointed second in command of the brig L'Enfant Prodigue (Lieut. de Vaisseau Victor André Hulot) then being fitted out at Lorient.

He undertook a voyage and subsequently followed his commanding officer to another brig, Le Bélier, on which he sailed in the Indian Ocean. On 22 December 1802 at 6 a.m. Le Bélier was involved in a naval action that never officially took place. Hulot approached and surprised a British merchant ship intending to board, but discovered, to his horror, that the ship was a British frigate, HMS Fox (Captain James G. Vashon RN) 32 guns.[17] Hulot decided to disengage from the ill-matched conflict whilst maintaining fire on the enemy. For the next seventeen hours the crew behaved magnificently and Le Bélier ultimately escaped. Hulot paid generous tribute to the members of the crew and in particular to Kergrist for 'his skill in executing the required dispositions'. The only casualty aboard Le Bélier was Sub. Lieutenant Desportes who was killed.

Kergrist's account of the action given some thirty years later was very different. According to family tradition, when Hulot recognized a frigate when he was expecting a merchantman, he lost his head and ordered Le Bélier to strike her colours. Kergrist refused to obey, arrested his commanding officer and locked him in his cabin. He then took command and directed the engagement himself, making the crew think that Hulot was either ill or mad. It would indeed seem to have been the first warlike action in which Hulot had been involved. After the engagement the relationship between Kergrist and Hulot remained as cordial as before and in a further action off Dieu on 22 December, Le Bélier drove a 14 gun coastguard ashore. On the following day Le Bélier captured the French corsair L'Espiègle (Captain Dubois), which was a British prize and sailed her to a French port, having taken the prize crew prisoners of war. Hulot docked at L'Isle de France on 3 February 1804 and found that he had been promoted Capitaine de Frégate substantive from 24 September 1803. As soon as he had berthed, Hulot submitted reports on his voyages. These are identical to the facts disclosed in the Officers' Service Records and the ship's muster roll. However the spaces for details of action and prize have been left blank. Sub Lieutenant Desportes is recorded as having died during the night of 22/23 December and not as having been killed in action. General Decaen, Commissioner General for French possessions in the Indian Ocean, was responsible for these strange omissions and also for failing to send in Hulot's reports to Paris. Consequently, the Admiralty never acknowledged that the actions of Le Bélier ever took place and the matter would never officially have come to light had not General Decean's papers been discovered at Caen City Library at the beginning of this century. Hulot died in 1809 and when Kergrist returned to France after the war, he applied for affidavits from five of his old shipmates on Le Bélier, to support his nomination for a decoration. Those affidavits were a confirmation of Hulot's report, and make no mention of the usurpation of command. However nothing was done because, according to French Admiralty records at the time, no such action had ever taken place. No attempt seems to have been made to seek confirmation of the action from British sources. An approach to the British Admiralty would have revealed that the log of HMS Fox records that at daylight on 21 December a strange sail was sighted heading south-east off the coast of Gujerat. HMS Fox made all sail to investigate the ship which proved to be a brig making short tack towards her. The brig was flying French colours and fired a gun to windward, being then five miles off to leaward of her. The brig was next seen to lower her colours and hoist English colours and also to make several signals. At 10.20 a.m. *HMS Fox* housed her guns and shipped the false half ports to give the impression of being a merchantman. The brig then hoisted French colours again and fired a shot, firing another shot at 10.30 a.m. At 10.50 a.m. the brig tacked and stood towards *HMS Fox* and fired several shots all of which overshot except for one which holed the topmast sail. This was no doubt intentional because Hulot, believing *HMS Fox* to be a merchantman, would not have wanted to sink her and would have been aiming at the masts and sails in order to incapacitate the ship, so as to facilitate boarding and capture. At 11 a.m. *HMS Fox* ran out her guns, hauled down her colours and opened fire scoring several hits. The brig cut away her boats from the stern and lightened the ship by throwing things overboard. *HMS Fox* continued firing whilst the brig fired back. The brig made all speed to disengage and by noon *HMS Fox*'s guns were falling short so she ceased firing. Pursuit continued until 7 a.m. on 22 December when *HMS Fox* lost sight of the brig.[18] The British account of the action would suggest yet another reason why Hulot's report was so defective. The French Admiralty may well have considered Hulot's attack on *HMS Fox* as being foolhardy and irresponsible and to have risked unnecessarily both the ship and the lives of the crew.

Le Bélier was laid up at Ferrol in 1804 and was sold soon afterwards. Hulot and Kergrist parted company when the latter was appointed second in command of the frigate *Guerrière* (Capitaine T. M. Hubert) 40 guns, which was on patrol off the coast of Norway with two sister ships, seeking to disrupt the British whale fisheries in the area. From time to time Kergrist commanded the *Guerrière*. A British squadron consisting of three frigates was despatched northwards to put a stop to the French action which had resulted in the loss of over thirty merchant ships, and on 18 June 1806, *HMS Blanche* (Captain Thomas Lavie RN), a fifth rate of 38 guns, sighted the *Guerrière* off the Faroe Islands. According to French accounts the *Guerrière* was in a deplorable state; foul in hull with some eighty men sick from the scurvy, to which thirty-six officers and men had already fallen victims. *Guerrière* tried to escape and at about 12.45 a.m. on 19 July *HMS Blanche* closed in and fired two broadsides. Although *Guerrière* returned fire she was quickly disabled, losing her top mast, and at 1.30 a.m. she surrendered having lost twenty killed and thirty wounded in the engagement. *HMS Blanche* hardly suffered any damage, with only four members of crew wounded, and subsequently Captain Lavie was knighted and his first lieutenant, Henry Thomas Davies, was promoted to Commander. *Guerrière* was added to the Royal Navy and served as *HMS Guerrière* until 1812, when she was captured by *USS Constitution* in the War of 1812. Many years later Kergrist referred to the loss of *Guerrière*, commenting that he 'had the misfortune to find myself in the same position as when on board *Le Bélier*. In this unhappy situation once again I did everything that a man of honour could but I did not this time take over command because I had reason to believe that my previous conduct on board *Le Bélier* had, in some way, been criticised because I had never been rewarded, although I had saved the brig. *Guerrière* was taken and I spent eight years as a prisoner.'[19]

Adapting to Peace

Kergrist's professional disappointment was compensated by the friendship he received from the people of Ashby-de-la Zouch and his total acceptance by the Kirkland family. His eldest child was baptized Thomas Louis Kirkland at St Helens Church on 17 June 1813. Following the peace Kergrist and Mary Ann sailed to France with their baby son and registered their marriage before the Tribunal Civil at St Brieuc, Brittany, on 25 January 1814. They returned to Ashby in 1817 for the baptism of their daughter Marie Thérèse Rose on 16 February, and this would seem to have been a particularly happy occasion because Captain Nicholas Kirkland's daughter Mary Ann was baptized at the same time.

Kergrist resumed his naval career after the war, being promoted Capitaine de Frégate in 1819. He suffered shipwreck in 1817 when commanding *La Caravanne*. He commanded various French men of war until his retirement in 1840 and although qualified for promotion to Vice Admiral, he never attained that rank. He died at Brest on 15 August 1859 having survived Mary Ann by three years. Young Thomas Louis Kirkland de Kergrist had an even more distinguished naval career than his father, attaining the rank of Vice Admiral on 8 October 1870, having served as Governor of Martinique and holding the Légion d'Honneur and other foreign decorations. The Kirkland and Kergrist families kept in touch throughout the nineteenth century, as is evidenced by the visit to Ashby in 1874 of Monsieur Deschard from Brest, and by the full list of descendants in the Admiral's funeral notice.*

If Mary Ann Kirkland found little difficulty in adapting to French life the same was not true of other Ashby wives of prisoners. Sous-Lieutenant Louis Jean was also taken at St Domingo, having been wounded in his right leg and suffering from asthma. In 1809 he married Elizabeth Edwards at St Helen's Church, Ashby[20] and joined the French prisoners Freemasons' Lodge in 1810.[21] In the same year he took the part of Valère in a production of *Le Medicin Malgré lui* by the 'French Gentlemen Prisoners of War – for the benefit of the poor' at the Society Theatre, Ashby. He was then fortunate enough to be exchanged in 1811 and returned to France with his wife Elizabeth. However, Elizabeth found life difficult in France and they were back in Ashby in 1814 where Louis carried on business in Wood Street as a watchmaker and jeweller until 1831. They then returned to France and Louis died in Calais in 1833. One of his daughters then met and married an Englishman named Hinton or Kinton. They lived in Leicester with Elizabeth. Louis's grandson was employed by J T Thorpe the author of the *History of Freemasonry in Ashby-de-la Zouch 1809–1909* and as a result Louis's masonic certificates and papers have been preserved.

The Earl of Moira

Thomas John's patron was Lord Rawdon later 2nd Earl of Moira, the 1st Marquess of Hastings (1754–1826), who had inherited all the estates of his uncle the Earl of Huntingdon (charged with various annuities) on condition he took the name and arms of Hastings[22]. Moira could not, of course, succeed to the title which remained in abeyance until claimed by Hans Francis Hastings in 1819. Moira greatly distinguished himself in the War of American Independence. At Bunker Hill (1775) as a Lieutenant of Grenadiers, he was one of only forty-seven who remained of his company and received two shots though his cap. General 'Johnny' Burgoyne remarked that Moira 'had that day stamped his fame for life.' He was mentioned in dispatches after the battle of Camden and defeated General Greene at Hobkirk Hill having attained the rank of Lieutenant

---

* The author has seen a watercolour portrait of Thomas Smith Kirkland with a note written in French on the back of the picture to the effect that it was originally given by Thomas Smith to his sister Mary Ann and presented to Lucy Bangham, daughter of Thomas Smith, by his cousin Le Normant de Kergrist in 1909 as a souvenir of a visit she had made to the family at Brest.

Colonel.[23] It is significant that Moira was Colonel-in-Chief of the 27th Foot when Thomas John's son Nicholas Smith joined that Regiment in 1804.

Moira was a skilful soldier and an able administrator but his political advancement was restricted largely as a result of his friendship with George, Prince of Wales and Prince Regent. Moira was a most influential nobleman nationally and locally and his liberal inclinations led him to move a Bill for the relief of insolvent debtors and to limit powers of arrest. Moreover Moira was Acting Grand Master of the Premier Lodge of English Freemasons and the friend of the royal princes who regarded Freemasonry as a means of mixing with the gentry, professional men, and tradesmen, on terms of limited informality. He it was who brought about the union after a long period of dispute of the Premier (or Moderns') and Antients' Grand Lodges. Moira had high ideals but his excessive vanity and luxurious way of living made him susceptible to flattery and deception.[24] Moira's life and career is of great interest and importance but it is not properly a subject for this work. Suffice to say that when Moira paid what proved to be his last visit to Ashby in 1823, the Leicester Journal reported that Captain Nicholas Kirkland when replying to the toast 'The Duke of York and the Army' took the 'opportunity of expressing his supreme admiration of the military tactics and general policy' of his Colonel-in-Chief 'in his public career and of his many domestic virtues.'[25]

Local Freemasonry

Thomas John was initiated a Freemason in the Tyrian Lodge No 379 at Derby on 2 August 1796 with Samuel Webster and Leonard Piddocke, two Ashby Attorneys.[26] His enthusiasm for this 'system of morality veiled in allegory and illustrated by symbols'[27] was such that on 26 June 1797 he held a great Masonic meeting in a large room in his house in Market Street. Welbourn Owston, a friend of Thomas John's and an auctioneer in Ashby, was initiated in the same lodge on 24 May 1796 and had his young son baptized Hiram Abif shortly after in a gesture of misplaced Masonic enthusiasm![28] Certainly in May 1799 John Simmonds, also a member of the Tyrian Lodge, recorded in his diary that 'he desired Mr T. Kirkland to mention my name as a subscriber to a society/masonic at which Earl Moira was in the chair on 6 May subscription ai/l *per diem* or a/a in advance annually.'[29] Owston, despite having no experience of the penal system, was later appointed Governor of the County Gaol and became Master of St John's Masonic Lodge No 348 at Leicester.[30]

Social Life

Thomas John was a popular man with a keen sense of humour. He reported to John Simmonds whose daughter was away at school, that 'he had been at Lichfield and seen our daughters who drank plenty of wine with him'. Again on 14 May 1800 John Simmonds recalls 'Mrs S came from Lullington and the same day Mr Brown, Mr Tunnicliff, Mr Hassall and Mr Thomas Kirkland dined at BH and a more delightful day JS never spent at Butt House.'[31]

Thomas John was also, however, not a man without prejudice. One gets the impression that James Richards of the Mansion House, Ashby, a Whig and a Dissenter, did not appeal to him greatly, although he supported him 'in green' with many other local gentlemen when he attended Leicester Assizes in March 1796 as High Sheriff. He was also greatly outraged at the extravagant 'shameful price of £120' incurred in the building of the iron and stone gates to Helens Churchyard in 1791.

Like his father, Thomas John was a keen musician, and records the first annual Cecilian meeting at the Queen's Head Hotel, Ashby-de-la Zouch, on 20 November 1793. He was a capable violinist. His social activities included membership of Brewins Club, whose meetings were transferred from the Bull's Head to the Lamb Inn on 17 October 1798 and the private Oyster Club, which held meetings during the winter of 1798–99 at various members' houses and public houses. Thomas John entertained them on 11 March 1799. Oyster Clubs flourished in other towns up and down the country and the records of such a Club at Preston, Lancs. have been preserved. The Oysters were despatched 'by fleet' from London between September and April and were consumed with 'best port' and sometimes with 'parched peas.' The Preston Oyster and Parched Pea Club existed from 1771 to 1841. The President was styled 'the Speaker' and other officers included one named 'Oystericus' who was responsible for ordering and maintaining the oysters in good condition, and a secretary, an auditor, a deputy auditor and a port laureate [sic] or 'rhymesmith'. Other officers were the 'celarius' who had to provide 'port of first quality', the chaplain, the surgeon general, the master of the roles (to see to the provision of bread and butter), the swig master, the clerk of the peas, a minstrel, a master of the jewels and a physician in ordinary![32]

The Lamb Inn was in Market Street where the Town Hall now stands, almost opposite to Thomas John's house. The hostelry was tenanted by Edward 'Ned' Sharpe and his wife Jane. Ned had married Jane Palmer at St Helen's Church on 5 May 1782 and the premises consisted 'of an old messuage 40′ front of timber and slate ... containing great accommodation as a market inn, stabling for sixteen horses, a barn, cow house, pig styes and garden.'[33] A local poet Thomas Hatton senior in *An original ode on ringing* dated 5 November 1844, wrote:

> then Ned Sharpe at the Lamb with good humour and wit
> with laughter and jokes your sides nearly split.

Ned died on 7 May 1794 but Jane continued to manage the inn successfully for many years. She died in November 1837 in her eightieth year.

The memorial to Thomas John in St Helen's Church records that 'a diligent and successful practice in his profession for many years and a scrupulous punctuality in all his dealings endeared as much to the public as his kind and affectionate conduct did to his family and friends.' His entries in the notes reveal a fine command of the English language and an estimable economy in the use of words. In a mere thirty words he paints a vivid picture of a bear running amok in Market Street on 4 June 1794, whilst his description of a mushroom party going to Foremarke on 18 August 1793 is altogether delightful. His entries were also strictly to the point, as when he writes, 'F. B. Davenport shot himself at Jos Taylor's Dog and Duck Stanton Tuesday January 23 1798.' Reference to the Leicester Journal for 2 February 1798 reveals the following version of the tragic event: 'Suddenly on the 23rd ult at the Dog and Duck Public House in Stanton Derbyshire Mr Francis Brewin Davenport.'[34]

The Apothecary

Although Thomas John was a surgeon, he was as an apothecary concerned with natural drugs, and refers to the production of English rhubarb at Oldecot Farm, Bretby, by Mr Burton in 1793, noting that 26lb by drying was reduced to 3½lb. When dried the rhubarb was kept in powder form and when mixed with magnesia and water it was used as a mild purgative. Medicinal rhubarb (*rheum officinale*) was first cultivated at Banbury Oxon in 1777 and is still grown there. The powder was produced from the dried roots. English rhubarb was kiln-dried as opposed to Turk rhubarb which was sun-dried. The notes also indicated that Thomas John's interest extended beyond the treatment of his human patients. He refers to the death of Mr Cattel's old horse, Rainbow, in November 1793 and in February 1799 to his surgeon brother James Bate Kirkland having a cow that calved three calves.

Thomas John also noted unusual medical circumstances, as when John Green was 'starved to death' on the night of 2 February 1799 in a snowstorm on the road between Ashby and Snarestone. He was sufficiently moved on 2 July 1799 to note that, 'W. M. Coxes' child drowned in the well,' and on 7 October 1800 that, 'Whyman's child drowned in Mr Newton's tan fat.'

Crime and Punishment

He was likewise involved with the administration of the criminal law and inquests at which he no doubt gave evidence. We learn that on 26 April 1794 at Inchy in Holland the 5th Irish Royal Dragoons, who had taken part in what Fortescue describes as 'the greatest day in the annals of British Horse,'[35] were quartered in Leicestershire, one troop being in Ashby. Unfortunately at between 10 and 11 p.m. on Monday 25 January 1796 a dragoon by the name of Timothy Dunn having spent the evening at The White Horse Inn, (where the Trustee Savings Bank now stands), and being the worse for drink, declared that he would strike down the first person he met on leaving the inn. True to his word he struck down a young woman named Mary Lakin, fracturing her skull. Mary died of her wound on the following Friday and Dunn was tried for wilful murder at the next Leicester Assizes. He was convicted and sentenced to death with three other members of his regiment, who had committed other capital offences at Syston. The Church service with sermon at Leicester Gaol on the Sunday before an execution was open to the public, and on this occasion an unseemly concourse disturbed what should have been a most solemn occasion and the *Leicester Journal* pronounced that such a disgraceful occurrence should not be permitted to recur. At all events, Dunn was duly hanged on the Monday morning having met his long-lost brother at the weekend

74

before his execution. Dunn and his comrades met their deaths with great courage and the *Leicester Journal* deplored the waste of fine young lives through the evil of drink. Dunn's regiment was disbanded with disgrace for mutiny, by General Order issued on 12 April 1799, and the officers were placed on half pay. It was a tragedy because the 5th Royal Irish Dragoons had served with distinction at Blenheim, Ramillies and Fontenoy. Dunn's body was returned to Ashby, 'and dissected in the town', in accordance with the sentence. No doubt Thomas John was the surgeon involved, (perhaps with that ingenious man, his distinguished father), and tradition maintains that the skeleton was articulated and retained by the practice. Certainly Mr Douglas Stewart, of New Packington, personally recollects, as a painter's apprentice, decorating No 15, Ivanhoe Terrace following the death of Doctor Williams, who had lived there in about 1926, and finding a skeleton in the cupboard. Unsure what to do, the decorators lowered it into an old well at the back of No 14, South Street and filled the well in. Scott declares that Dunn's body was exposed to view after dissection in the White Horse for three days. Scott relied much on word of mouth tradition and he may not be accurate. However, the 4th Earl Ferrers was so exhibited in Surgeons' Hall thirty-five years before, and Thomas Kirkland senior would have been well aware of what happened then.

The Surgeon's Practice

In matters of surgery we note that Thomas John inoculated for the cowpox: the first children in the town were so protected on 11 July 1800. Edward Jenner (1749–1823) had vaccinated a boy named James Phipps with lymph taken from the cowpox vesicles on the finger of a dairymaid, named Sarah Nelmes, on 14 May 1796. The boy developed a cowpox pustule. On 1 July, Jenner inoculated the boy with smallpox matter, and he did not develop smallpox. Jenner's ambition was to wipe out smallpox everywhere, but this could not be done by inoculating cowpox matter, because cowpox was a rare disease, and it was essential to have a constant supply of fresh cowpox matter available. Jenner proved that when an individual had been inoculated with cowpox matter taken from a cow, matter from that inoculated person could be used successfully to inoculate another individual, and thus through other individuals indefinitely. In July 1798 Jenner published his results in, *An enquiry into the causes and effects of the variolae vaccinae.*[36] Within two years the practice was spreading rapidly, and by 1800 it was first adopted by Thomas John in Ashby. As surgeon to the French prisoners of war depot at Ashby, Thomas John would appear to have given evidence at the inquest held by Mr Charnel Bateman, the Derbyshire Coroner, another member of the Tyrian Lodge of Freemasons, at Packington on Capitaine Fort Denègres, who had been found dead in a field near Packington, on 6 December 1808. Denègres had been taken at San Domingo and had been at Ashby since 1804. He lodged in the town, and had been expecting an urgent message. As no letter had arrived by 4 p.m., he left his lodgings in haste. At about 5 p.m., a labourer found the body of Denègres covered by his military cloak. The body was still warm. The medical evidence was that a sword had entered the breast between the fourth and fifth ribs and on the right side had passed through the lungs and pierced the heart; the left hand was slightly wounded between the second and third fingers. Neither the cloak nor the waistcoat of the deceased had been pierced. From this it seemed clear that Denègres had been killed in a duel, and the jury returned a verdict of wilful murder against some person or persons unknown. He was buried in Packington Churchyard on 9 December, and the following entry appears in the Packington Parish Register of burials: 'Denèrges Monsr fort Denerges [*sic*] a French prisoner from Ashby-de-la Zouch, buried 9 December 1808, by me R T Andrews curate.' No-one was ever charged with the crime.[37]

Little mercy was shown to sexual offenders. Watts, the postman at Ashby, was convicted at Leicester Assizes in April 1812 of committing an unnatural offence at Ashby. He was sentenced to two years imprisonment, and to be set in the pillory for one hour at Leicester, and once at Ashby, for the same time. The Leicester Journal reported that, 'Watts . . . made his appearance on Saturday last surrounded by an immense concourse of spectators . . . For several minutes after he was put in there appeared no disposition on the part of the populace to annoy him – nor was anything thrown at him until by his gestures, 'Peep fool, peep, peep at your brother, etc' he seemed to brave their resentment – he was attacked immediately after with all the filth that could possibly be collected, but of which there was evidently a scarcity – on being liberated he kicked the dirt in the face of the Sherriff's officers and conducted himself throughout with greatest impudence. Within a month he is again to stand in the pillory at Ashby-de-la Zouch, how he may fare we know not, but here he certainly had not half that he deserved.' In a later edition of the same paper we read, 'Watts who stood in the pillory here three weeks since, is to make his appearance at Ashby-de-la Zouch tomorrow where it is hoped he will meet with his deserts.'[38] The pillory stood in Market Street opposite Mill Lane.

Economic Depression

Thomas John was an interested observer of the social change and disturbance that accompanied the Industrial Revolution, and the depression caused by the Napoleonic Wars. There were riots in the town in October 1793 and September 1800, as a direct result of the high cost of bread. On the first occasion, colliers from Coleorton and Swannington created disturbances which caused great apprehension among those responsible for the maintenance of law and order. There was an understandable nervousness, because of the bloody massacres being reported from France. Samuel S. Perkins JP of Orton Hall, Orton-on-the-Hill, caused the military to be called out from Nottingham, and on Sunday 3 November a detachment of troopers from the Queen's Regiment of Light Horse rode into the town and restored order without bloodshed. The Reverend J. Cole Galloway JP committed to the County Gaol John Streets, junior, charged with, 'damning the constitution, the Duke of York and all his forces, and using other seditious expressions.' Mr Perkins committed John Williamson of Thringstone, Richard Jenks and Samuel Read of Coleorton, to prison charged with, 'riotously assembling in the neighbourhood of Coleorton on the 7th ult. and committing divers unlawful acts.'[39] In 1800 bread had risen to a higher price then had ever been known before, and serious riots had broken out in Nottingham, where a baker's shop had been attacked in the city.[40] A mob of colliers assembled in Ashby on 10 September of that year, but no serious harm was caused. Thomas John also records the first general navigation meeting, held at the Queens Head on 7 February 1792. This meeting led to the building of the Ashby-de-la Zouch canal, which was constructed under statutory powers between 1794 and 1804. It commenced at the reservoir on Ashby Woulds, and continued through Moira, Donisthorpe, Oakthorpe, Measham, Snarestone and Shackerstone joining the Coventry canal beyond Hinckley without a single lock. The Canal was intended to pass through Ashby, but shortage of capital caused the plans to be modified to provide a mineral railway from Willesley basin to Ticknall and Breedon-on-the-Hill. The canal was never profitable, and was sold with its tram roads to the Midland Railway Company in 1846 for £110,000.

Murder at Bilstone

A shudder passed through the local population early in 1801, when John Massey assaulted and killed his wife on the road between Bilstone and Sheepy Magna, having previously attempted to throw his ten-year-old step-daughter into the mill dam towards the end of 1800. Massey was, 'a remarkably stout man about fifty-four years of age, esteemed punctual in his dealings and industrious in his business . . . but much addicted to passion'. He was a cruel man of great physical strength, and when young had been a champion wrestler earning for himself the nickname, 'topsey turvey'.[41] The Trial took place at Leicester Assizes, when Massey was convicted of murder. He was sentenced to death and his body was ordered for dissection. However, Massey petitioned the Judge that he should be buried between his two wives, to both of whom it was said he had behaved with great cruelty. The Judge then ordered that he be hung in chains as near to the scene of the crime as might be convenient. He was duly hanged on 23 March, and exhibited in the gibbet erected by the roadside. Eighteen years later the skeleton was still intact. The gibbet post is still standing there today.[42]

The Blue Coat School

In many local matters Thomas John followed closely in his father's footsteps. They served together as trustees of the Blue Coat School Charity, which had been founded in 1699 by Isaac Dawson. There is a tradition that Isaac, when training to be a Barrister-at-Law, was robbed by Highwaymen whilst on a journey. One version maintains that he was travelling into Lincolnshire whilst another records that he was going to York. He described his adventures in a letter to his father which reads as follows:

Hond father, these may satisfie you that I am through Mercy safe returned from York, which jorney has been

78

somewhat difficult; for about half a mile from Nottm
I overtook three highwayman, with whom I travelled
about three mile, when they stopped me and tould me
they must have my moneys, which they took from me
with my watch etc, horse and whip and gloves, and tyed
my hands behind me and my legs together – so left me;
but I quickley loosed myself and pursued them. When
I had gone about seven miles a foot, I mett with one of
their horses, which I mounted; and when I came to ye
next town I got 3 men to go along with me in pursuit
of 'em, but they haveing fresh horses ouer-red me so yt
I was forced to go by myself. When I came almost to
Blyth I mett one of ye 3 men coming back again, who
told me ye other 2 went 2 several ways in pursuit of 'em
but they both returned home without takeing 'em. When
I came to Blyth I borrowed wt money I thought shd
want, so went forwards for Bautry, where I tooke post
for Donkaster, and, from thence to Ferry-bridg; but in
the way to Ferry-bridg there is a town called West Bridg,
where I happened to hear of 'em, so called assistance and
sizd them. The next day went with 'em before a Justice
who committed 'em to York gaol. I hope shall see you
hear next week; then shall give you a more perticuler
acount. I am wt Duty to self and love to Br and Sisr
your Obd Son I Dawson.
Nott January 5 1714/15.[43]

The highwaymen were tried at York Assizes, convicted and hanged.
Dawson was entitled to receive the sum of £40 for his services to the
community. But, no doubt, feeling it to be blood money, he applied
it towards the school foundation and the preaching of an annual
sermon. The school house to the east of Lower Church Street was
purchased in 1721 at a cost of £45. Funds were raised by public
subscription in the town, and by 1764 the school was sufficiently
endowed. The master was required to instruct twenty-six boys
who were clothed in blue coat, waistcoat and trousers, with
cap and bands. In 1769 the Green Coat School was founded by
Alderman Newton of Leicester for twenty-five boys, who each
wore a green coat, waistcoat, and trousers, with cap and bands.
The two schools became united and the school was sufficient for
150 pupils. Admission was restricted to boys from Ashby whose
parents were parishioners of St Helen's Church. They were taught

reading, writing and arithmetic and provided with stationery.[44] The school closed early in this century and the endowed funds were transferred to the Grammar School. By 1895, 161 children were attending the school. In 1799 a new Master had to be appointed and the trustees had to decide between two candidates. One was a Mr Orme of Melbourne, the other Thomas Chapman, who was a nephew of Thomas John and must have been very young for the office. Orme was appointed by five votes to four, but any question of nepotism does not seem to have occurred to Thomas John who voted for his nephew. It was sad that Chapman was not appointed because he subsequently became commissioned in the army, attained the rank of Captain and died of fever in the West Indies in 1808. The schoolroom has now been fully restored and serves as a lodge room for Ashby-de-la Zouch Freemasons.

The Lords of Willesley

The 'young Ascanius' of 1752 had grown up to be a great joy to his father Francis, Earl of Huntingdon, who had purchased a commission for him in the 12th (Suffolk) regiment in 1770. Charles Hastings served at Gibraltar as an ensign and was promoted to Lieutenant in 1776. He was a close friend to his cousin Lord Rawdon and when the War of American Independence broke out, he volunteered for service in America with his cousin. He received permission to serve as a Lieutenant in the Light Infantry Company of the 23rd Regiment (Royal Welch Fusiliers), then in America. He was present at the taking of Fort Washington and in the battles of Pelham Manor, White Plains, Danberg Powder Mills, Brandywine and German Town, in the course of which he was wounded twice. During his service in America he was appointed ADC to General Sir Henry Clinton (1738–1795) and General the Earl of Percy. Returning to the 12th regiment at Gibraltar, he was promoted Captain in 1780 and was present at the siege of the Rock from 1779 to 1782 by the joint French and Spanish forces. General George Augustus Eliot (1717–1790) conducted the heroic defence and Hastings covered the retreat of the sortie with the Grenadiers and Light Infantry, and was mentioned in Orders. He returned to England in 1782 as Major in the 76th (Hindoostan) Regiment, but was placed on half pay when peace was signed with France. Shortly after this he purchased, in 1783, a Lieutenant Colonelcy in the 34th Regiment, then in Canada. He served there for two years and was commandant of Quebec before returning to England. His health had been impaired by continuous service, and this coupled with his father's death in 1789, caused him to go on half pay again. He married Parnell Abney on 2 June 1788. She was the daughter and sole heiress of Thomas Abney of Willesley Hall, who was the son of Sir Thomas Abney Kt, one of the Justices of the Common Pleas. Charles and Parnell had three children. The eldest son Charles Abney Hastings, was a member of Parliament for Leicester, but lost his seat at the time of the Reform Bill in 1832, and then opted out of public life. He died in 1856. A daughter died in infancy. The younger son, Frank, joined the Royal Navy, serving as a boy of eleven at the Battle of Trafalgar. After fifteen years service he had attained the rank of Commander when he sailed into harbour at Port Royal, Jamaica, in the survey ship *Kangaroo*. The flag ship of the West Indies Station was already there and the Captain (according to Frank's report), 'thought proper to hail me in a voice that rang through the whole of Port Royal, saying "You have overlaid our anchor – you ought to be ashamed of yourself – you damned lubber you – who are you?" ' Frank felt so insulted that a few days later he challenged the Captain to a duel. This resulted in Frank being court-martialled and dismissed the service. He then volunteered to serve with the Greeks in the War of Greek Independence, in which he was greatly admired by the Greeks for his personal bravery and lack of self-interest. He served the Greek cause for six years, asking for nothing and receiving nothing from the Greek Government and generously expending his own small fortune on the venture because he thought that the Greeks were worth it. He manned the steam ship *Perseverence* and sailed her to Greece with a crew of volunteers. Very few steamers at that time had ever sailed so far, and no-one at the Admiralty believed that an Iron ship could ever take part in a naval engagement. The *Perseverence*, re-named *Karteria*, flew the Greek flag and ultimately, at the battle of the Bay of Salona, more than justified Frank's faith in her when he sank four large Turkish ships and two brigs.[45] In 1828 he was wounded and died of blood poisoning. He was a highly successful Philhelline.

Hastings purchased again into the 61st Regiment as a Lieutenant Colonel, and served in England and in Jersey, achieving the rank of General in 1813, having been created a Baronet in 1806. He became Colonel-in-Chief of the 12th Foot on 15 October 1811. He comments rather sadly, 'I regret much not having been more employed, but think it a duty incumbent upon me to state most humbly that it was more my misfortune than fault as I have never failed seizing every opportunity that offered to make a tender of my services.'[46]

He spent his latter years at Willesley Hall, corresponding at great length with his cousins Warren Hastings, and the Marquess of Hastings. In 1815 when Napoleon surrendered himself to the British, Hastings had written to Warren Hastings suggesting that Napoleon should have shot himself rather than surrender. Warren Hastings took him strongly to task, writing, 'I generally prefer your judgment to my own on questions of a political nature; but I do not absolutely assent to your doctrine of applying a loaded pistol to the case of a desperate fortune. It is very Roman indeed and it is not English and it is, with very few cases excepted, selfish.'[47]

Hastings, (then Sir Charles), was living in retirement at Willesley Hall, whilst maintaining a London house and keeping himself closely informed of political and military affairs. Miss Moore, the illegitimate orphan daughter of General Sir John Moore, was still residing at Willesley Hall.[48] It would seem that Sir Charles, perhaps obsessed by his own illegitimacy, sought to care for others suffering from a similar handicap.

There was a great occasion in Ashby on 4 August 1823, when the Marquess of Hastings returned after his retirement as Governor General of India, greatly honoured and respected. 'The venerable Marquess was joyfully received by the inhabitants of the ancient town of Ashby-de-la Zouch, who testified their respect by every demonstration of gladness and festivity. The principal street was tastefully ornamented with boughs, flowers, and emblematical devices, while crowds on horseback and on foot rendered the scene altogether a picture of animated and enthusiastic joy.'[49] However, Sir Charles was not present, and as soon as he could get away, the Marquess went to Willesley Hall to take tea with his old kinsman and comrade.

Although there is no hint of it in the notes or the local newspapers, Thomas John was very likely to have been summoned urgently to Willesley on 30 September, because on that day Sir Charles shot himself in his bedroom as he thought Napoleon should have done, being, in his own words, 'in peace with all mankind'.[50] Mr Charnel Bateman, still the Derby Coroner, on '2 October 1823 went to Willesley to view the body of Sir Charles Hastings Bt, who shot himself, being at the time in a state of temporary derangement, twenty-one miles £1.15s.9d.'[51] The following unusual directions with regard to his funeral were contained in Sir Charles's Will: 'I desire that my body may be opened after my death and buried

82

without a coffin on the spot marked by me wrapped up in either woollen or oiled cloth or in such perishable materials as will keep my body together until deposited in my grave by six of my most deserving poorest labourers; that several acorns may be planted over my grave that one good tree may be chosen and preserved so that I may have the satisfaction of knowing that my body will serve to rear a good English Oak. The tree to be watched and watered by the gardener who must now and then be rewarded.'[52] A tree can be seen in Willesley Churchyard growing out of the iron railings around a grave: possibly this is Sir Charles's Oak!

Thomas John did not survive long himself. On 4 August in the following year, he died at Ashby aged sixty-four, still under the shadow of his famous father. His obituary read 'Mr Thomas Kirkland Senior Surgeon, son of the late Thomas Kirkland MD. As a professional man he ranked high in the estimation of the public and his benevolence and philanthropy were too conspicuous to need any eulogy.'[53] By his Will (and a Codicil), he appointed John Nicholas Hanson, of Burton-upon-Trent, and The Revd William M'Donall, Vicar of Ashby, his Executors, and after leaving his wife Mary a legacy of £200 and all his furniture and effects, he left his estate to his wife for her life and on her death to his four children in equal shares. His medical instruments were bequeathed to his medical sons Thomas Smith and William Henry.[54] All the contents of the house, including the museum, were sold by public auction, without reserve, within four weeks of his death and his widow, Mary, moved to Warrington, where she took up residence near or with her surgeon son William Henry and his wife Elizabeth. They both died in 1833, but Mary survived until 1845.

Thomas Smith Kirkland (1785–1869) – Tom the Third

The Sporting Doctor

Thomas Smith Kirkland was born on 14 May 1785. In view of his grandfather's and father's regard for Dr Prior, it would seem likely that he was educated at Ashby-de-la Zouch Grammar School. However, by the end of the century, Prior's health was failing and the school was reduced to three or four boys.[1] Certainly, his brother Nicholas Smith was admitted to Repton School, Derbyshire, in October 1800, under its new headmaster, Revd Thomas Boultbee Sleath, who had succeeded William Bagshaw Stevens.[2] Thomas John's decision to send Nicholas Smith to Repton may have been influenced by the fact that the Earl of Moira was a Governor of the School. Thomas Smith was apprenticed to his father Thomas John. In 1800 he had started making entries in the notes in place of his father. In April 1813 he gave notice to the St John's Masonic Lodge that he would be leaving the country. There is no evidence that he ever did, apart from an absence of any notes written between August and December 1813. If he did volunteer his services as an army surgeon he does not seem ever to have been accepted into the service. He married firstly Mary, the daughter of Richard and Mary Harrison, of Packington, but she died on 21 April 1820 at the early age of twenty-two. Secondly, he married Hannah, daughter of Richard Faux, of Merrivale, Leicestershire. Thomas Smith lived and practised through years of great scientific advance in medicine, and during his life his grandfather's dream of the unification of the physicians and surgeons was brought to pass by the Medical Act

1858. Thomas Smith, himself a surgeon, thus became entitled to be addressed as Doctor Kirkland as his grandfather had been. If, however, Thomas Smith was interested in all this, no evidence of it can be found in the notes. Thomas Smith seems to have been a competent local practitioner with no ambitions towards the medical distinction of his grandfather. He comments regularly on the weather, and in 1833 rejoices that, 'the winter so mild that hunting was not interrupted by the snow or frost one day.' Horse riding was Thomas Smith's great interest, and he served on a committee set up in 1835 to express the gratitude of the steward and organizers of the Ashby-de-la Zouch races to William Eames, of The Elms, Leicester Road, for allowing his land to be used for the event. A silver salver was presented to Mrs Mary Eames, who was a daughter of Thomas Cantrell, of Hill House – another surgeon. These were the first races to be held in Ashby during the nineteenth century and about 10,000 people attended the meetings. The races continued every year thereafter until 1845, when the Burton to Leicester railway-line was laid across the racecourse. The course ran parallel with the Upper Packington Road as far as the brook. It then followed the brook to Leicester Road, returning to the finishing post near to the Leicester Road, Upper Packington Road junction.[3] A grandstand was built near the finishing post, and the charge for admission to the stand was 2s. 6d. Well known members of the nobility and gentry served as steward for the races, including Sir George Howland Willoughby Beaumont, Bt, of Coleorton Hall (1836), John Storey, Esq. (1837), George Moore, Esq., of Appleby Hall (1838), Captain Farnham, MP, of Quorn Hall (1839), Sir W. W. Dixie of Bosworth Park (1841), Viscount Curzon (1842), Hampton Clement, Esq. (1844), and C R Colville, Esq. MP (1845).[4]

Thomas Smith believed in early rising, regular exercise and outdoor pursuits, as essential to good health. He delighted in old English sports and pastimes and especially in fox-hunting. In the hunting field he was regarded not only as a good sportsman, but a daring and intrepid rider. When incapacitated by old age he still enjoyed attending the meets and viewing the horses and the hounds.[5]

Local Life and the Baths

Thomas Smith was not a very enthusiastic freemason and resigned from the St John's Lodge in 1817. However he was one of the founders of the new Ivanhoe Masonic Lodge No. 631 at Ashby in 1836, but little was done to ensure that the Lodge was well supported. The Lodge met at the Royal Hotel on the first Monday of every month between May 1836 and October 1841. Thereafter meetings ceased to take place, and the Lodge was erased from the roll of Lodges by Grand Lodge in 1851. The failure of the Lodge was thought to be caused by excessive cost and unbusinesslike management; each meeting was followed by a 'champagne banquet' and subscriptions were comparable to those in prosperous old established London Lodges.[6] Another factor may have been the sudden death in 1840 of Revd John Heyrick Macaulay, Headmaster of Repton School and a very keen member. Entries in the notes were scarce between 1823 and 1832 although important events were taking place both nationally and locally. In Ashby, the Baths had been built and completed in 1822. The spring from which the Baths were supplied was at the Moira Colliery some three miles away. A source had been discovered in 1805 at a depth of about 700 feet from the surface during mining operations. This water had been analysed by an eminent London Chemist and found 'to contain saline ingredients in valuable proportions'. In fact the analysis had been carried out by Dr Daubeny, Professor of Chemistry at Oxford University, in 1829. Subsequent analyses were carried out by Dr Andrew Ure MDFRS in about 1850, and by Dr B. Paul, of Victoria Street, London in the 1880s. Apart however from agreeing that the Ashby mineral water was saline, the compounds identified by these three official analyses differed considerably.[7] The Royal Hotel (originally named the Hastings Hotel), was built in 1826 to accommodate the numerous visitors consequent upon 'the popularity which the water speedily acquired'[8] and Edward Mortimer Green, a young attorney, who had set up in practice at Ashby in 1828 and had subscribed £200 towards the cost of the new hotel, added the following postscript to a letter dated 29 December 1831 to a local solicitor: 'I made several inquiries for you last May but without effect. I hope you have not formed an unfavourable opinion of our Baths and accommodation in general.'[9] The treatment available to patients and others seeking the waters must have resulted in a busy professional life for the local physicians, surgeons, chemists and druggists. Thomas Smith is listed among the surgeons of the town in Wayte's guide, (1831) together with Messrs T. Cantrell, N. Ingle, J. Beavington and S. W. Mousley. By February 1838 and prior thereto Thomas Smith was practising in partnership with Charles A. Dalby, surgeon, who had been appointed union surgeon for the Ashby-de-la Zouch district in about 1837. The name of the practice was Kirkland and Dalby. They practised from Market Street and numbered Sir George H. W. Beaumont Bt, of Coleorton Hall, among their distinguished patients. In the year to 31 December 1838 Thomas Smith attended at Coleorton Hall on thirty-five occasions, always charging a fee of 5s. His remedies included a Bolus, mixture, drafts, apperient mixture, plaster, powder, pills and leeches. The surgeon's bill, amounting to £24.18s. 3d, was rendered at the end of the year and paid nine months later! The partnership continued until after 1850.[10] After this Dalby left the town and died at Southampton in 1855. The town was attractive because of its wide and handsome main street. It was noted that there were two other streets running parallel to Market Street on either side. Significantly, the cottages of the poor were to be found between these streets and access to them was provided by entrances or courts by the side of every alternate house in Market Street.[11] This defect in town planning was to have very serious results on the future of Ashby as a Spa town. Perhaps the most important factor in the town's growing popularity was the publication of Sir Walter Scott's romantic novel *Ivanhoe* in 1830, which features the town prominently.

Public Sanitation

An entry in February 1832 reflects Thomas Smith's anxiety concerning Asiatic Cholera, which first reached the United Kingdom in October 1831. In 1831–1832 there followed a very deadly epidemic resulting in 16,000 deaths. Nothing was known about its cause, and it was often regarded as evidence of divine displeasure. However, Dr J. Kennedy MB, the resident physician to the Ashby Baths, who lived in Rawdon Terrace, delivered a public lecture entitled *The nature, causes and prevention of Cholera*, at the Ivanhoe Baths Rooms on 17 September 1832 at 12 noon. Tickets cost 2s. 6d each[12] and the lecture was arranged by the Board of Health for Ashby-de-la Zouch. At this time a Cholera Provident Society was set up in the town. In 1832 many practitioners did not accept that the disease was capable of transmission from one person to another. Cholera was believed to be caused by 'sudden transitions from heat to cold, great fatigue or muscular exertion in the sun, indigestable food, acid fruits, melons, cucumbers or the inhalation of noxious gases'.[13] The belief was fast growing, however, that most infectious diseases were caused by filth. Bacteriology was still not understood and it was not until the early 1880s that Robert Koch succeeded in discovering the *cholera bacillus*.[14] However, Thomas Smith lived and practised through the carbolic age – a period when every energy was exerted to abolish dirt, bad smells, and nuisances. We now know that the theory was mistaken, but the 'sanitary revolution' that resulted had great and beneficial effects on the health of the nation. Consequently, when a case of infectious disease occurred in any house, the first action to be taken was to inspect the drains, and in particular it was long believed that diphtheria was caused by bad smells. Thomas Smith, like his father and grandfather before him, was a miasmatist, holding that the transmission of disease in cases where these were clearly not contagious, was effected by a miasma which emerged from the earth, causing fever whenever an epidemic was rampant.[15] We find that Thomas Smith notes the establishment of a Board of Health under 'the Sanitary Act' (the Public Health Act 1848), and the commencement of the draining of the town in 1852.

This all arose because of a near disaster for the town. The Baths were no longer being patronized because of the offensive smells pervading the Bath Grounds caused by the filthy state of the Gillwiska Brook, whilst the mortality rate among infants of under one year, as revealed by the official registration of births and deaths, which had been recorded since 1837, was one in six, as against one in nine in Smisby and in the remainder of the Union of Ashby-de-la Zouch. When compared with Smisby, 'every individual born in the town of Ashby loses nearly two years of life and ... every adult loses nearly 10 years.'[16] This was the result of Ashby-de-la Zouch having asked the General Board of Health for an inspection under the provisions of the Public Health Act. The General Board carried out inspections in 192 places in England and Wales which had petitioned it for help in the first year after the Act came into force. For this it was necessary for at least 10 per cent of the rate payers to petition for an inspection. The population of Ashby had increased from 2,674 in 1801 to 5,691 in 1851 and no steps had been taken to provide services for such an increase. There was no public supply of water although individual houses had the use of springs. Most of the inhabitants had to depend on unreliable and often contaminated public wells. The inspection was carried out by William Lee, the Superintending Inspector, who was accompanied during his inspection by the following local persons:

C. A. Dalby, Union Surgeon for the Ashby District.
(Thomas Smith's partner)

Joseph Kidger, Land Surveyor.
Robert Chaplin, Architect of the Ivanhoe Baths and the
Royal Hotel.
Edward Mammatt, Geologist, Musician and Organist,
totally blind since he was eight years of age.
John Mammatt, elder brother of Edward, Marquess
of Hastings's agent who had built the Manor House
in 1831–1832.
William Dewes, Solicitor and Clerk to the Justices.
Thomas C Dewes.
John Knight, Clerk to Edward Mortimer Green,
Solicitor, and described as 'Lawyer' in the notes.
John Salisbury, builder of the Leicester Road Railway
Bridge.
Mr Usherwood, a tax collector.

Very frank evidence was adduced from these witnesses, although
the Inspector was concerned at the differing testimonies he received from John Mammatt, the Lord of the Manor's agent and
the Reverend Marmaduke Vavasour, the Vicar of St Helen's,
concerning 'the state of burial grounds.' John Mammatt gave the
following testimony:

> I reside at The Manor House near the Parish Church
> burial ground. The Churchyard is in a very crowded
> state; additional room is absolutely necessary. I see
> graves open frequently; in nine out of ten cases the
> remains of the dead are disturbed and exposed. I am of
> opinion that interments ought not to continue amidst
> the dense population of the town. The graves vary from
> 4 to 8' deep. The soil for a depth of 4' is a rich loam;
> below that a stony shale at least 30' thick. In the lower
> part of the churchyard the graves are wet, in the upper
> dry. In 1812 a faculty was obtained by which half an
> acre was added to the burial ground of the parish. There
> is a drain through the part added in 1812 but it existed
> before that time. In the new part there are some spaces
> left between the graves but this has not been done in any
> systematic manner nor with any definite object. There is
> a burial ground connected with Trinity Church but the
> interments are not numerous there. The ground has only
> been opened about six years. There are no burial grounds

attached to any of the dissenting places of worship. The sights frequently presented by the parish churchyard are of a very painful character. There has been no proposal for the formation of any public cemetery.

The Revd Vavasour was prevented from attending the hearing but he subsequently sent the following communication to the Inspector:

The parish churchyard contains, exclusive of the Church, about an acre and a quarter and Trinity Church one rood and a half. The annual number of interments in the former will average eighty-three. The soil is very good and dry in the parish churchyard and lies rather upon an elevation. The burial ground at Trinity Church is at present wet. The depth of the graves are from 4 to 6' never less than 4' from the surface. No offensive effluvia arises from either of the graveyards. Corpses generally remain from twelve to fourteen years undisturbed in the parish churchyard; in Trinity Churchyard but few interments have as yet taken place. There have been no interments in the parish church itself of late years.

William Dewes had this to say:

For a few years the baths were well frequented; there was a considerable influx of company to the town and great benefit was derived from it by the inhabitants. After that time the visitors decreased, until now it can scarcely be called a bathing place. I attribute this mainly to the disagreeable state of the atmosphere in the immediate vicinity of those buildings, and to the effect generally produced by it on the town. The drainage and sewerage of the town is most defective, the town is infinitely worse than if it had no drains.

In his report, the Inspector referred to the Bath Grounds and to Turks Head Yard (at the rear of Stone's Fruiterers), in the following terms:

. . . a sluice appears to have been put down about 7 years since for the irrigation of the meadows in front of the public Baths above the railway and complaints were made that when the process of irrigation was going on there, the whole of the drainage of the town was pent up as far as the old stone yard on the upper side of Market Street. On examination I found the brook is contracted just below the Ivanhoe Road and, at the grooves of the sluice, it is 6' wide and 4' deep. This was stated to be full when the meadows were under irrigation. Immediately above are two public drains, one of them from the baths and adjacent houses. When these outlets are closed, the water is dammed up, and the refuse stands in them for a great distance, and the foul gases are driven back into the buildings, and through the gratings of the streets. Another consequence of this sluice is, that 12" deep of solid refuse requires to be taken out of the brook course every year, from thence to the mill below.

The brook adjoins Turks Head Yard, and amidst there an intolerable stench; privys are built so as to empty their soil into it. Under one of them about half a cubic yard of night-soil lay exposed in the bottom of the brook. Mr Dalby stated there had been several cases of fever in the Yard.

The Inspector had more to say on 'the evil construction of privys.'

In many parts of the town privys are constructed under sleeping rooms. In a majority of those which came under my notice, there is neither drain, cess pool, nor ash pit; and on inquiring how they were emptied, I was informed that the only means available was to scoop out the soil from under the seat and carry it away in buckets. I have already adverted to the numerous instances of privys emptying their contents directly into the brook.

Mr Dalby gave a sombre report in his capacity as Union Surgeon for the Ashby District. He said that the four Law Commissioners' returns showed a large proportion of epidemic disease for a town in a position naturally so healthy as Ashby.

'In the year 1844 Typhus Fever prevailed in Ashby to an alarming extent. I am not aware of any extraordinary circumstances to which that unusual extent of fever could be attributed. It commenced in autumn and continued through the winter. The number of cases was great, but the intensity of the disease was not more than common. The disease became in some sense endemic, and has continued to the present time in a somewhat mild typhoid form, but with occasional instances of intensely active and fatal character. During the last and present winters we had some cases among the more opulent classes, the wife of my Partner was one,* and the year previously his female servant. On the south side of Market Street several cases of typhus have occurred among the wealthy inhabitants. About this time last year, there was one of the most virulent I ever witnessed, near the upper part of Market Street, and also near the drain which passes under the houses lying between Market Street and Ivanhoe Road. During the present winter a bad case of typhus occurred in the same street, about midway between the two cases previously named, and also adjoining to the same drain. Besides this there have been many of a milder form. From the brook, up past my own house in Kilwardby Street, and about me, is the most unhealthy part of the town. I have had much sickness in my own family since residing there.

There is a very offensive drain connected with the Vicarage in Upper Church Street. The Revd Mr Vavasour, the Vicar, has had several cases of typhus in his own house. About the Green, and all along the line of the brook, also in the Courts already alluded to, between Market Street and Ivanhoe Road, there has been much typhus and low fever of a constant kind with diarrhoea and general debility, especially among the women, who are mostly confined to the houses.

I attribute these diseases to the noxious emanations arising from the want of better sanitary works and regulations, and I am clearly of opinion that the causes of the above diseases which I have enumerated as existing in the town, are removable by improved

---

* This would have been Hannah Kirkland.

drainage, water supply, ventilation etc.; I believe that
all my medical brethren here coincide with me in
this opinion.'

The work of the clergy was illustrated by the evidence of The Revd
Thomas Fell, Minister of Holy Trinity Church who said:

> I have been called in to see a dying man, and could
> not bear to enter the room until it had been ventilated
> for half an hour. As a general rule, one meets with
> the least welcome in the dirtiest houses. The social
> position of the people thus depressed is in a direct
> ratio to their physical and moral condition. They
> become careless and indifferent. There are many
> lodging houses for tramps in Ashby-de-la Zouch. I
> am in the habit of visiting them; they are generally
> unhealthy places. The people in them herd together
> without distinction of sex, and the greatest immorality
> prevails. That immorality is connected with the filthy
> condition of the houses, bedding, and persons of
> the occupants.

The Report never seems to have been published and the proceedings
of the local elected board were held in camera. However, immediate
steps were taken to improve the sanitary condition of the town and
the *Leicester Chronicle* reported that economic conditions had so far
improved, that public improvement was 'the order of the day' and
Leicester which had fallen behind other towns because of its 'laud-
able desire to get out of debt' was now able to follow the example of
other large towns. Liverpool was about to spend 2 million pounds
on the assize courts, Manchester had embarked on the opening up
of confined courtyards and the provision of parks; Edinburgh had
its public baths, while 'Birmingham, Sheffield, Preston – and to
come nearer home, even Ashby-de-la Zouch – are all actually on
the stir or about to be so, to add to public health comfort and
convenience by arrangements for improving their streets buildings
or suburbs'.[17]*

---

* Although the drainage of the town was completed in 1852 or 1853,
the cost of connecting up the houses to the new sewers was more
than the tenants could afford or the landlords were prepared to outlay.
Consequently earth privies continued in use until the end of the century.

Harsh Discipline

It is interesting that Thomas Smith makes reference to Private John White of the 7th Royal Hussars being killed as a result of military flogging at Hounslow Barracks on 15 June 1846. Thomas Smith's grandfather was aware of the danger of shock in the practice of surgery and it would seem that he disapproved of public punishments of this nature. Public opinion had been hardening against military flogging since 1835 when a marine died after receiving 245 lashes. On Easter Sunday 1841 Lord Cardigan (subsequently of Balaclava fame) ordered a defaulter to receive 150 lashes at Hounslow Barracks in the same room and immediately following Divine Service. Great national indignation was expressed in the press and Lord Melbourne, the Prime Minister, advised that Cardigan be removed from the command of the 11th Hussars. Cardigan was saved by the Duke of Wellington, who advised that no military offence had been committed.[18]

Gas comes to Ashby

Among the snippets of local news noted by Thomas Smith is the building of the gas works on 11 July 1833 and the laying of pipes. Progress was so rapid that the gas was lit and operating that same year. The Ashby Gas Company had been formed in 1833 with £2,000 capital divided into shares of £25 each. In 1847 an additional £5 per share was called up. By 1852 the venture had proved to be consistently profitable paying an annual dividend of 5 per cent. The practical consequence of all this was that a gas lamp was put up in the Doctor's yard and lit on 8 September 1834.

At this time a new pinfold and prison with an adjoining house for the Gaoler was built on the Green. The building served the town until 1861 when the Police Station in South Street was built. The prison had an impressive gateway capable of admitting the black maria with an exercise yard and cell block on the northern boundary. Sadly it was demolished in 1989.

Nineteenth Century Poverty

The short but busy reign of King William IV saw the implementation in 1836 of the Poor Law Act and the election of the first trustees. The 'House of Industry' had been built on Nottingham Road ten years previously. It was 'a spacious brick building with two receding wings accommodating about 100 paupers.'[19] Up to that time the Poor Law System introduced in the reigns of Queen Elizabeth and King Charles I had afforded the poor 'a means (with proper industry) to feed and clothe themselves.'[20] Scotland and Ireland had no statutory provision for the poor at all. The old system operated on a parish basis and the harshness that often resulted in practice had been illustrated by a case involving an Ashby pauper in 1817. A little girl, by name Ann Sutton, from Stretton-en-le-Field when ten years of age was bound apprentice by that Parish until she was twenty-one to Messrs Pilkington and Webster, of Ashby, who were cotton manufacturers. We remember Mr Webster having his children inoculated against the cowpox in 1800. The manufactury was in Bath Street and the employees lived on the premises and wore particular dresses provided by their employers. In November 1813 Pilkington and Webster went out of business and Webster went over to Burton-upon-Trent to see a Mr Peile, who had another cotton manufactury there. He proposed that his apprentices be assigned to Peile but he did not mention their names or their number. Peile agreed to take them and Webster made application to Magistrates to get the assignment of the apprenticeships completed. The Magistrates objected that this could not be done without the consent of the several parish officers. Webster then told Peile that he could do no more than rely on the verbal agreement, which was that Peile should take over all his apprentices. Ann Sutton was at that time still with Pilkington and Webster. About eighteen of the apprentices were sent to Peile at different times and on each occasion one of Pilkington and Webster's servants was sent to deliver them to the overlooker of Peile's manufactury. However many of the apprentices did not go to Peile, but went where they wanted to and got situations elsewhere. After it was found that the parish apprentices could not be formally transferred, Ann Sutton's mother asked Webster to have her discharged as she wanted to get her a place elsewhere in service. Webster gave his consent and Ann Sutton left with his knowledge to get a place elsewhere. However, Ann did not obtain her expected work and after she had been at home about five weeks, Webster called on her mother and recommended that she should take her to Peile at Burton where she could get employment. About three weeks later Ann went to Peile with another girl, wearing their ordinary clothes and not taking their indentures with them. They were both hired as servants for fifty-one weeks by Peile's foreman, who did not know that they were apprentices. Ann continued in Peile's service until she was removed because she was expecting a child and had become a pauper and a burden upon the parish. The Magistrates made an order for Ann to be removed from the parish of Burton-upon-Trent to that of Ashby, because her indenture of apprenticeship had never been formally assigned to Peile at Burton. Ashby appealed to the Court of Kings Bench, where the case was argued before Lord Ellenborough, the Lord Chief Justice, Mr Justice Bayley and Mr Justice Abbott, on 12 November 1817, who quickly decided that the Magistrates were correct and that Ashby would have to bear the cost of maintaining Ann Sutton and her child. It would be interesting to know whatever happened to Ann Sutton. It shows, however, how much time and expense the parish was prepared to involve itself in to avoid maintaining just one poor child and her baby.[21] The House of Industry, or the Ashby-de-la Zouch Union Workhouse on Nottingham Road, was originally purchased for £2,000 and was considerably enlarged during the nineteenth century. An infirmary was built adjacent to it in 1843 at a cost of £752. By 1877 about ten acres of land was attached to the workhouse of which three acres was cultivated by the able bodied paupers. The profits from the land for the year to March 1876 amounted to £202.18s. 5d. There was then accommodation for 300 paupers and the large boardroom also served as a chapel. The staff comprised a resident master and matron with a clerk.[22] The workhouse was demolished during the 1939/45 war and the site now forms part of an industrial estate.

Failure of the Bank

Messrs Fishers & Co. was the local bank which had been founded under the auspices of Joseph Wilkes. The day to day running of the bank was in the hands of Edward Mammatt, of Overseal, who was also the agent for the Marquess of Hastings. Mammatt died suddenly on 15 January 1835 and an immediate loss of confidence and a run on the bank resulted. Mammatt's son John (of the sanitary report), and the other directors, J. N. Fisher and J. Simmonds, endeavoured to maintain the credibility of the bank, but failed to do so. Difficult creditors' meetings were held, and ultimately 13s 4d in the pound was paid out to the creditors. However, as late as 21 July 1840, J. N. Fisher was writing to Mammatt indicating that settlement would be made to five particular shareholders on 24th of that month.[23]

Queen Victoria's Coronation

Queen Victoria's coronation in 1838 was celebrated in Ashby with customary patriotic enthusiasm, and for the first time the poor women sat down to tea in the North Street's school playground. The organizing committee were regaled at the Royal Hotel two days later, and it is interesting to note that Edward Mammatt was in the chair, and among the tradesmen were Peter Servantie, formerly Pierre Servantie, French prisoner of war, batman to one of the French officers, who had settled down and married in Ashby and had set up business in the town as a barber. In 1837 he was tenant of a house and garden in Wood Street from the Marquess of Hastings.[24] This note dated 20 June 1838 mentions the Royal Hotel, the name having been changed from the Hastings Hotel in 1836, seemingly in honour of Queen Adelaide, consort to King William IV. The Queen was a frequent visitor to Earl Howe at Gopsall and at Sudbury.

Church and State

The building of the new Holy Trinity Church was hastily recorded but the details of the price, the date, and the personage who laid the foundation stone, were all left blank and never completed.

Thomas Smith records the setting up of the first small claims court in Ashby. Prior to the building of the Courthouse in South Street in 1861 the County Court was held monthly in a large room at the Royal Hotel known as 'the Public Office.'

Medical Limitations

We are reminded of the limitations in medical treatment when we read of the fearful sufferings of Thomas Smith's old horse who had been 'taken ill on the first days hunting after the frost'. Believing that the main treatment for all diseases was a spare diet, blood letting and purging, the poor horse was subjected to bleeding and purging, and 'he never ceased purging after and was shot at Mr Draper's Melbourn in about two months after being reduced almost to a skeleton.' Henry Menion Hawksworth, who was one of the witnesses to Thomas John's will, lost three wives between his first marriage in 1837 and his own death in 1852, at the early age of forty-five. The hopeless resignation of the patient to the terminal nature of so many diseases is illustrated by a verse of doggerel, popular among the monumental masons of the period. The author has found two such in Swepstone Churchyard, one dated 1785 and another as late as 1867, which read as follows:

> *A lingering sickness did me seize*
> *and no physician could me ease*
> *I sought for rest but all in vain*
> *till God did ease me of my pain.*

Queen Adelaide

Queen Adelaide, now the Dowager Queen, seems to have been the only member of the Royal Family to ever have visited Ashby officially since the seventeenth century. On 26 October 1839 she was met by local gentlemen on horseback on the Measham road. They formed a procession to escort the dowager Queen to Holy Trinity Church, then in course of construction, approaching the church through Hill House grounds from Wilfred Place. She visited the Castle ruins and the Ivanhoe Baths and returned to the Royal Hotel for tea. She came to Ashby again on 4 August 1840 to see the Holy Trinity Church shortly before it was consecrated. She also patronized Measham, being present at the opening of the National School and giving her name to Queen Street in the village.

Advances in Transport

When Thomas Smith succeeded to his father's practice in 1824 a journey to London was still long and difficult. The 'Sovereign' coach departed from the Queen's Head at 11.30 p.m. on its eight hour journey, staging at Leicester, Welford, Northampton and Dunstable, on the road to London. The journey north started at 12 midnight and the coach called at Burton-upon-Trent, Uttoxeter, the Potteries, and Warrington, en route for Liverpool. A revolution in transport was accordingly brought about by the extension of the Midland Railway from Swannington to Burton-upon-Trent, which was completed in 1845, and the first train ran on 1 March. This rendered desirable a new road from Ashby Station to Packington and beyond, now known as Lower Packington Road. This was a toll road, and the notes record that the first tolls were collected at the Toll Gate Cottage near Laundry Farm on 6 April 1843. The railway provided the shortest and cheapest route from the town to Manchester and Liverpool, and the line was operating before the railway station had been built. Temporary buildings were 'run up' at Ashby and other stations to meet the immediate need. Soon picnic parties were making use of the railway on a regular basis.

Mid-Victorian Ashby

The Gillwiska brook was culverted in March 1855 by Sprigg and Orchard and the course of the mill brook was diverted. In the same year the Doctor's grandson was being pushed around the town in the 'first patent perambulator' ever seen in the locality.

In 1856 the Lamb Inn, which had been made so famous by Jane Sharpe, was demolished and the new Town Hall and market was built on the site. It was built as a private speculation, the Town Hall Company having raised £4,000 by the issue of 400 £10 shares. Originally it comprised a reading room and refreshment room immediately fronting Market Street, with a large room for public meetings above. The market house extended backwards to Ivanhoe Road (South Street) and was 100 yards long, 12 yards wide and contained 22 butchers shops.[25]

Sir Charles Abney Hastings died on 30 July 1858, a bachelor, and his estates at Willesley and Packington passed to his kinswoman Lady Edith Maud Abney Hastings, Countess of Loudoun. A loyal address was presented to her on 13 October. Shortly afterwards she took up residence at Willesley Hall with her husband Charles Frederick Clifton later first Baron Donington. The avenue of trees that can still be seen leading from Willesley to Ashby Castle was planted at that time. It was to her memory that the Loudoun Memorial was erected in 1878 containing an epitaph in her praise by Benjamin Disraeli, Earl of Beaconsfield.

Thomas Smith mentions the building of the new Police Station and Police houses in South Street in 1861. Ward, the Police Superintendent, called on him as a near neighbour and gave him details of prisoners confined in the new cells. In addition to the Superintendent, the Ashby Police Station had a staff of one Sergeant and eight constables.[26]

Henry Weynsford Plantagenet Hastings the 4th Marquess, described by the late Mr J G Shields as the 'rackety Marquess,' whose gambling and extravagance all but ruined the estate, commenced his short but colourful reign as Lord of the Manor with a 'sumptuous dinner' at Moira to celebrate his coming of age on 21 July 1862. Lady Florence Paget (1842–1907), a daughter of Henry Paget and granddaughter of the great Marquess of Anglesey, who was engaged to be married to Henry Chaplin (1842–1923), friend of the Prince of Wales, eloped with the 4th Marquess in the great society scandal of 1864. The 'rackety Marquess' died on 10 November 1868, at the early age of twenty-six, and the tradesmen of Ashby closed their shutters as a token of respect.

Thomas Smith died on 15 August 1869, at the patriachal age of eighty-four and was buried in Ashby Cemetery. One year previously his grandfather's house in Market Street was pulled down by Charles Matthews, the chemist and general factotum: Matthews, who was churchwarden of St Helen's for many years, lived and carried on business at 63 Market Street.

Thomas Smith's widow, Hannah, lived in Ivanhoe Terrace until her death on 27 August 1883. Thomas Smith's last entry was made on 31 March 1868. Thereafter newspaper cuttings abound, interspaced with interesting local events that require no detailed commentary.

Thomas Smith left no male heir, but his younger daughter Lucy did the next best thing and married a surgeon. Her husband, Dr Francis Bangham, practised as an assistant with Doctors Kirkland and Dalby and succeeded to the practice after Thomas Smith's death. Bangham resided at 62 Market Street and was 'highly respected by all classes'.[27] He was appointed Public Vaccinator and Medical Officer for the Union. He retired in 1875 because of ill health and left Ashby. However, he returned to the town and died at 4 Rawdon Terrace on 19 February 1882 aged sixty-four. He was succeeded as Medical Officer and Public Vaccinator by Doctor Charles Roberts Williams MB CM, who also practised from 15 Ivanhoe Terrace. Williams was a member of the first Ashby Golf Club founded in 1895 and was a scratch player.[28] He died on 7 December 1925, still assisted in his practice by the articulated skeleton of Timothy Dunn!

The End of an Era

After the death of Doctor Bangham the only male successor to the Kirklands of Ashby-de-la Zouch, was his son Thomas Kirkland.

Much had been hoped of him and after taking his degree at Jesus College, Cambridge, he had decided to be ordained. However on 10 February 1879 he was returning from a day's shooting at Bishopton, Warwickshire, with his companion and friend, Rev J. Phillipps, Curate of Shottery and Vicar of Bishopton, who was carrying in his left hand a bag containing two ferrets. Bangham was the guardian of the day's sport – four rabbits. When they were about 400 yards from Bishopton Church they stopped to secure the ferrets, which had bitten a hole in the bag. Phillipps held the bag in front of him, whilst Bangham tried to make the bag secure. At this moment, Phillipps inadvertently loosened his hold of the gun on his shoulder, which was capped and loaded with the triggers down. The weapon fell backwards onto the ground and the charge exploded. The local newspaper reported that, 'both gentlemen were instantaneously in great peril, as they stood facing each other; but it is miraculous to think that the charge passed between the legs of Mr Phillipps, and entered the left leg of Mr Bangham inside the calf, just under the knee joint shattering the bone entirely, blowing part of it away, and leaving a hole in its place. Mr Bangham, who bore the injuries most bravely, at once cried out, "I'm shot" and in answer to another enquiry, he replied, "In my leg." Mr Phillipps, as quickly as possible procured some stimulant (which Mr Bangham refused) and also a four wheeler belonging to Alderman Kendall, and drove the injured gentleman at once to the Infirmary . . . '29 Bangham's left leg was amputated above the knee.

One is tempted to ask why Phillipps was carrying a loaded gun in the first place. It is to be hoped that he was a more competent clergyman than he was a handler of fire arms.

Bangham lived at Erdington and married Maria Constance Jagger on 29 September 1880. He died eleven years later without issue. Thomas Smith's daughter, Lucy, lived on into the Edwardian age, actively concerning herself in Church and social affairs. She presided over her surviving daughters Alethea, Mary, Edith and Florence and outlived her daughter Elizabeth, who had married Samuel Morris, the Superintendent of the Great Western Railway at Exeter. Lucy lived to be eighty-three. After her death the entries became intermittent with only one reference to the 1914–1918 war. Time eventually accounted for her daughters all of whom maintained to the end that family pride centred upon Thomas Kirkland MD.

The Kirkland Notes (1789–1931)

Notes of Thomas John Kirkland (TJK), Thomas Smith Kirkland (TSK), Hannah Kirkland (HK), Lucy Bangham (LB) and Alethea Bangham (AB).

The interpretation of the Notes may be assisted by the following short description of Ashby-de-la Zouch in the eighteenth century.

The fortunate discovery in 1950 of the Earl of Huntingdon's Estate map prepared in 1735 by William Gardiner, a land surveyor, reveals in great detail the features of the town in which the Kirklands lived and practised. The map shows the courts between Market Street, North Street and South Street which would have been thickly populated. Persons of quality and substance had servants, coachmen and grooms living in their houses and the surgeons, in particular, often received patients into their own houses for treatment and convalescence. Ashby was a coaching town on the London to Liverpool road with a population of about 2,500 and all the noise and smell of inns, hostels, stables, manure and rubbish. The Gillwiska Brook flowed open across the cobbled Market Street, just west of the island[1] and was spanned by a stone bridge with three arches.[2] The brook provided power for two flour mills, one on what is now Lower Packington Road, and the other at Laundry Farm.[3] Nearly the whole of the town and the surrounding land belonged to the Earl of Huntingdon, the other principal landowners being Thomas and James Richards, of the Mansion House, the Ashby Free School Trustees, Simeon Ashe (whose family founded the Ashe Charity and an exhibition at Emmanuel College Cambridge[4]), and

The Revd Peter Cooper MA, Vicar of Ashby-de-la Zouch, and proprietor of the Glebe Lands. Strangely some property to the south of Market Street, (then Kilwardby Street) and now the site of Kwik Save, was half burgage tenure: this was a tenure in socage, which was a system of holding land in return for services rendered to a superior landlord, and probably a relic of a Saxon liberty that survived the Norman Conquest. Burgage tenure was found where houses, or land formerly the site of houses, in an ancient borough, were held of some lord in common socage at a certain established rent.[5] This might seem to indicate that Ashby-de-la Zouch was in Saxon times a borough, although there is no direct written evidence of this, and the place name Ascebi is undoubtedly Danish. There was a fine Jacobean octagonal butter cross in Market Street, east of where the Town Hall stands, which Throsby refers to as the finest in the county. Just west of this on the north side of the street, immediately to the west of Hussey's shop on the site of 63 Market St, Messrs German's sales office and Renée Jane's shop, was Kirkland's house, from whence he carried on his practice as a surgeon. The garden was to the rear, whilst the land to the north of North Street, now the site of the former Church of England Infant School, was the Doctor's shrubbery. The road to Derby passed through Callis Town and into Woodcote Lane, both names of medieval origin, following the southern side of the winding brook. There was a bowling green on the site of the Burton Road (C of E Primary) School, bounded by the Holywell Stream, on its course from Holywell Farm to The Green. The streets of the old town were much as today (1990) except that Kilwardby Street (then Killerby Street) extended to the Gillwiska Brook, and there was no development beyond Market Street, Kilwardby Street, Bath Street, Hill Street, The Green, Wood Street and Leicester Road.[6] The sloping fields opposite the Mansion House, in Kilwardby Street, were named Dyers Close and Tenters Close, probably because these fields had been used for pegging out linen, after washing, to achieve the whiteness produced by the dew. Hill House (then Hill Top) was a considerable farm. The field names are of interest, and in particular Musson's backside, and Grainger's backsides, indicate the antiquity of some of the surnames of the present day inhabitants. Travelling was difficult, expensive and often dangerous. There were Toll Gates at Boundary, New Packington, Loughborough Turn, Tamworth Road (Midland Garage), Five Lane Ends, Norris Hill and Upper Packington Road.[7]

Although Ashby Castle had not been the residence of the Lords of the Manor, the Earls of Huntingdon, for over one hundred years, the location of the parks are shown on the survey as the Little Park, Prestop Park and the Great Park. The Little Park extended south from the Castle Grounds, to the brook separating Ashby and Packington. This had been used for red deer. The Little Park is mentioned by John Marston in a masque performed at the Castle in August 1606, on the occasion of the first visit of the Countess of Derby to her son-in-law Henry, 5th Earl of Huntingdon, and entitled 'The Lorde and Ladye of Huntingdon's Entertainment of their right noble mother Alice Countess Dowager of Derby.' At the close of the drama a shepherd sings 'a passionate ditty at my lady's departure; he then presents the Countesse with a scarf and adds;

Farewell Farewell
Joy love peace health
in you long dwell
with our Farewell Farewell

so the Countess passed on until she came through the Little Parke where Niobe presented her with a cabinet and so departed.'[8]

In 1735 the Upper Packington Road and Nook Lane were the only roads leading from Ashby to Packington. The Lower Packington Road was not laid down until October 1842. It was completed and the first tolls taken on 6 April 1843. It would in any case have passed directly across the Little Park.

Prestop Park on the hill where Burton Road leaves the town retains its ancient name, perhaps meaning 'Priest's Hill.'[9] Prestop Park was anciently for fallow deer whilst the Great Park (now known as Old Parks) was 'ten miles in compass'.[10]

The road to Burton passed up Kilwardby Street and Hill Street (then called Rosemary Lane).[11] The present Burton Road Hill was too steep for horse drawn traffic and was known as Clap Lane. Travellers for Burton approaching from Tamworth Road seemed to have had an alternative road available to them. There is an eminence on the Moira Road approaching Shellbrook with the ancient name of Nobs Grave. By leaving Tamworth Road near to the Willesley Lane turn and crossing the Moira Road at Nobs Grave, it joined the Burton Road at the foot of Prestop Park Hill. The fields between Moira Road and Burton Road were named 'Crossways'.

The Nottingham Road proceeded by way of the Town Common Land which was not enclosed until twenty years later. Wood Street was called in the enclosure award 'Woodengate Street' and the estate plan shows the gate across the road near to the Hollies. A bridge over the stream near to Featherbed Lane was called 'Tottering Bridge' no doubt for good reason.[12] On 26 June 1748 a labourer by name John Dent was buried at St Helens Church having been 'killed in ye Wood Street by the crush of a cart'.[13]

The Bath Grounds were known as Hall Meadow and the Tamworth Road followed Wilfred Place, joining the modern road near to Midland Garage. The houses at Lyons Well were built to front onto that road, as was a house known as a Paragon House and recently demolished. The road to Tamworth may not have been too salubrious as one field is named Beggars Bushes and another Dirty Ditch.

The civil Government was administered locally, as it had been since the time of King Canute,[14] by three petty law officers comprising a Constable and two Headboroughs, who were appointed annually at the Court-Leet for the Manor of Ashby-de-la Zouch held under the authority of the Lord of the Manor. In 1747 Francis 10th Earl of Huntingdon was Lord of the Manor and the Lord's Bailiff presided at the meetings which in 1775 took place at the Angel Inn (now the Queen's Head). The town water supply consisted of several springs, notably Holywell in the Callis, Lyons Well in Wilfred Place, and Perrins Well at the site of the Loudoun Memorial.[15] Houses in the town had their private wells but all water had to be carried into the houses.

Fire prevention left much to be desired. On 12 July 1753 fire destroyed 150 bays of buildings whilst twenty years later five houses were burnt down as a result of a fire which started in Mrs Reasons' hatters shop.

The town had a Cavalier tradition, the Castle having been one of the principal royalist strongholds for King Charles I during the Civil War. Stories would still have been told of how the royal army of 6,000 Cavalry and Infantry under Lord Astley and Sir Marmaduke Langdale quartered in the town on 27 May 1645 on its march from Uttoxeter to Leicester, which it captured on 30 May. Following the King's defeat at Naseby, the remnant of that same army passed through Ashby again, and it was firmly believed that the village blacksmith had shoed King Charles I's horse at the Castle Inn, Hugglescote, and had seen the Royal insignia on the horse shoe. It was not surprising therefore that politically the town was Tory. The franchise was limited to freeholders and in the by-election of 1719, of forty-seven voters in Ashby, only four voted for Lord William Manners the Whig candidate. In the general election of

1775 the Whigs collected twelve votes against forty-four for the Tory candidate. Kirkland voted Tory in this election and never seems to have altered his allegiance. However, Mr Pochin, the Whig candidate was elected in 1780 largely because the expense of the previous election had been more than the town could afford.[16]

Political events created interest in the town such as when John Thelwall (1764–1834), a fashionable lecturer and secretary to the radical Earl Stanhope, passed through on 17 November 1797. He had stood trial for 'constructive' treason in October 1794 with Hardy, a shoemaker and secretary of the London Corresponding Society and Horne Tooke, the genial ex-cleric, and although all were acquitted they had received sentences of imprisonment on lesser counts. Ashby-de-la Zouch was a self-sufficient market town, largely untouched by the Industrial Revolution that was to follow, proud of its Grammar School and tradition of independence and addicted to gossip. The town suffered from the coarseness of 18th century society and the Revd W. B. Stevens recorded that in 1792 the Revd John Dewe, headmaster of Appleby School, a sensitive and religious man, would 'not ride through the town of Ashby because a foolish wench had been treated at an ale house, in a drunken frolic, by some Bloods of the Place, with brutal indecency'. He also commented that 'the People of this Place live in a nook of the world very much among themselves. They are indeed a Peculiar People, zealous of good eating'.[17]

The Kirkland Notes

At Easter Fair on Monday and Tuesday, 1 and 2 April, 1793 the fall of snow was so great that few people could get. (TJK)

In 1813 four fairs were held annually in Ashby-de-la Zouch; there was also a Statute Fair for hiring servants and a weekly market plentifully supplied.[18]

By 1831 *'The fairs of which there is generally a good show of horses and cattle are held on Shrove Monday, Easter Tuesday, Whit Tuesday, the last Monday in September and 10 November. It has also a Statute Fair for hiring servants on the first Tuesday after 21 September. The market is held on Saturday and is well supplied with meat, poultry, butter, eggs, vegetables and fruit.'*[19]

By the end of the nineteenth century fairs and markets were held at Ashby-de-la Zouch on Shrove Monday, Easter Tuesday, 10 November and one on the first Tuesday after 21 September for hiring servants.[20]

During the twentieth century the only fair has been the annual Statutes Fair which is still held on the first Tuesday after 21 September. It is now extended however to include the preceeding Friday evening, Saturday and Monday. The Statutes Fair may be a Patronal Fair as the Patronal Feast of the Parish Church was held on Holy Cross Day (10 September) which would have fallen on or near 21 September prior to the alteration of the calendar in 1752.

Rejoicing at the Queen's Head for the Restoration of King George III, 18 March, 1789. (TJK)

The Queen's Head occupied the site of the Midland Bank. It was transferred to its present site, then the Angel Inn, subsequent to 1812.

The symptoms of King George III's illness were recorded in the greatest detail. It is now believed that the Royal malady was Porphyria.

Post from Loughborough began to go everyday Monday 10 June, 1793.
Post from Atherstone everyday began Sunday 30 November, 1794.
Post from Burton everyday began 1 May, 1801. (TSK)

By 1831 the mail from London and the South arrived at 9.30 a.m. It was collected for London at 4.30 p.m. The Northern mail arrived at 4.20 p.m. and left at 9.45 a.m. All post was delivered to the Post Office at 10.00 a.m. and at 5.00 p.m.[21]

An earthquake at half past eleven at night on Wednesday 18 Nov., 1795 at this place. (TJK)

This earthquake was officially recorded as occurring at 11.00 p.m., on 18 November, 1795. The shock was felt from Leeds to Bristol and from Norwich to Liverpool. It was particularly severe at Derby and Nottingham and was described as 'a smart shock of an earthquake felt in the neighbourhood' of Mansfield.[22]

Earthquakes of this type have been recorded recently. On 11 February, 1957, a tremor caused damage to buildings and the cross to fall from the Loudoun Memorial in Bath Street. The epicentre was at Diseworth. It was recorded at 3.6 on the Richter scale. On Wednesday 30 May, 1984 at 3.55 a.m. a tremor recorded at 2.7 on the Richter scale was felt in Ashby-de-la Zouch deriving on the Thringstone fault.[23] On 24 April 1990 the town was shaken by an earthquake centred on Wrexham reaching 5.2 on the Richter scale.

Gibb's Subscription Horse bought of Mr Green Saturday 15 Aug., 1795 then just turned four years old, price ten guineas. (TJK)

A Mr John Gibbs died 4 February, 1797. A subscription horse was so named when various individuals agreed to subscribe money for the siring and rearing of the horse.

108

Mr Jno Mee began to new-front his house Wednesday 29 Aug. 1792. (TJK)

Jno Mee was a shoemaker. 'New-fronting' involved the construction of a contemporary front to an older building.

Mr Wilkes' weaving building built in the year 1792. (TJK)

Joseph Wilkes of Overseal (1732–1805) industrialist and inventor. Pioneer in communication. The cotton industry was developed in Measham by Wilkes. In 1802 Messrs Wilkes and Jewsbury were negotiating with Boulton and Watt for a steam engine. The Measham mill was on the southern side of Measham on the site of the motor auction sale ground. Wilkes also operated a brickyard where 'jumbo' bricks were manufactured in order to reduce the tax on bricks.[24]

Mr William Miles robbed between this town and Mrs Nicklinsons Jany 19, 1793. Mr Charles Rowel of Snarestone robbed the same night and supposed by the two same men between here and Measham. (TJK)

In 1802 Mary Nicklinson was the tenant of a farm and ninety-six acres at a rent of £120. The farm 'lies very contiguous to the town, is not made the most of or well-managed by the present occupier'. The farm would seem to have been where Rotherwood now stands.[25]

20 Feb., 1793 English rhubarb from Mr Burton's Bratby twenty-six pound which by drying was reduced to three pounds and a half. (TJK)

Bratby was Bretby, Derbyshire. The Burton family farmed Oldicotes Farm to the north of the Burton-on-Trent golf course. The local practitioner prepared many of the medicaments which he prescribed. When dried the rhubarb was kept in powder form.

First general navigation meeting at the Queen's Head. Friday, 7 Feb., 1792, second meeting Saturday, 22 Sep., 1792.
First spade dug in the canal by Mr Hall of Shackerstone on Thursday, 2 Oct., 1794. (TJK)

James Richards Esq. refused the faculty for his seat Tuesday, 25 June, 1793. His hounds went for the first time of their ever hunting and found on the Woulds 1 Oct. 1795. Killed a hare. Disposed of part of his pack latter end of 1797 and the remainder the beginning of the year 1799.

Appointed Sherriff in Feby. 1796 the assizes on Wednesday 16 March when he was attended from this place by forty-six gentlemen out of which the following were in green.

Mr Pestel	Ashby
Mr Farnel Junr	do
Mr Shaw	do
Mr Lapley	do
Mr Sleath	do
Mr Webster	do
Mr Evans	do
Mr Jos Snelson Junr	do
Mr James Kirkland	do
Mr Thos. Kirkland	do
Mr Thos. Green	do
Mr Evan's Atty	do
Mr Robt. Chapman	Ashby
Mr Slater	do
Mr Sam Beadsmoore	do
Mr Harry Blinkern	do
Mr Thos. Kirby	do
Mr Thos. Dalby	do
Mr Wm. Bott	do
Mr James Goode	Normanton
Mr Wm. Pycroft	Overseal
Mr Michael Buckley	Normanton-on-Sore
Mr Vinrace	Ashby

(TJK)

The Sheriff or Shire-Reeve was the Chief Officer within the County. It was his duty to see that the orders of the Court were duly executed. He was accompanied by Foresters or Bowmen dressed in green and supported by a retinue of local gentry, often colourfully attired.

Ellis Shipley Pestell was a solicitor with an exclusive practice in the town and much respected. In 1802 he lived in a large house (now 53 Market Street) situated in High Street, rent £25 per annum.[26] Described by Rev WB Stevens as 'A strutting little attorney of Ashby'.[27]

Joseph Farnell had a shop on the north side of High Street, 38 feet front. He was a banker and died on 7 December 1802. Mr Farnell Junior would probably have been Joseph Farnell who died in March 1850. This Joseph Farnell is likely to have been the Government Agent who was responsible for the French prisoner of war depot at Ashby paying them each per week. He was a party to two deeds of reinfeoffment dated 10 December 1813 and 9 May 1828 and a mortgage dated 29 January 1845 concerning Ashby-de-la Zouch Free School properties.[28] In 1821 he was living at 71 Market Street and carried on the business of a grocer. The shop was later occupied by Arthur Byatt, a draper, milliner and mantle maker.

Samuel Webster was a solicitor and a tenant of 'good messuage brick and tile three storeys and modern sash front and bow window at the corner of High Street'.[29] This is the shop on the corner of Market Street and Lower Church Street. The rent was then £10.10s. Webster was a solicitor to the Ashby-de-la Zouch Association and a Freemason being a member of the Tyrian Lodge, Derby. His tombstone is in St Helen's Churchyard.

James Bate Kirkland (1753–1821) son of Thomas Kirkland. (See page 54)

Edward Evans was an attorney. He marked as examined a deed relating to property in Market Street on 25 June 1775.

Thomas Green was a liquor merchant and another member of the Tyrian Lodge.

Thomas Dalby was a solicitor. He was articled to E S Pestell in 1788. He was appointed solicitor to the Ashby-de-la Zouch Association on the death of Samuel Webster in 1813. 1803 he was a partner in Piddocke and Dalby solicitors of Ashby.

James Richards was a landowner and squire residing at the Mansion House. He was an old friend of Thomas Kirkland. There is a small watercolour of him by Thomas Dalby in Dalby's scrap book. He married Elizabeth Bacon (*née* Kirk) widow of Joseph Bacon of Bunby, Lincs on 30 November 1792.

William Pycroft was a banker and joint Treasurer of the Ashby-de-la Zouch Canal Company with Joseph Wilkes.

A bear broke out of the White Lion stable unmuzzled, ran down

111

the Mill Lane, up the back lane, down the market place, and was taken near the Woulds, Saturday 4 June, 1794. (TJK)

There is no record of a White Lion Inn in Ashby. The bear was no doubt part of a travelling circus. The animal ran down Mill Lane, up back lane (North Street) and back into Market Street. It was recaptured near Moira.

Coffee Room opened on Christmas day 1794 and papers received for the first time. (TJK)

Coffee houses filled the place now occupied by the Club. It was cheaper and more informal and with a greater admission of strangers. Such houses were also the centres for news, as newspapers were few and expensive.

The Union Inn Measham Chaise passed through this town for the first time Thursday 7 May, 1795. (TJK)

A chaise is a two wheeled, one horse carriage. The Union Inn stood at the corner of High Street and Atherstone Road, Measham. The building was demolished in March 1969. It was built in the late 1780s by Joseph Wilkes. It was known as Wilkes's large Posting Inn and had a cannery consisting of ostlers' houses and stables for thirty-eight horses. It was built of jumbo bricks.

Mr Cattel's old horse Rainbow died middle Nov. 1793. Mr Cattel slept for the first time at his new house Wednesday 30 July 1794. (TJK)

John Cattel, baker, died 2 June 1801.

On Monday evening Jany. 25 1796 between the hours of 10 and 11 o'clock Mary Lakin was struck on the head with a sword by Timothy Dunn, a soldier belonging to the 5th Regiment of Irish Dragoon Guards, which fractured her skull and she died the Friday morning following. Dunn was executed 21 March and dissected in this Town. (TJK)

The Assize Judge was Mr. Justice Rooke. Lakin was a common name in Ashby. In 1802 Richard Lakin was tenant of a cottage on the green and Nathaniel Lakin of a 'neat messuage situate in the High St 30ft. front'.[30] The Regiment was the 5th Royal Irish Dragoons.

112

Francis Tenth Earl of Huntingdon (1729–1789) by kind permission of the Rt. Hon. the Countess of Loudoun. *Photo John Bowker.*

Louise Madeleine Lany (1733–1777). 'La Lanilla'. By courtesy of Bibliotheque Nationale, Paris.

Selina Dowager Countess of Huntingdon. *Photo John Bowker from a contemporary print.*

Extract from John Prior's map of Leicestershire 1777. *By kind permission of the Leicestershire Record Office.*

Calke Abbey, Derbyshire (c.1734) A painting showing the South Front.

Earl Ferrers shooting John Johnson. *From a 19th century print.*
Photo John Bowker.

Battle of Bunker Hill 1775. From the British Martial Register 1806
Photo John Bowker.

Francis Rawdon 2nd Earl of Moira
1st Marquess of Hastings (1754–
1826). *From an early 19th century
print. Photo John Bowker.*

Laurence Shirley 4th Earl Ferrers
(1720–1760). *By kind permission
of the trustees of the William Salt
Library, Stafford.*

Maggy's Cottage, Lount, Leics. John Johnson's house. *Photo John Bowker.*

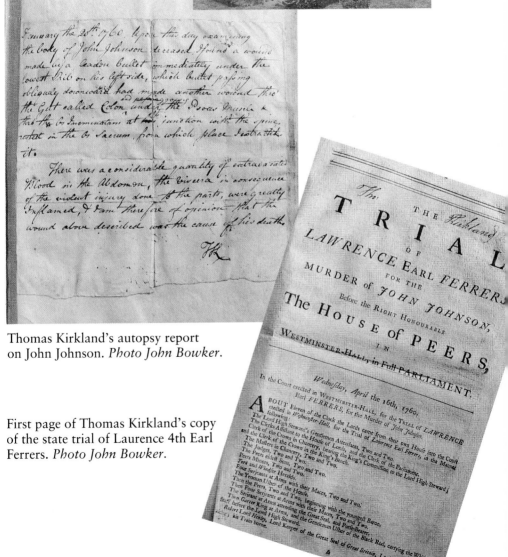

Thomas Kirkland's autopsy report on John Johnson. *Photo John Bowker.*

First page of Thomas Kirkland's copy of the state trial of Laurence 4th Earl Ferrers. *Photo John Bowker.*

Execution of Laurence Shirley, 4th Earl Ferrers. *By kind permission of the Trustees of the William Salt Library, Stafford.*

Thomas Kirkland's signed copy of the execution of Laurence Shirley, 4th Earl Ferrers. *Photo John Bowker.*

Execution of Laurence Shirley, 4th Earl Ferrers. *By kind permission of the Trustees of the William Salt Library Stafford.*

Earl Ferrers in his coffin at Surgeons Hall. *By kind permission of the Trustees of the William Salt Library Stafford.*

Thomas Kirkland M.D.
(1722–1798). *Mezzotint by
John Raphael Smith (1794).
Photo John Bowker.*

Erasmus Darwin M.D. by
George Stubbs. Painted in
enamels on an oval
Queensware plaque. Dated
1783 and fired by
Wedgwood. *By courtesy of
the Wedgwood Museum
Trustees, Barlaston, Stoke-
on-Trent, Staffs. England.*

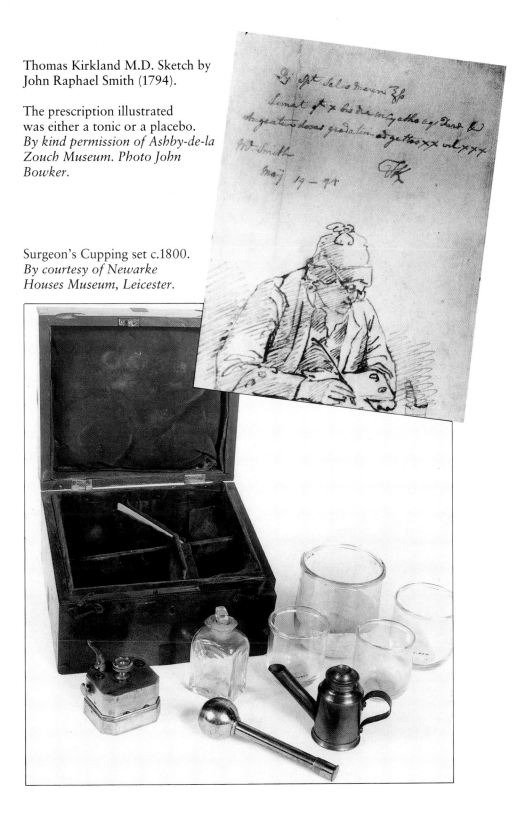

Thomas Kirkland M.D. Sketch by John Raphael Smith (1794).

The prescription illustrated was either a tonic or a placebo. *By kind permission of Ashby-de-la Zouch Museum. Photo John Bowker.*

Surgeon's Cupping set c.1800. *By courtesy of Newarke Houses Museum, Leicester.*

Capture of Guerrière by H.M.S. Blanche. *By courtesy of the National Maritime Museum Greenwich, London SE10 9LF.*

Capture of H.M.S. Guerrière by U.S.S. Constitution. *By courtesy of the National Maritime Museum Greenwich, London SE10 9LF.*

Thomas Kirkland's house, Market St., Ashby-de-la Zouch.
Photo John Bowker from an old print.

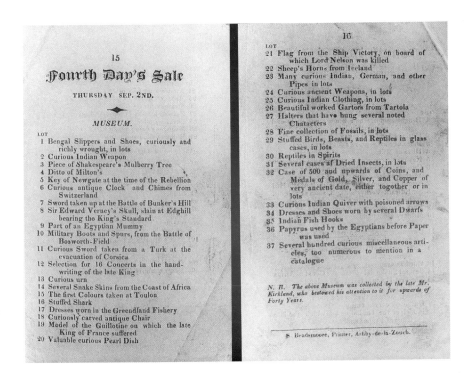

15

Fourth Day's Sale

THURSDAY SEP. 2ND.

◆

MUSEUM.

LOT
1 Bengal Slippers and Shoes, curiously and richly wrought, in lots
2 Curious Indian Weapon
3 Piece of Shakespeare's Mulberry Tree
4 Ditto of Milton's
5 Key of Newgate at the time of the Rebellion
6 Curious antique Clock and Chimes from Switzerland
7 Sword taken up at the Battle of Bunker's Hill
8 Sir Edward Verney's Skull, slain at Edghill bearing the King's Standard
9 Part of an Egyptian Mummy
10 Military Boots and Spurs, from the Battle of Bosworth-Field
11 Curious Sword taken from a Turk at the evacuation of Corsica
12 Selection for 16 Concerts in the hand-writing of the late King
13 Curious urn
14 Several Snake Skins from the Coast of Africa
15 The first Colours taken at Toulon
16 Stuffed Shark
17 Dresses worn in the Greendland Fishery
18 Curiously carved antique Chair
19 Model of the Guillotine on which the late King of France suffered
20 Valuable curious Pearl Dish

16

LOT
21 Flag from the Ship Victory, on board of which Lord Nelson was killed
22 Sheep's Horns from Iceland
23 Many curious Indian, German, and other Pipes in lots
24 Curious ancient Weapons, in lots
25 Curious Indian Clothing, in lots
26 Beautiful worked Garters from Tartola
27 Halters that have hung several noted Chatacters
28 Fine collection of Fossils, in lots
29 Stuffed Birds, Beasts, and Reptiles in glass cases, in lots
30 Reptiles in Spirits
31 Several cases of Dried Insects, in lots
32 Case of 500 and upwards of Coins, and Medals of Gold, Silver, and Copper of very ancient date, either together or in lots
33 Curious Indian Quiver with poisoned arrows
34 Dresses and Shoes worn by several Dwarfs
35 Indian Fish Hooks
36 Papyrus used by the Egyptians before Paper was used
37 Several hundred curious miscellaneous arti-cles, too numerous to mention in a catalogue

N. B. *The above Museum was collected by the late Mr. Kirkland, who bestowed his attention to it for upwards of Forty Years.*

B Beadsmoore, Printer, Ashby-de-la-Zouch.

Extract from sale particulars Thos. John Kirkland deceased 1824.
Photo John Bowker.

Willesley Hall c.1820. Photo John Bowker
from a print.

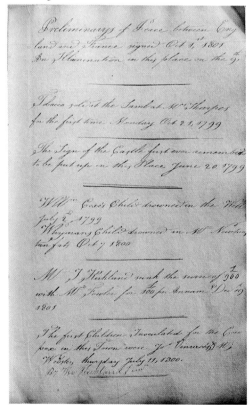

Page from Kirkland notes in
the handwriting of Thomas
Smith Kirkland. *Photo John
Bowker.*

Colonel (later General)
Louis Francois Baron
Lejeune (1775–1848).
*From Lejeune's Memoirs,
courtesy of the Cambridge
University Library. Photo
John Bowker.*

Dowager Queen Adelaide (1792–1849). From a contemporary publication. *Photo John Bowker.*

Extracts from Ashby-de-la Zouch race cards showing Capt. Beecher's participation. *Photo John Bowker.*

32 Horses Octr 3 1837

ASHBY-DE-LA-ZOUCH RACES.

TUESDAY, OCTOBER 3rd, 1837.

To Start precisely at Eleven o'clock.

JOHN STORER, 239, STEWARD.

THE PRIOR PARK STAKES.

Of 7s. 6d. each with £6 added for Maiden Ponies not exceeding 13 hands. Weight for inches. 12 hands, 5st. 7lb.—under, catch weights. Heats, One Mile. The second Pony to have £1 out of the Stakes.

Mr. T. Woodwards b. p. Matilda, 6 yrs old, green and red cap
Mr. Pilkington's br. p. Fatima, 3 yrs old, white and pink cap
Mr. J. Briggs Jun. bl. p. Creeping Jane, blue and yellow cap
Mr. S. Elstead's ch. p. Tommy Roach, purple and yellow stripes
Mr. J. Bradley's br. p. Paddy Carey, 5 yrs old, blue and white cap
Mr. H. Woodhouse's cream col. p. Effie, 3 yrs old, black & white stripes
and black cap

THE BATH STAKES,

Of Ten Shillings each with £12 added, for Maiden Galloways not more than 14 hands. Three-years-old 7st.—Six and aged, 9st. with 7lb. allowed for every inch. Heats, One mile and a-half. The second Galloway to receive £2 out of the Stakes

Mr. J. Briggs's Jun. bl. m. Kitty, aged blue and r. and white cap
Mr. S. Rose's g. m. Lilly of the West, aged pink & blue and blk cap
Mr. J. Potter's b. h. Pickpocket, aged blue and white cap
Mr. Spencer na. g. h. Mount Eagle, 4 yrs old blue & yellow & blk cap
Mr. N. W. Ingle's b. m. Sparrow Catcher, 4 yrs. old, purple and gold
and black cap
Mr. T. Shaw's g. f. by Chance, 4 yrs. old, blk. & white stripe & blk. cap

A HURDLE RACE,

Of Three Sovereigns each with Thirty Sovereigns added, for Horses not tho-rough-bred. Heats, Two miles. Four Leaps in each Heat. The Hurdles to be 4ft. high. Four years-old, 10st. 7lb. Five, 11st. Six and aged. 12st. Gentlemen Riders. The Second Horse to carry 7lb. extra, and if twice a winner 10lb. ner of any Race or Steeple Chase, to receive £5 out of the Stakes. A win-

Mr. Grace's bl. g. Indiaman, 6 yrs old, purple and gold, 12st.
Earl of Chesterfield's b. h. King of the Valley, 5 yrs old, crimson and purple and crimson cap
Mr. Pearce's br. g. Vampyre, 6 yrs old, pink and purple cap
Mr. Ouseley's b. h. Conservative, 6 yrs old, blue and black

The Lamb Inn, Ashby-de-la Zouch. Jane Sharpe's Posting Inn.
Photo John Bowker from an old print.

Thomas Smith Kirkland as a young man.
Photo John Bowker from an oil painting.

Thomas Smith Kirkland in
old age. *Photo John Bowker
from an old photograph.*

St. Helen's Church & Castle ruins at Ashby-de-la Zouch showing the old Assembly Room (demolished in 1830). *Photo John Bowker from a print in T. Wayte's Guide to Ashby-de-la Zouch & the Neighbourhood.*

Rev. Thomas Fell. First vicar of Holy Trinity Church, Ashby-de-la Zouch. *Photo R.O. Jones from a contemporary photograph.*

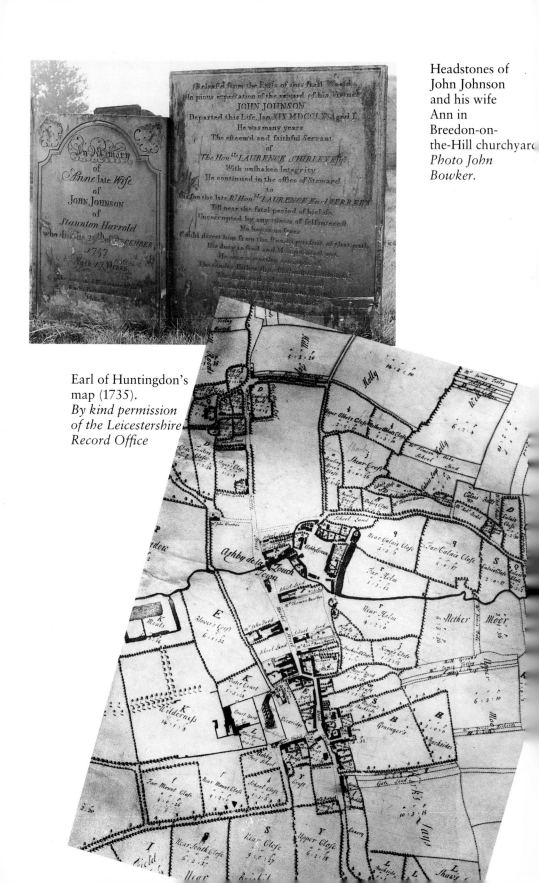

Headstones of
John Johnson
and his wife
Ann in
Breedon-on-
the-Hill churchyard
*Photo John
Bowker.*

Earl of Huntingdon's
map (1735).
*By kind permission
of the Leicestershire
Record Office*

A County meeting called at Leicester by the Earl of Moira to meet P.A. Curzon Esquire respecting the Navigation on Monday 23rd September 1793. (TJK)

Rode my black horse given me by the doctor for the first time to Mr Webb's Donkhill Pitts 19 Sept 1793 which horse I also rode 24 Feby 1794 to the same place being the last time he was rode he was taken ill on his return and died 2 March 1794. (TJK)

A Mr Webb had stables at Pown's Mill near Lichfield which were reported as being burned in December 1793. Donkhill Farm is near Catton, Alrewas, Staffs.[31]

Mr Owston went to his house at the corner to sleep for the first time Friday 19 June 1795.
Saml. Beadsmoore opened his new shop by Sleath's 2 July 1793. (TJK)

A mushroom party went to Formark Sunday morning early 18 Aug. 1793 a quarter before 3 o'clock and returned by 8 o'clock. Thos. Kirkland, Thos. Bedford, Saml. Beadsmoore Jnr., Charles Rice, Master Smith Kirkland Servt. Boy gathered in weight 61 pound. (TJK)

7 Feby. 1799 Mr James Kirkland's cow calved three calves. (TJK)

30 July 1795 Stamford of this place received sentence of death for breaking into the dairy of Jon Simmonds Esq., Butt House, but was reprieved for seven years transportation. (TJK)

Butt House Blackfordby. Stamford stole four tablecloths.[32]

Mr. Timms over Mill rob'd of upwards of 10 pounds on Friday night about 9 o'clock 1 Nov 1793.

In 1802 Samuel Timms was the tenant of Ashby Mills comprising a messuage brick and tile and overshot water grist mill with two pairs of stones, drying kiln, barn, granary, two stables, cow house, dove house with sundry sheds, timbered, tiled in good repair on which the tenant stated he had lately spent upwards of £200. He also occupied another brick and tiled building and overshot water grist mill with three pairs of stones and a windmill. He also occupied 73½ acres of land at a rent of £225 per annum.[33]

113

Sunday 3 Nov 1793 between sixty and seventy of the Queen's 16 Regiment of light horse came here from Nottingham to quell a riot amongst the Colliers at Coleorton: part of them returned on Thursday the 7th and the remainder on Saturday 9th. (TJK)

The first annual Cecilian meeting at the Queen's Head on Wednesday 20 Nov. 1793. (TJK)

28 Nov. 1793 two men taken up at the White heart by the names of Horner and Simpson on suspicion of being Highwaymen but acquit the next day by Justice Hall. (TJK)

Mr Elkington took a level for a Conduit Tuesday 3 Dec. 1793. (TJK)

The Iron and Stone Church gates erected 1791 which came to the shameful price of 120 pounds – Mary Ratcliff died 4 Oct 1791 and after living twenty-six years in a house adjoining the old Church Gates was the first corpse carried through the new gates, aged fifty-three. (TJK)

The old houses above Mr Richards took down in Nov. and Dec. 1793 and the new wall built in Jany. 1794.

Presumably the wall that now divides Glenridding from Strawberry Hill, Kilwardby Street. The old footings of the wall near the road are of stone.

On Saturday night 2 Feb. 1799 the snow was deep and weather so severe that John Green was starved to death on road between here and Snarestone. (TJK)

The register of burials at St Helen's Church contains the following entry under 1799 'Feb 6 John Green'.

Mr Gibbs organist died Saturday Feby. 4, 1797. Buried Tuesday 7. Pall bearers Mr Cattel, Owston, Webster, Robt. Chapman, Thos. Kirkland, Bedford, Concert for his widow the next day. (TJK) *An anthem was sung at his funeral by Mr James Kirkland, Mr Saml. Beadsmoore and two others. The organ was in repairing. A piano lute was taken to the organ loft from which Mr T K Glazebrook at that time in the seventeenth year of his age accompanied the choir.* (LB)

Thomas Kirkland Glazebrook was the son of Dorothy Kirkland (1748–1834) and the Reverend James Glazebrook, Vicar of St James' Latchford. He was the secretary of the first Warrington Board of Health, established in 1831 to make plans against the threatened cholera epidemic which broke out there in June 1832. In this fascinating and amazingly detailed report he makes passing references to his grandfather Thomas Kirkland MD. In 1831 Glazebrook was secretary to the Warrington Dispensary. He died at Southport, 18 January 1855, aged seventy-four.

Mr Webster, Leo'd Piddocke, Thos. Kirkland Junr. initiated Masons at the Tyrian Lodge, Derby No. 379 Tuesday 2 Aug 1796. Mr Thos. Kirkland passed to Fellow Craft Wednesday 24 with Mr Webster and Mr Wm. Evans. Mr Thos. Kirkland raised to Master by himself 22 Nov in the same year. (TJK)

Mr. Thos. Green initiated Mason Tuesday 28 March 1797. (TJK)

The accuracy of all the above entries are confirmed by the minutes of the Tyrian Lodge now no. 253 at Derby.

June 26 1797 Mr Thos. John Kirkland entered his thirty-eighth year and had a great Masonic meeting on the occasion. Copied from the diary of Mr John Simmonds of the Butt House, Ashby-de-la Zouch, dated to commence Jany 29 1796. The Masonic meeting above referred to was a Lodge held in a large room in Mr Kirkland's house. My father Mr Thos. Smith Kirkland had table glass with Masonic device made for that occasion in his possession. (Lucy Bangham) [In margin] *The 26th was his birthday* (LB)

The stagecoach from Birmingham to Nottingham passed through this place for the first time Monday 30 Oct 1797 turned over in the street Thursday 13 Dec 1798. (TJK)

Thelwell passed through this place Friday 17 Nov 1797. (TJK)

F B Davenport shot himself at Thomas Taylor's Dog and Duck, Stanton Tuesday, 23 Jany 1798. (TJK)

Francis Brewin Davenport was a freemason and member of St John's Lodge no. 348 at Leicester. He was appointed Provincial Grand Secretary on 18 June 1793 and must have been well acquainted with the Earl of Moira.[34] In the Derbyshire Quarter Sessions accounts for 1798 he is described as 'Gentleman a Lunatic'.

Robt. Pemberton taken before a Justice for stealing a kettle from Mr Salisbury, bricklayer, 4 Dec. 1798 and committed to prison at the Sessions following brought to trial but no Bill found. (TJK)

A carriage called the Sociable to hold twelve inside passengers came to the George Inn for the first time and the first that was ever known here Wednesday 11 April 1798. (TJK)

A Sociable is an open carriage with two seats facing each other.

Duke of Rutland passed thro this place 5 Septr. 1798.

Duke of Bedford passed thro this place 7 Septr. 1798 Friday. (TJK)

John Henry 5th Duke of Rutland KG (1778–1857) Lord Lieutenant of the County of Leicester, Recorder of Grantham, Cambridge and Scarborough, Colonel of the Leicestershire Militia. Francis Russell 5th Earl of Duke of Bedford (1765–1802); he was a Foxite Whig.

Cross repaired in April and May 1798.
A part of the street belonging to the Earl of Moira paved in Nov. and Dec. 1798 and 7 Jany. 1799. (TJK) Do. in 1830 (TSK)
The Causeway in the south side in 1829. (TSK)

The Market Cross was a handsome octagonal Jacobean structure in the centre of Market Street opposite to the entrance to the Town Hall. The exact position is clearly marked on the Earl of Huntingdon's estate map, 1735. The Foundations were revealed when repairs to Market St were being carried out in October 1990.

Ashby Infantry marched to Church in their uniform for the first time 29 July 1798. (TJK)

Wednesday 5 Septr 1798 the Leicestershire Regiment of Militia was conveyed thro this place in waggons attended by the Duke of Rutland for Ireland. Friday 7 Septr. the West Suffolk and Saturday Septr 8 the South Lincoln. (TJK)

The two estate's one left by my Father to my Brother Frank and the other by my aunt Kirkland Loughbro to my Brother John the annual income of each being £60 were sold to Mr Fisher, Castle Donington 26 Nov. 1798 for £4,257. (TJK)

On Sunday 10 Febr'y 1799 about half past one o'clock, as Mr Muncey of Impington was coming to Cambridge, he observed a handkerchief upon a snow drift, and on approaching the spot, heard the sound of a human voice, upon which he called a shepherd who was then in the field, and they found that the person under the snow was Eliz'th Woodcock, who had been missing since Saturday evening the 2'd inst. The shepperd whose name was Stittle, on coming to the spot, called out 'Mrs Woodcock' and was immeadiately answer'd. 'J'no Stittle I know your voice: for God's sake help me out.' Mr Muncey then ran for her husband who came with assistance and after considerable labour extricated the poor woman from her miserable situation, and conveyed her to her husband's house at Impington.

On enquireing into the circumstances of her being lost, she said that she was returning from market between seven and eight o'clock on Saturday evening; about half a mile on this side of Ipington her horse started; and threw her off together with her basket, that the horse ran from her and she wander'd, with her basket a considerable distance from the road, till she was almost exhausted, having lost one of her shoe's in the snow, when she sat down under a bush in expectation of the snow abateing. Being very much fatigued it is conjectured that she fell asleep, and the wind being high, the snow drifted over her to the height of several feet and there she remained for eight nights without any sustenance except what she received from eating the snow. She said she heard the bell ring for church at Ipington, Histon and Chesterton on Sunday the 3'd, that she frequently heard people passing near. She had beat down the snow as far as her hands could reach, which formed a space for her more easily breathing; and she says it was so light as to enable her frequently to read in an almanack which she had with her. Her basket with the meat etc. was not more than two yards from her; but her legs being buried in the snow were so benumbed that she was unable to make any effort to get it: she perceived the snow waste on Saturday the 9th when she slipt off a branch from the bush under which she had taken shelter, and finding she could thrust it thro the snow above her, fortunately thought of tying her handkerchief to the top of the branch by which means she was providently discover'd.

Mrs Wood is the wife of a small farmer at Ipington four miles from Cambridge: she is about forty-five years of age, and has five children to one of which she gave suck at the time the accident

117

happened. When first taken out of the snow her voice and pulse where as strong as in full health, her legs appeared like those of a drowned person and a partial mortification has taken place.

(Leicester Journal, *Feby 22'd 1799*)

On Tuesday 19 Febr'y 1799 a most unfortunate and distressing circumstance occurred on the forest line of the Leicester Canal, near Sheepshead. In consequence of the thaw, the water swell'd so rapidly in the Reservoir as to occasion the middle part of the head for about thirty yards, the Aqueduct and large embankment to give way; – the violence of the water carried away in its progrefs the whole of Mr Chester's house and premises, a small house near Black Brook, several stacks of Hay and Corn, about fifty head of sheep, and the fences and roads are torn up and the land injured to an extent of near six miles; happily no lives were lost.

(Leicester Journal, *Friday Feby 22'd 1799*)

The Cross pulled down 1827

The Church altered 1829 (TSK)

Mr Danl Mendoza the celebrated Pugilist exhibited in this place, Tuesday Dec 11 and Saturday 15th 1798 dined with me on 11th and supped at the Tripe Club on the 14th. Sparred at Ashby with a man by the name of Peter from Normanton Wednesday Jany 2 1799. (TJK)

Brewins Club removed to Mr Sharpe's at the Lamb Wednesday 17 Oct 1798 and the first club night was on the Monday following. (TJK)

Mr Ralph Orton's house, the sign of the Bear, sold to Mr Shakespear on Thursday 13 Dec 1798 price 654 guineas. (TJK)

1 Augt 1798 Admiral Nelson obtained a great Victory over the French Fleet off the Mouth of the Nile, an illumination at this place. 4 Oct. 1798, a riot happened with some of the Anglesea Militia on Tuesday the 9th at a Ball at the Old George. (TJK)

Mrs Sharpe's new cellar began Monday 29 Oct 1798 first cask tapped Jany. 1 1799. (TJK)

Private Oyster Club 1798 first night Monday 10 Dec at Mr Thos. Green's 2nd – Tuesday 18 Dec James Kirkland's 3rd – Monday 25

Dec at Mr Sleath's, being Mr Jno Nichlinson's night; 4th – Monday 31 Dec at Mr Cattels, 5th – Tuesday 8 Jany. 1799 at Mr John Ingle's, 6th – Tuesday 15 Jany. at Mr Timm's Mill, 7th – Tuesday 5 Feby. at Mr Handley's, 8th – Tuesday 19 Feby. at Mr Owston's, 9th – Monday 11 March at Mr Thos. Kirkland's, 10th – Tuesday 2 April at the Lamb being Mr Robt. Chapman's night, 11th – Tuesday 23 April at the Bulls Head, being Mr Richard Shaw's night.

On Thursday 31 Jany and Friday 1 Feby 1799 the fall of snow was much greater than had been known here for many years and the road so drifted that there was no passing 'till they were cut: another fall on Saturday the 8 Feby. (TJK)

The sign of the Wheat Sheath kept by Mr Farmer, and the houses adjoining pulled down April and May 1803. (TSK)

The Wood Street gravelled beginning of the year 1803 and the Market place paved in May and June the same year. (TSK)

Mr Abney gave a dinner to the Infantry Wednesday 28 Dec 1803 (TSK)

Robt. Abney of Lindley near Nuneaton, Sheriff of Leicestershire, 1777 married Elizabeth widow of James Richards 8 Septr. 1800 living at Ashby-de-la Zouch 1804.

A meeting of the Trustees of the Blue School Charity was held at the Queens Head Inn on Friday 3 May 1799 for the purpose of electing a Master when Mr Orme, then schoolmaster of Melbourne, was chosen.

For Mr Orme five votes	*For Mr Chapman*
James Richards Esq.	*Mr Thos. Kirkland*
Reverend Jno Prior	*Mr Beavington*
Reverend Jno Piddocke	*Mr Newton*
Mr Dewes	*Mr Hudson*
Mr Farnel	(TJK)

Mr Orme open'd his school June 10th 1799. (TSK)

Lord Moira review'd the Cavalry and Infantry on the Woulds 24 July 1799. (TSK)

Captain Needham gave an entertainment to the Infantry at the Lamb, Wednesday 10 July 1799. Expenses –

Supper 70 at		1s
		——
		£3.10s
Liquor		£4.10s
		——
		£8.00s (TSK)

Preliminarys of peace between England and France signed 1 Oct 1801. An illumination in this place on the 9th. (TSK)

Tobacco sold at the Lamb at Mrs Sharpe's for the first time Monday 21 Oct 1799. (TSK)

The Sign of the Castle first ever remembered to be put up in this place 20 June 1799. (TSK)

Wm. Coxe's Child drowned in the Well 2 July 1799.

Whymans Child drowned in Mr Newton's tan vats 7 Oct 1800. (TSK)

Mr T. Kirkland sunk the sum of £900 with Mr Fowler for £100 per annum 19 Dec 1801 (TSK)

The first children inoculated for the Cowpox in this Town were Jos. Vinrace's and Mr Webster's Thursday 11 July, 1800 by Thos. Kirkland Junr. (TSK)

A Buck, given by Earl Moira to the Ashby Cavalry and Infantry, cooked at the Queens Head 12 Aug, 1799 and another, to the Measham Infantry, cooked at the Union the same day, except one haunch which was sent to Ashby Infantry. (TSK)

A Mob of Colliers in this Place in consequence of the dearness of provisions Wednesday 10 Sept, 1800. (TSK)

James Richards Esq., Captain of the Ashby Cavalry died Friday 30 Aug, 1799 aged fifty-three. Buried with Military Honours Thursday 5 Sept. (TSK)

Richards lived at the Mansion House.

A Fox killed in Mr Sleath's yard by Sir Henry Harper's hounds 22 Jan, 1801. (TSK)

This 'kill' would seem to have taken place at Repton School. The Revd W B Sleath was headmaster and Nicholas Smith Kirkland was a pupil. Sir Henry Harpur (1764–1819) was described by Rev W B Stevens as 'the isolated baronet'.[35] He took a lady's maid as his mistress and then spurned the conventions of the time by marrying her!

Massy who is in Gibbits near Bilson was hung Monday 23 March, 1801. (TSK)

The officers of the Ashby, Loughborough and Measham Infantry dined with Earl Moira Monday 24 Oct, 1799. (TSK)

The first meeting for inclosing the Woulds held at the Queens Head, Monday 18 Nov, 1799. (TSK)

This meeting was in connection with the inclosure of the Ashby Woulds.

The Revd. M'Douall came to Ashby 17 Jany, 180— and preach'd his first Sermon on the 21st. (TSK)

The Reverend William M'Douall MA was appointed to the living of St Helen's, Ashby-de-la Zouch by Francis Marquess of Hastings in January 1804. Thomas John appointed him an Executor of his Will. According to Mr Gerald McDouall, of New Zealand, a direct descendant, the vicar was incumbered with a club foot and declined an Archdeaconry because he would have been unable to wear gaiters.

Mrs Walker, daughter of the late Mr John Sowter, drown'd herself in Ansel's Well 25 Sept 1807.   Ansels Well is Annswell.

Marlow order'd for transportation 9 Oct 1805 sent off on the 23rd and The Revd J Piddocke appointed one of His Majesty's Justices of the Peace 8 April 1807. (TSK)

Mr Dinwoodie opened the free school 17 April 1804.

Mr Rossel appointed second master 23 Aug 1804.

Mr Field appointed to the blue school 7 April 1806 and opened on the 16th. (TSK)

Dinwoodie was appointed Master of Ashby Grammar School in succession to the Reverend John Prior following his death in 1803. Prior had not been a distinguished Headmaster despite his many other accomplishments. His failing health impaired his effectiveness as a schoolmaster and it is said that shortly before his death the number of boys had fallen to three or four. During Dinwoodie's time (1803–1812) important changes happened, including the building of the new school house, at a cost of £600. This building, now known as the Hood School, was described in 1818 by Carlisle as 'a modern, handsome building of two storeys' about 60 feet in length. The ground floor was divided into two rooms, one of which was used by the Headmaster for the Classical School and the other by the Trustees'. The upper storey consisted of one room where the English School was held.[36]

Thomas Chapman received his Commission 4 March, 1807. Set off for the West Indies 30 March, appointed Lieut. 27 April, 1808. See the Globe Paper for Wednesday 27 April, his death in the Army List Sept, 1808. (TSK)

Lieut. Thomas Chapman was the son of Thomas Fowler Chapman and Jane Kirkland and a brother to Jane Chapman who was still living in 1870.

Mr Robt. Chapman received his Commission 15 November, dated 31 October, 1807, set off to join his regiment 26 December. (TSK)

Robt. Chapman was another son of Thomas Fowler Chapman and Jane Kirkland.

Monsieur Denegres, a French prisoner, killed in a duel Tuesday 6 Dec. 1808. (TSK)

Sold our estate at Peckleton 4 Nov., 1808 to Mr Boultby of Tooley 53 acres, two roods at £50 per acre received our half after paying the expenses £1320. 0s. 0d. (TSK)

Peckleton is a small village between Leicester and Hinckley. Tooley Park was within the Parish and in 1871 contained 630 acres.

First French prisoners came Friday 21 Sept., 1804. Forty-two officers. Forty more 3 Novr. and about thirty merchants Friday and Saturday 22 and 23 of Novr. 1805.

Forty-seven French and Dutch prisoners came 11 September, 1809.

Ten Dutchmen sent back 6 Novr.

13 Jany., 1810 Four Prussians (received from Ashbourn as prisoners) in the French Service. Thirty one French prisoners that were taken at St Domingo sent home March the first and second 1811, and eleven 7 Augt., 1812. (TSK)

This entry is very incomplete. Apart from St Domingo and the Walcheren expedition of 1809 French prisoners had also been captured at Badajos and after the Battle of Vittoria in Spain in 1812.

Dial put up on the North side of the Church November 1809, six feet four inches in diameter. Dial regilt 1835. (TSK)

Watts the Postman put in the Pillory in this town 23 May, 1812. (TSK)

Crib and Molineaux fought Saturday 28 Sept., 1811 at Crown Point; won by the former at eleven rounds. (TSK)

Sir Sidney Smith passed through this place Wednesday 17 Oct., 1810 and was drawn from the first gate going to Measham to the Queens Head by sixteen men. (TSK)

Sir William Sidney Smith (1764–1840) Admiral of the Fleet. Smith was MP for Rochester in 1802 and had returned to England in the summer of 1807. In 1799 his Defence of St Jean d'Acre thwarted Napoleon's ambitions on India. After he had retreated Napoleon said 'if it had not been for you English I should have been Emperor of the East. But wherever there is water to float a ship we are sure to find you in the way'.[37]

The theatre built in Vinraces yard in March and April 1812.
Played in for the first time by Chas. Stanton's company 8 May 1812, and the last night for that season 17 June.
Theatre in Cotton Mill Lane built. (TSK)

Vinraces yard is thought to be in Kilwardby Street between the Mansion House and the Congregational Church. The theatre in

Bath Street was built in 1828 by a Mr Bennett, the Manager of the Worcester Co.

1830. The old Assembly Room pulled down Decr 1830. (TSK)

1832. Manor House built in the years 1831 and 1832 (TSK)

The Manor House was built by John Simmonds Mammatt (1805–1851), Steward to the Marquess of Hastings. The old assembly room was an early seventeenth century building to the north of Ashby Place, having access to the Churchyard.

Miss Mary Chapman set off for Dublin 10 Sept. 1810 and Miss Jane Chapman 10 Decr. 1810. (TSK)

These were two of the children of Thomas Fowler Chapman and Jane Kirkland.

The new part of the Church Yard taken down in the middle of the summer 1810. The seats in the Church made shorter and the middle aisle made wider in Oct. 1810. The new wooden Church Yard Gate by the School put up Oct. 1810. The new Pulpit put up at the latter end of May and the beginning of June, price £120. Preached in the first time Sunday 16 June by the Revd Mr Ferriman. The new velvet cloths put round the Pulpit 25 Dec, 1811 given by Lady Lowdon.
Church altered and flues laid in 1829. (TSK)

The double decker pulpit was removed when the Church was restored 1877–1880. The sounding board is now used as the vestry table. According to Hextall the church underwent considerable alteration and was given new pews in 1829. It seems that the pews and the floor were old and the gallery projected too far into the body of the church from the west end. Two side galleries were erected and hot air apparatus was constructed near to the north door from whence flues conveyed warmth to all parts of the building. The alterations cost about £1,200 which was raised partly by subscription and Church Rate and the other part by rent of pews.[38] Lady 'Lowdon' was the Marchioness of Hastings and countess of Moira.

The trees in the Wilderness by the side of the Mount Walk planted by Earl Moira's children 17 Apl., 1811. (TSK)

The Earl's children were (1) Flora Elizabeth, later Lady Flora Hastings of Queen Victoria's bedchamber scandal; (2) Francis George Augustus who died an infant; (3) Francis George Augustus born 4 February 1808; (4) Sophia Frederica Christiana, born 1 February 1809; (5) Selina Constantia, born 15 August, 1810; (6) Adelaide Augusta Lavinia, born 25 February 1812.

The old bridge taken down that crosses the street and the two new culverts built in Jan and Feb 1812. (TSK)

Mr Clarke's houses pulled down to build a meeting house Feby. 1812, preached in for the first time Sunday 16 Augt 1812 by the Revd Mr Benson. (TSK)

The 'Westley Society' had been tenants of buildings consisting of a brick and tile building used as a dissenters' meeting house in Kilwardby Street and let to Samuel Clarke at a rent of 7s, per annum. According to Wayte the Wesleyan Methodist Chapel in Kilwardby Street had been built opposite to Clarke's licensed house.[39] According to tradition Wesley preached in a yard to the east of the 'meeting house'. It is now the area between the library and Hendon House.

1813. Wednesday 1 Dec. an ox and four sheep roasted to celebrate the Glorious Victories attained by the British and Allied Armies. Numbers at dinner at the Queens Head 44, ditto at White Hart 52. (TSK)

News had reached Britain of Napoleon's defeat at Liepzig and of the Prussians reaching the Rhine. In November Wellington had commenced the invasion of France over the Pyrenees. This event was reported in the *Leicester Journal* of 10 December 1813 as follows: 'A patriotic feast for the working people of the Town – Sir Charles Hastings of Willesley Hall offered a fat bullock. The bullock and four sheep were roasted in the Market Place and divided into joints which were distributed to the different ale houses in the town according to the numbers entertained at each. Above 500 people were regaled with beef, mutton, bread, potatoes and ale and the remains were distributed by two members of the Committee stationed at each ale house, to any who were ready to receive them. Later nearly 300 women were entertained to tea.'

At 5.00 p.m., 'a most handsome dinner' was served at the Queens

Head and White Hart to the subscribers themselves and their numerous friends. The Revd M'Douall took the Chair. A toast was drunk to Lord Wellington and his Army and 'especially our townsman Captain Kirkland'. Mr Kirkland returned thanks for his son.[36]

1818. Mr John Joyce of Blackfordby shot himself 10 July, 1818. (TSK)

There is a tombstone to John Joyce in Blackfordby Church Yard. He was the son of John and Ruth Joyce and died when he was 53 years of age.

1823. The Marquess of Hastings visited Ashby 4 August, 1823. (TSK)

British Summary and Weekly Intelligence 17 April, 1819.
Our National Debt in £1 Bank of England notes taken at the round sum of £800,000,000 will be found to amount to the enormous weight of 698 tons 2 quarters and 9lbs. Allowing 2cwt. 2 quarters to each man it would require upwards of 5,00 ablebodied porters to carry it away. Two hundred and thirty waggons, with four horses to each, would scarcely be sufficient for that purpose. This calculation is made at the rate of 512 Bank of England notes to the pound. (TSK)

1832. The Epidemic Cholera appeared on the Thames and in London Feby 1832. (TSK)

Lord Rawdon the son of the 2nd Marquess of Hastings came to Ashby for the first time on 18 Septr. 1832. (TSK)

This was Charles Paulin Serlo, later 3rd Marquess of Hastings. He died on 17 January 1851 aged 19 when serving as an Ensign in the 52nd Regiment of Foot. He was drowned when he fell into the Harbour at Dublin.

1833. Gas works began 16 July and began to lay down the pipes 30 July. Lit same year. Winter so mild that hunting was not interrupted by snow or frost one day. (TSK)

1834. Lamp put in the yard and lighted with gas 8 September. Pinfold built and New Prison with a house adjoining on the Green September 1834. Farmers old house pulled down July 1834. (TSK)

126

1835. Messrs Fisher's & Co. Bank stopped payment 17 January, 1835, declared bankrupt Feby. Paid in the whole 13s. 4d., in the pound.

A piece of plate (a silver salver) given to Mrs Eames as a Tribute of respect to her Husband for his generous conduct in permitting the Races to be run over his ground; they were the first races at Ashby in the Nineteenth Century and about ten thousand people attended. The Committee consisted of the following Gentlemen; Mr N Ingle, Mr Spencer, Mr H Woodhouse, Mr T Kirkland. (TSK)

1836. 28 June First Election under the new Poor Law Act. Mr Brown's List. Benj Cheatle, Wm Usherwood and Wm Hood. Mr Simmonds List. Mr Eames, Mr Guest and Geo Germain. The National School built on the ground formerly part of Dr Kirkland's Shrubry. (TSK)

1837. 22 March Ashby Steeple Chases postponed this day in consequence of the ground being covered with snow. A great fall of snow at night the ground covered a foot deep on the 23rd and a severe frost at night which continued every night, very severe until 11 April and snow more or less every day. 15 April the ground covered with snow this morning; it continued to snow heavily all day. Hay selling at £10 to £12 per ton. The Steeple Chases were run on 31 March Mr John Capenhurst beating in both races the celebrated rider Captain Beecher. Capenhurst rode two of the Earl of Chesterfield's horses. (TSK)

1838. 6 Jany. Severe frost set in and continued till The Spring so backward that the Ash Trees were not the least in bud until June and only going in leaf in the middle of the month. 10 January Royal Exchange London entirely burnt down.

Mr Hextall purchased Miss Worstall's houses and new fronted them in June 1838. (TSK)

28 June. This being the Queen's Coronation the poor men and women of Ashby were regaled with roast beef and plum puddin at six o'clock in the evening Poor Women sat down to tea in the National School room and yard. (TSK)

20 June. A Party of Gentlemen and tradesmen about   sat down to dinner at the Royal Hotel, among the company were Mr Edward

Mammatt (in the Chair), Mr Peter Servantie etc etc (TSK)

August. The weather being very wet and the harvest so late that I have for the last 14 years got my hay at the latest by 4 July, this year it was not got until 11 August. (TSK)

The new Church contracted for by Cooper and Lilley for the sum of   and began this month the first stone above the foundation laid by   on the   of   (TSK)

The Church was designed by Henry Hugh Stevens of Derby. The first stone was laid by Earl Howe on 25 August 1838. The entire cost of the building was £3,643. 4s. 4d.[41]

1838. August. The Ashby Small Debts Court came into operation this month. (TSK)

In 1832 the County Court was held Monday in a large room at the Royal Hotel known as the Public Office.

13 Oct. A heavy fall of snow. A severe frost commenced 2 and 3 of Jany and continued about seven week. My old horse taken ill the first days hunting after the frost; was bled and had a purge given him, he never ceased purging after, and was shot at Mr Drapers Melbourn in about two months, after being reduced almost to a skeleton. (TSK)

1839. 14 May. Cold weather and several snow storms during the day. (TSK)

1840. The Dowager Queen visited Ashby 4 August. The Bishop of Peterborough came 4 August. (TSK)

The Trinity Church consecrated by the Bishop of Peterborough August 13/40. (TSK)

A Bazaar held for the benefit of the Trinity Church 29 September and 30th/40 collected £910.

Mr Bell the new Curate preached Novr 29th/40

Wednesday 9 December, 1840 a sharpe frost at night Earl Chesterfield's Stag hounds were to have met at Coleorton on Friday 11th, but could not on account of the frost, rained at night. Hunted *with Lord Hastings on Saturday about one o'clock at   . Frost continued to the end of the year and until 16 Jany, 1841. (TSK)*

Decr. had two horses bad of the Distemper (Influenza) towards the end of the month. (TSK)

1841. This year commenced with a severe frost which continued until Saturday, 16 Jany. Snow began on Saturday 2 January and continued on the ground to Saturday 16 March on Monday very severe frost on Tuesday and Wednesday the 19th and 20, 21, 22 January 25, 29, 31 and snow which continued on the ground to 11 Feby with severe frost. 7 Feby the thermometer 12 degrees below freezing.

5 The Grey Mare bad of the Influenza.

Frost continued nine weeks and one day.

March.
Plate glass used for shop window for the first time in Ashby by Mr Welch, Draper.

Mr Cape's front building pulled down and rebuilt with stone front in August and September. (TSK)

1842. Mr Davys' house new fronted August September October. October begun a new road to the Mill and Packington. (TSK)

This was the Packington Road.

1843. Toll taken on the new road to Packington for the first time 6 April.

April. Steeple Chases and Hunt Dinner at the Hotel, 57 dined.

8 April Marquess of Hastings Hounds met at the Hotel.
The Revd S B Sweet preached his first Sermon in Ashby 10 September. (TSK)

1844. The new Royal Exchange opened in London by the Queen Monday, 28 October. (TSK)

1845. The clock of the new church put up October. (TSK)

1846. Death from Military Flogging. 15 June Frederick John White, Private in the 7 Royal Hassars was flogged and died 11 July. He received 150 lashes with a cat delivered by two Farriers giving 25 lashes each in their turn. Colonel Whyte and Dr Warren of the Regiment being present at Hounslow barracks. (TSK)

1847. The Railway commenced June. (TSK)

1849. The Railway opened and two trains each way on 1 March. (TSK)

1850. First Picnic Party at Ashby on 3 June by railway from Leicester and Burton. Numbers of passengers from Leicester:

First Class	59
Second do	557
Desford and Bagworth do	30
Passengers from Loughborough and the stations north of the town	150
	796
Passengers from Burton and other stations	400
	1196 (LB)

1852. A Board of Health established and commenced draining the town under the Sanitary Act. (LB)

1854. The Ashby and Sparkenhoe Agricultural and Horticultural Exhibition held in the Bath and Castle grounds 4 and 5 Oct (TSK)

1855. Tuesday 16 Jany 1855 a severe frost set in with snow. Very heavy rain on Monday 5 Jany the wet did not get in the turfland owing to the hardness of the ground. Snowed heavy on Monday evening the 5th. Frost continuing. A heavy fall of snow on Thursday night 22 February. Rained and thawed on Sunday afternoon, frost continued more or less the greater part of March.
19 March Sprigg and Orchard commenced arching the Brook over between Ison's and Bostocks down to the back lane. Carried on to Mr Bindley's Factory by the same Contractors and finished November 1855 and the old brook in part filled up. (TSK)

This arch now supports Union Passage. Ison's is now W H Smith's and Bostock's is Stones.

The first patent Perambulator (Childs Carriage) brought to this Town 22 November for Master T K Bangham. (TSK)

Thomas Kirkland Bangham (1855–1891) was the eldest grandchild of Thomas Smith.

6 November. Frost commenced until the 13th.

19 November. Severe frost until the   (TSK)

1856. The Lamb Inn finished being pulled down 3 May to make room for the New Market House etc. Began to put the Glass Roof on, on Wednesday 5 November. (TSK)

The Town Hall and Market area still stands. It presents a handsome stone front to Market Street. In 1879 there was a reading room on one side and a refreshment room on the other. The market area contained 22 butchers shops. To erect the building £4,000 was raised by the issue of 400 shares of £10 each.[42]

1857. Mr Linforth the first person buried at the new cemetery Sunday 18 October (TSK)

He was an assistant master at the Ashby Grammar School. His memorial is a broken column.

1858. Julliens Concert in the Bath grounds 7 July. (TSK)

On Wednesday 13 October an Address from the Inhabitants of Ashby was presented to Lady Edith Maud Abney Hastings on her Ladyship's accession to the Estates of Willesley and Packington. (TSK)

Sir Charles Edward Abney Hastings only surviving heir of General Sir Charles Hastings Bt died without issue leaving his estates to Lady Edith Maud who was the sister to Henry Weysford Charles Plantagenet Hastings later 4th Marquess. She was required to adopt the name 'Abney' and since that date the Loudoun family has been known as Abney Hastings.

1859. Severe Frost Commenced 23 October the thermometer as low as 11½ on the 23 and 24 at night. a Snow storm on the 22nd. (TSK)

1860. 17 November Snow fell all this day, a severe frost at night and continued to (TSK)

A fire in Hardwicks Cellar about 2 o'clock on Sunday morning 18 Nov. (TSK)

In 1875 William Hardwick lived at the Elms, Upper Packington Road.

The Rifle Corps attended Divine Service in Trinity Church 2 Dec. (HK)

1861. The New Prison for Criminals and the three houses for the Police commenced the second week in July. (TSK)

These houses stood in South Street West of the Police Station and were demolished in 1963. The Police Station was erected in 1862 at a cost of about £2,000. In 1878 the Police Force consisted of a Superintendant, a Sergeant and eight Constables.[43]

1862. Ward, the Superintendant of Police came to his house in December last, and prisoners confined in the New Lock up the first week in January three persons besides Mrs Severn there on 16 Jany. (TSK)

1863. Mr Spencer's House (late School property) pulled down in September; the houses on each side propped up being in a very bad state (HK)

The coming of age of Henry Weysford Charles Plantagenet Hastings 4th Marquess of Hastings celebrated with great rejoicings at Donington and Ashby 22 July. Also a sumptuous dinner given at Moira on the 21st to celebrate the same. (HK)

1864. 5 July Mr Robt Knight began to take down his house to rebuild it. (TSK)

1865. 26 Jany On the night of this same 26th snow fell which blocked up the roads and put a stop to traffic and snow falling at intervals continued on the ground till 24 Feb. (HK)

132

1868. May. Mr C Matthews took down the old house Dr Kirkland lived in and began to build a new one on the site. (HK)

Charles Matthews Chemist and Druggist of 63 Market Street. He was Church warden of St Helen's Church for many years.

26 September The poor old favourite Black Horse killed. (HK)

1871. A severe frost set in 14 Decr 1870 and continued till Feby 1st/71 (HK)

A New Clock with Chimes put up in the old Church 3 Feby. (HK)

1872. 3 May Fan a favourite and faithful dog died. (HK)

1873. 9 May Athletic sports held in the Bath Meadow by the Boys in the Latin school. (HK)

September. Line of Railway opened from Nuneaton to Ashby. (HK)

1874. 1 Jany Line of Railway opened to Derby by Melbourne.

23 April The weather like Midsummer that fires were not required and herbage so forward that the grass on the lawn in the front of the house was mown for the first time this year. (LB)

The house was 15 Ivanhoe Terrace, South Street.

28 Feby 1874 Monsieur Deschard from Brest came to visit us. (LB)

M A Déschard was a direct descendant of Louis François dc Normant Kergrist and Mary Ann Kirkland. In 1895 he was Commissaire Général de la Marine.

21 Nov 1877 Lady Flora Paulyn Barbara Hastings daughter of the late Countess of Loudoun and Mr Abney Hastings married to Henry Fitzalan Howard Duke of Norfolk at the Brompton Oratory, London. (LB)

Henry Fitzalan Howard KG PC GCVO 15th Duke Premier Duke and Earl (1847–1917). The Duchess of Norfolk died without issue in 1887. The wedding was celebrated in fine style in Ashby. There was a splendid banquet at the Town Hall given by Mr Abney Hastings to over 400 tenants and tradesmen.

1878. 19 May The last service was held in the Parish Church and Collections made before the restoration. In the morning the Rifle Corps attended. In the afternoon the School children and in the evening a crowded congregation to whom the Vicar the Revd John Denton preached. (LB)

The Revd John Denton MA 1830–1903 formerly Vicar of Holy Trinity.

1879. 30 July and 31st The Leicestershire Agricultural Society held their Show in the Bath grounds. (LB)

2 Augst The Leicestershire Volunteers encamped in Willesley Park till Friday the 8th when they were reviewed and left. Their first night in camp was remarkable for a heavy storm of thunder and lightening with rain that flooded the tents. (LB)

1880. The Parish Church of Ashby-de-la Zouch was re-opened after being closed for Restoration on 31 March 1880. (LB)

During the period of Restoration services had been held at the Town Hall.

1881. 18 Jany A severe snow storm visited England blocking many lines of rail with drifts and stopping tunnels in London. Many animals reported to have died from the severity and several persons frozen to death. The frost lasted about a fortnight and then for a few days mild weather set in. Thermo at Leicester about zero. The Thames, Servern and Mersey were frozen. (LB)

1882. A Bazaar held at the New Grammar School to aid the fund restoration of St Helen's Church £1600. 8s. 11d, was raised by it. (LB)

1883. The Dome taken down from the Bath Room being considered unsafe at the beginning of the year. The Baths were built in 1822. (LB)

1884. The Baths closed this year and the building falling to decay. (LB)

1885. Lord Donington restored the Ball Room and exterior of the Baths. (LB)

23 Sepr, 24th, 25th a Bazaar held in the Ball Room for the restoration of the Tower and rehanging of the Bells of the Old Church. (LB)

1 Novr Service held in Ball room during the repairs of Trinity Church. (LB)

1886. Trinity Church reopened 3 March. Bazaar for repairs of Trinity Church 21st, 22nd and 23rd of July in the Ball room at the Baths.
28 Oct Consecretion of Bells of St Helen's by Bishop Mitchenson: they had been recast at Loughborough. (LB)

1887. The Queen's Jubilee kept in this town (Ashby Z).

Tuesday 21 June The poor men had dinner in the Street, the women and Children tea. A torchlight procession to the Windmill Hill where a bonfire was lighted.

Wednesday 22nd The gentlemen of the town had a dinner
Thursday 23rd the Ladies had a Ball

Friday 24 A Masquerade torchlight procession to Windmill Hill.
A Company formed to take the Bath Grounds and Hotel and to put the same into order and good repair. (LB)

1888. 24 July The Saline Baths restored and reopened by a Company, who also have the management of the grounds and Royal Hotel. A Gala day in connection with the grounds in the Autumn, a Baloon ascent and various entertainments. (LB)

1890. On Tuesday 23 Decr Bishop Mitchinson of Leicester dedicated the Tubular Bells of Holy Trinity Church Ashby which were presented by the family of the late Samuel Ratcliffe to his memory (LB)

The Right Revd and Venerable John Mitchinson MA DCL DD (1833–1918) Scholar of Pembroke College, Oxford, First Class Mods 1853. Headmaster of The Kings School, Canterbury, 1859–1873. Bishop of Barbados and Windward Islands 1873–1881. Rector of Sibson, Leicestershire 1881–1899. Archdeacon of Leicester

1886–1899. Master of Pembroke College, Oxford and Canon of Gloucester Cathedral 1899. He died at Gloucester on 23 Sept 1918. Samuel Ratcliffe lived at Highfields House.

A severe frost set in about 25 November and at the end of it two sheep were roasted on the Thames at Walton and during a large fire in London the water frose in the fire engine's hoses and so did the fireman's beards. The frost lasted with very slight thaws until 23 January 1891 (LB)

1892. Leicestershire Banking Co 25 Feby the new building built on the site of Old Bank & house of Thomas Smith Kirkland belonging to Trustees of the Grammar School was opened by Lord Donington who drew the first cheque of £5 which he gave to the Vicar Canon Denton to be given to the poor of Ashby de la Zouch. (LB)

1895. 15 Feby An Explosion of Gas at the Railway Station which blew up the floors of the booking Hall, & the large windows & Clock of the same. Three men were injured not very badly. The severe frost had caused the main pipe to burst under the floor.
The Frost set in about 12 Jany & continued till about 11 March. Water had to be taken to the houses for 6 or 7 weeks & much trouble from pipes bursting in the mains. (LB)

1895. Very hot weather in Septr – 21 Oct frost and on Sunday 27 Octr snow about an inch deep. Thaw set in on the 31st. The frost again which continued many weeks: water carried to the houses for six weeks. (LB)

1896. Trinity School & Mission Room opened by the Bishop of Peterborough 15 Jany. A tea in there and some entertainments the next night. 26 May 1896 Bishop Mitchinson held a dedication service at the Parish Church in consequence of the Gift of the new Clock and chimes by Mr & Mrs Robt Davenport. Shock of earthquake felt on 17 Decr. (LB)

Robt Davenport Watchmaker and Jeweller lived at 38A Market Street.

1897. At the end of May a portion of the top stone work of the Royal Hotel fell down in the middle of the night.

136

5 June Saturday Fall of stone at the Royal Hotel obliging the building to be refaced with red brick edged with stone. 7 June Annual Gala Fete in the Bath grounds on Whit Monday. Tuesday 22nd Jubilee Celebration of the Queen's reign of 60 years, Dinner in Market Street to men and women, Teas, Sports, Torch-light procession & Bonfire. Jubilee Celebration Thursday 24th at the Workhouse. Jubilee Celebration in the Callis on Wednesday 30 June July Wednesday 21st Flower show (severe thunderstorm) (LB)

6 Octr Wednesday Death of Miss Kirkland, Funeral on the 11th at the Cemetery. (LB)

Novr. Sunday 28 Heavy Gale. (LB)

29 Decr Wednesday An entertainment was given at the Trinity Mission room to help pay off some of the large debt remaining on the building. It was called a Japanese Cafe Chantant, and about 40 young ladies dressed as Japanese waited at the tea tables on the visitors who were also entertained with music, singing, dancing etc. It was a success. (LB)

Catharine Kirkland, elder daughter of Dr Thomas Smith Kirkland.

On Thursday morning 10 Decr ult the Old Bulls Head Inn, Ashby de la Zouch one of the oldest landmarks in the Midlands was seriously damaged, the gable roof being blown down. This involved the destruction of the ancient heraldic device of the Hastings family, an interesting object to visitors. The Inn is closely associated with the old Castle which was dismantled by order of Parliament in 1648 and Cromwell is said to have stayed in the house at the time that it was the temporary abode of William Bainbrigg to whom was deputed the demolition of the Castle. (LB)

This newspaper cutting is out of a Birmingham paper in the summer of 1797 – the Birmingham Weekly Mercury.

REMARKABLE INSTANCES OF LONGEVITY
Last week died at Ashby-de-la Zouche, Hannah Sturges, aged 106; she well remembered the rejoicings at the Peace of Utrecht in 1713, when she was twenty-two years old, and that booths were erected in the town, and barrels of ale wheeled about and distributed to the poor inhabitants. What is remarkable to happen in the same family is

that an elder brother died two years ago, at Clifton near Ashbourne, at the age of 109; and another sister at Ashby about twenty years ago at the age of 80. So that the united ages of a brother and two sisters was 295 years. Lately also died at Ashby, a horse of Mr Hudson's, upwards of 40 years old; and a Spanish gander, which had been kept by Dr Kirkland upwards of 25 years, and it is supposed was near five years old when the Doctor first had it. Joseph Hollingsworth, an old servant of the Doctor's and now in his service, had driven the gander regularly every day to and from pasture for twenty-five years together.

It was sent to Lucy Bangham by a lady who knew that I was a great-granddaughter of the Dr Kirkland here mentioned (LB)

1898. Water from Milton brought to supply the town of Ashby & first used. (LB)

Jany Wednesday Trinity Church Sale of Work. (LB)

Rummage Sale Shrove Tuesday 22 Feby (LB)

19 April Terrible fire in the Whitwick Colliery 36 lives lost (LB)

Whitwick Colliery disaster: see Memorial in Christ Church Coalville.

Diamond Wedding of Old Mr & Mrs Smith, Wood Street 6 May. (LB)

Wednesday 27th, 28th & 29 Grand Bazaar in the Bath Grounds for the Parish Church restoration of Vestry & room over. (LB)

1899. Quorn Hounds met in the Market Place Ashby-de-la Zouch 25 Nov 1899.
October 1899 Spire of Holy Trinity Church taken down owing to it being unsafe. Cost £105 to remove.
19 Oct 1907 The Honble Paulyn Francis Cuthbert Rawdon Hastings died at the Manor House and was buried 23 Oct in the Chapel of the Castle at Ashby-de-la Zouch. (LB)

Paulyn was the younger son of Baron Donington and the grandfather of the present Countess of Loudoun.

138

1900 – Newspaper cutting:
   '*Mr Justice Joyce, the new Chancery Judge, will take his seat in court for the first time on Thursday.*
                           Daily Mail, *29 October 1900* (LB)

The Honble Sir Matthew Ingle Joyce (1839–1930) is buried at Breedon-on-the-Hill.

1901. 5 Volunteers returned from the war in South Africa on Tuesday 24 July. They were met by their comrades, the Town Volunteers & Band, with others of the townspeople & went in procession round part of the town, & into the Bath Grounds where they had a short service & nice address from the Revd H B St John & Revd Basset after which Silver watches with the name & an inscription were presented by Mr Adcock to each of the returned men. Later they were entertained at a dinner in the Ball room. (LB)

The Revd Henry Beecham St John, Vicar of Holy Trinity 1882–1904.

1902. The Coronation of King Edward the 7th was fixed for 26 June decorations and festivities were arranged for that day in the town of Ashby-de-la Zouch but on the 24th a shock came upon the nation of the King's dangerous illness, obliging him to undergo a severe operation; it caused deep sorrow on the Nation but in accordance with the King's wish that his people should not be disappointed, a dinner was given in the Street. (LB)

Sir Francis A Laking, a Physician in ordinary to the King had diagnosed appendicitis. Peritonitis set in but the King still refused to postpone the Coronation. Finally Sir Frederick Treves (the Surgeon who befriended the 'elephant man') was called in and operated on the King, who was laid out on the billiard table at Buckingham Palace and held down during the administration of the anaesthetic by Queen Alexandra and three strong men as he struggled and threw his arms about.)[44]

Then the children had tea, & after that the women all had tea in the Street. The town was beautifully illuminated at night & the decorations extensive & elegant. The King & Queen were subsequently crowned in Westminster Abbey on 9 Augst & after that he went a cruise round Great Britain & stayed at Balmoral to thoroughly establish his health. (LB)

1902. On 16 Sepr the new building for the Girls Grammar School was opened by the Marquess of Granby a tent was erected on the grounds in which speeches were made & a golden key presented by Mr Barrowcliffe the Architect to the Marquess, Canon Denton as Chairman, in his speech, gave a History of the foundation of the Ashby Schools from the time of Edward the 6th. The Marquess responded, Miss Hogg the Head Mistress, Sir C B Mclaren & many others spoke, after which the company went to inspect the new building that is fitted quite up to date with rooms to teach cookery, chemistry etc. Previous to going to the school the Marquess was met at the Station & then lunched at the Hotel with the lady and Gentlemen Governors. (LB)

1903. Canon Denton died 12 June aged 73. He was rural Dean & had been connected with Ashby as Curate Vicar of Trinity & after, Vicar of the Parish Church. Under him the Chancel of Trinity Church was enlarged & the Vicarage built. The Parish Church enlarged by adding two side aisles. He was much beloved. (LB)

1904. On 6 March Canon Denton was succeeded by The Revd Preston who came to the vicarage towards the end of the year. (LB)

At Holy Trinity Church Ashby-de-la Zouch the Institution of the Revd W Fowler by the Bishop of Peterborough took place on Friday 9 Decr 1904. (LB)

1905. Mrs Denton the widow of Canon Denton died 1 Feby 1905, her kindly presence much missed in the town. (LB)

Mr Sawyer succeeded Mr Preston as Vicar of the Parish Church. (LB)

1906. A very long & cold spring with but very few days of warm sunshine, attributed to the earthquake which had been terrible in Italy & San Francisco; also to large ice floes in the Gulf Stream kept quite cold till
The first electric car made a trial trip on Saturday 19 May into the town at 4 p.m. from Burton to Ashby. (LB)

20 Dec The Honble Paulyn and Lady Maud Hastings celebrated their silver wedding at the Manor House. (LB)

1908. A cold April snow fell on the 22 & storms continued till the

26 drifts in many parts of the country being many feet deep. (LB)

*1915. Lt Edward Rawdon Hastings died in France of Enteric fever 15
Sept 1915. News received in Ashby 19 Oct 1915 that Capt Reginald
Rawdon Hastings had been killed in action.* (AB)

*1917. The Duke of Norfolk died 11 Feb 1917 was buried at Arundel
Castle 15 Feb 1917*

*Mrs Hubert Rostron née Isobel Hastings died 15 July 1917 buried
in the vault at the Castle 19 July 1917.* (AB)

*1918. Lady Shaw née Florence Edith Denton buried in the Parish
Churchyard 25 Aug. She died in Dublin 21 Aug after an accident
of falling thro a window in Dublin Castle.* (AB)

*1915. Dreadful cyclone at Packington devastated the farmyard of
Mr Oakey.* (AB)

*1920. 17 May 1920 Charles Edward Hastings Abney Hastings 9th
Earl of Loudoun passed away at the Manor House Ashby-de-la-
Zouch Friday. He was buried at Loudoun Friday 22 May 1920*
(AB)

*15 June 1920 The first wedding that took place in the Ch of our
Lady of Lourdes was celebrated between Miss Cecily Creagh of
Grangewood Lodge Lullington & Mr G C Maxwell RE, of Bispham
Lancashire.* (AB)

*12 June A fearful thunderstorm broke over Ashby struck 2 houses,
& killed a cow by lightening.* (AB)

*1925. 18 May 1925. A cloud burst over Ashby and in a very short
space of time North St, Market St, South St, the Green, Derby Road
& Bath St were flooded and became a raging torrent. The walls
adjoining the Police Station collapsed & the Courtyard was a scene
of desolation. There was a great deal of damage done to property,
estimated at thousands of pounds. Men swam across Market St. It
was quite impossible to get to either post office in the Town.* (AB)

*1930. 29 Nov to 6 Dec. Great shopping week in Ashby. The Street
decorated with festoons. 6 Dec 1930 An ox was roasted in the Street
behind the War Memorial. Alderman John German cut the first slice
off the ox.* (AB)

1931. A Memorial was unveiled on Wednesday 11 Feb to the late Duchess of Norfolk, née Lady Flora Hastings in the Church of Our Lady of Lourdes. The Memorial is given by the present Duchess of Norfolk. The tablet is placed over the great West doors, it is flanked by the armorial bearings of the late Duke & Duchess & surrounded by the ducal crown. It was unveiled by Monsignor Vincent Bull. Rev Hugh Duncan Hanford Instituted and Inducted to the Living of St Helen's Church Ashby-de-la Zouch 9 July 1931. (AB)

Deaths*

A

Ashpinshaw Mr (White horse) 6 Decr 1794 Aged
Ashpinshaw Mrs Edwd. 10 May 1795 Aged
Abney Mrs 22 May 1798
Alt Mrs 30 June 1799
Adams Mrs Castle 11 April 1802
Adams Mrs his second wife 19 Dec. 1806
Ansel Mr Baker April   1808
Ansel Mrs his wife April   1808
Almy Miss Eliz.
Almy Miss Molly 20 May 1808
Allamond Mrs 5 May 1809
Adams Mrs Shoulder of Mutton 20 July 1810
Allsop Mrs 5 April, 1811
Addams Mrs James third wife 19 Sept. 1813
Alt Mrs Post office 21 November 1814
Adcock Mr Thos. Schoolmaster 27 Augt., 1815
Allamond Mr 4 December 1817 Aged
Atkins Mrs 28 March, 1821
Adams Mr Tho 30 Decr., 1822
Abney Mrs 27 November, 1830 Aged 90

---

* The entries in the Deaths and Marriages do not always follow in strict
alphabetical sequence. The entries are transcribed as they appear.

Armstrong Mr Quartermaster 7th Inniskillen Dragoon*
    Died 5 November, 1832 Aged 62
Armstrong Mrs 16 October 1840
Ashpinshaw Mr 29 August 1844 Aged 57
Armstrong Mr John 11 February 1855 Aged 41
Armstrong Mr Elliot 13 February 1866 Aged 48
Allen Mr James Auctioneer 10 May 1879 Aged 34
Abel Miss died 11 May 1898
Adams Miss Sarah died 20 Feby. 1902 Aged about 80.
Allen Miss M 12 Dec 1927

B

Beadsmoore Mr Jno. Senr. 30 July 1792 Aged
Beadsmoore Mr Jno. Junr. 28 Novr. 1795 Aged
Beavington Mr Thos. Surgeon Senr. 19 Novr 1792 Aged
Beavington Mr Thos. Son of William B 3 July 1796 Aged
Buckerfield Mr Thos. 23 April 1787 Aged
Bishop Mr James (Waggon & Horses') 22 April 1797 Aged
Bannister Mr Thos. at Mr Edwd. Sharp's (Lamb) 26 June 1793
    Aged
Bodel James 2 Augt. 1799
Brown Mr Cutler 1 December 1799
Beavington Mrs 22 Jan. 1801
Beadsmoore Mr Saml. Senr. 23 April 1803
Beavington Mr Willm. 13 Augt. 1803 Aged
Beadsmoore Mrs Ashby Senr. 20 Sep. 1803
Brewin Mr Thos. (late of the Bull's Head) 3 Dec. 1803
Brooks Mr 7 April 1804
Blenkarne Mr
Beadsmoore Mrs wife of Mr Saml. B Stationer 6 March 1808
Brooks Mrs Shoemaker 23 July 1808
Buck Molley late off Mr Pratts 24 Oct. 1808
Beavington Mrs Benj. 18 March 1810 Aged
Buckerfield Mr Jos. Kings Head 4 April, 1811
Blunt Mr Loughbro. 25 May 1811
Blenkarne Mr Jas. Baker 30 Oct. 1813

---

* William Armstrong (1770–1832) served in the 6th Inniskilling Dragoons
and was quartermaster from 1809–1814 being the first NCO to hold
that appointment. He was commissioned and became Adjutant in 1827
as Lieutenant. He was Riding Master prior to his discharge. He was
Paymaster in 1815 and a 'Waterloo man.'

Buckerfield Mrs Jos. Hatter 11 Sept. 1813
Bailey Mrs Taylor 29 April 1814
Beadsmoore Mr Saml. Stationer 23 Octr., 1819
Beavington Mr Benj. 16 Feby., 1832 Aged 50
Beavington Mrs T 23 Dec. 1834
Bindley Mrs John 18 Decr. 1836 Aged 23
Burton Mrs 3 Feby., 1837 Aged 66
Bradford Mrs 8 February 1853 Aged 53
Bradford Mr 11 February 1858 Aged 58
Barney Mr Timothy Quorn 4 Feb 1837
Boyer Mrs 2 September 1834
    (*Charlotte wife of Rev. John William Robert Boyer.*
    Rector of Swepstone at Aberystwyth Aged 54)
Buller Mr John 13 Augt. 1838 Aged 23
Beavington Miss Sarah 16 July 1840
Bott William 20 October 1842
Barker Miss Augst. 1848
Beavington Mr John 25 Jany. 1855 Aged
Beavington Mrs Ben Decr. 16/50 Aged 68
Beavington Mr John Jany. 1855
Buller Mrs 17 June 1860 Aged 80
Bindley Mr 25 Sep. 1862
Beavington Mr W 29 Jany. 1864 Aged 71
Bagnall Mrs 24 March 1865 Aged 76
Bird Mr Jany. 1866
Bobart Mr 9 June 1867 Aged 66
Buller Mr G (destroyed himself) 4 Feb. 1870 aged 47
Bullen Miss 24 April 1870 aged 56
Bindley Miss Margaret 10 June 1870
Bagnall Mr (Late of the Old George Inn) 13 Decr. 1871 Aged 84
Beadsmore Mrs 19 July 1872 Aged 73
Bagnall Mrs (widow of J Bagnall Painter) Oct. 1872 Aged 82
Brown Mr (Solicitor) 10 July 1874. Aged 82
Bagnel Mrs (at the King's Head) 20 March 1877 Aged 63
Bosworth William (Seedman) 27 March 1877 Aged 58
Bangham Francis (Surgeon) 19 Feby. 1882 Aged 64
Blood Mrs   1887
Bagnall Mr (King's Head) 2 Oct. 1887 Aged 72
Bangham Lucy Catharine 18 June 1885
Barker Mr John Stationer died 16 March Aged 78
Bangham Lucy widow of the late Francis Bangham died 10 June
    1909 Aged 83 years.

Bartlett Mrs 24 Oct. 1927

Betts Miss Elizth. died 21 Jany. 1888 Aged 76

Bott Mrs (the plumbers wife) 13 Jany. 1889

Bangham Thomas Kirkland 10 June 1891 at his residence New Oscott Erdington Birmingham Aged 36. He was the only son of Francis Bangham Surgeon of Ashby-de-la Zouch

Bodington Lucy widow of Robt. Bodington Kenilworth Chase died 28 June 1889 Aged 78

Baker Miss Elizth. 1 July 1899 Aged 76

Brown (Sexton) died at the Cemetery Lodge 21 Oct. 1905 Aged 74

Baker Miss Hannah died 3 Oct 1906 Aged 76

Bangham Lucy 10 June 1909 Aged 83

Brown George 4 March 1922

Bullen Ebenezer 25 Jan. 1924 Aged 73 yrs.

C

Chapman Mr Thos. Senr. 23 Jany. 1793 Aged

Chapman Miss Elizabeth 4 Novr. 1799

Cattel Mrs John 2 August 1799

Cattel Mr John, baker, 8 June 1801

Clarkstone Mr Abrh. 28 Aprl. 1800

Clarkstone Mrs his mother 26 Nov. 1801

Clarke Mr Saml. 8 Jany. 1803 Aged 73

Cheatle Mr Thos. 19 Feb. 1806

Cutter Mr Chals. 17 Feb. 1808

Chapman Mrs Senr. 1 May, 1808 Aged 83

Cutter Miss 28 Feb. 1811

Cantrell Mastr. Willm. 18 April, 1811

Chapman Mrs Boarding School 24 Dec. 1815

Clarke Mr Saml. Hosier & Framesmith 8 June 1816

Crossley Miss Teressa 28 Augt. 1816

Cantrell Mast John 30 Jany. 1817 Aged

Crossley Mrs 13 March, 1818

Charlesworth Mr Thos. Hosier 25 March, 1818

Cheatle Mary 30 March 1818

Cheatle Mrs Eliz. 23 July Buried 25th 1818 Aged 55

Chapman Miss Schoolmistress 24 March, 1823

Chapman Mr Auctioneer 16 May 1823

Choice Mr John (late of Normanton)   Sept. 1823

Crossley Mrs (2nd wife of Mr T Crossley) 24 Dec 1830

Chapman Mr Michael 21 April, 1831 Aged 48
Cheatle Mr Benj.   1834
Cheatle Mrs 18 September 1834
Chapman Mrs 10 Octr. 1835 Aged 80
Cantrell Mrs 12 December 1837 Aged 63
Cheatle Miss Ann died 7 Feb. 1839 Aged 28
Cape Mrs died 20 March 1839 aged 21
Canttrell Mr Jos. November 1839 Aged
Cheatle Mrs Richd. Jany. 1840 (London)
Cooper Sir Astley Paston Bart. 11 Feby. 1841
Crossley Mrs Leod. Burton 9 Feby.
Chapman Miss 24 Novr. 1843
Cope E 10 December 1848
Cantrell Mr 20 Feby. 1849 Aged 78
Cheatle Mr Ben. 1 Nov. 1850 65
Crossley Miss Jane 16 May 1857
Cradock Mr Edward 18 January 1853
Cape Lieut. Jonathan Murdered at Lucknow 21 March 1858 Aged
    19
Campion Mrs 21 August 1861 Aged 43
Cheatle Mr James (Butcher) 28 Nov. 64 Aged 74
Crisp Mr (Independant Minister) 12 Jany. 69 Aged 86
Cotton Mr 5 April 69 Aged 68
Cheatle Mrs daughter of Mr T Ragg 22 Jany. 71
Chapman Miss Jane 2 Decr. 1870 (at Loch side) Aged 92
The Revd. Archibald Creighton Vicar of Stallingborough died
    4 March 1871
Crisp Mrs (widow of the Independant Minister) Oct. 1872 Aged 90
Cox Thomas Bricklayer 17 April 1881 Aged
Coote Michael MD born 22 November 1841 died 17 Nov. 81 Aged
    39
Carman Mary Mrs 10 April 1905
Cheatle Mr Wm. Senr. (Mount House) 28 Jany. Aged 81
Cheatle Mrs widow of Richard Cheatle (P Clerk) Nov. 1874
Cradock Mrs Ed. 25 March 1876 Aged 69
Cockayne Mrs
Chubb Mr Auctioneer 28 July Aged 76 1883
Cheatle Mr James died 1891 Aged 73
Revd. Charles Clarke BA Baptist Minister died 20 Jany. 1905 Aged
    71
Creighton Mrs widow of the Revd. Archibald Creighton Vicar of
    Stallingborough died 4 Feb. 1909 Aged 92

D

Dale Mrs 12 June 1800

Devenport Mrs 30 July 1803

Dewes Mr Benj. Junr. 18 July, 1806

Devenport Mr John Flaxdresser 14 Sept., 1810.

Dewes Mr Geo. April 1811

Dinwoodie Mr Schoolmaster 14 March, 1812

Dewes Mrs Benj. second wife 18 April 1814

Dalby Mr Attorney Donnington 1 Jany. 1817 Aged

Dalby Mrs Castle Donnington 23 May 1818 Aged

Dale Thos. Senr. Baker 11 Decembr., 1818

Denstone Mrs 9 June 1819

Dalby Mr Thos. Attorney 15 July 1819

Dewes Mr Benj. Senr. 18 January, 1820

Dewes Mrs Henry died at Caldecote 16 July 1839

Dale Mrs   Dec. 1842

Dalby Miss   Novr. 1846

Davidson Mr C drowned at Swarkestone 15 July 1847 aged 20

Dalby Master Frank 11 Jany. 1855 Aged 14

Deavenport Mr James Aged 80 21 March 1856

Dalby Mr Charles Surgeon died at Southampton 6 Oct. 1855

Dalby Mrs Charles died at Southampton 25 Sep. 1856

Davys Mr Thomas High Field Ashby died 17 Sep. 1856

Dewes Mr Henry 24 Febry. 1858 Aged 64

Dewes Mrs Henry 2 May 58

Davys Mrs Thomas 17 Augst. 1860 Aged 64

Dewes Mr Thomas Condale 20 Sep. 1861 Aged 69

Dalby Mrs Widow of Mr Thos. Dalby Solicitor 16 Jany. 1862 Aged 81

Davenport Mr John (Clerk to the Board of Guardians) 17 July 1864 Aged 84

Dewes Mr Thos. Cardale 15 Oct. 1864 Aged 78

Dewes Mr W Solicitor 18 Nov. 1866 Aged 70

Dewes Mr Charles I 18 Jany. 1868 Aged 41

Davys Mr J 14 Nov. 1872 Aged 81

Davenport Mrs William Oct. 1872 Aged 95

Dalby Mrs Thos. B 1 Feby. 1873 Aged 68

Dalby Mr John at Swannington 26 Augst. 1873

Dewes Mrs Widow of W Dewes (Solicitor) 8 Oct. 1873 Aged 76

Dicken M D 12 April 1875 Aged 63

Davys Mrs J 30 March 1876. Aged 64

Davenport Mr John 15 March 1877 Aged 65

Dalby Mr Thos. Burgh (Lawyer) 27 Jany. 1878 Aged 69

Davenport Mr Thomas 24 July 1878 Aged 55

Dewes Mr William (Solicitor) 15 Sep. 1880 Aged 58

Daniel Fred died 17 Jany. 1881 Aged 31

Dalby John died 18 Feby. 1882. Aged 46 (Lawyers Clerk)

Dyer Mr (plasterer) died 24 April 1888 aged 62

Donington the Rt. Honable Lord died Wednesday 24 July at Donington Park and was buried in the family Vault of the Hastings at the Parish Church. Aged 73 1895

Dunicliffe Mr Thos. (retired grocer) died 17 Oct. 1895 Aged 76

Dresser Jane Althea at Bournemouth 27 Feby. 1896 Aged 42

Dalby Mrs Thos. widow of Mr T B Dalby (Lawyer) died 2 Augst. Aged 80

Denton Henry St Aubyn at Aligarti India 2nd son of Canon Denton died 8 July 1898 Aged 36

Daniel Mrs widow of John Daniel 14 Jany. 1900 Aged 85

Denton the Revd Canon Vicar of St Helens Ashby-de-la Zouch died 12 June 1903 Aged 73

Denton Mary Elizabeth widow of Canon Denton 1 Feb. 1905

Davenport Mr J W Wine Merchant died 27 April 1906 Aged 51

Davenport Mrs (mother of the above) died 14 June 1906 Aged 80.

Dewes Mrs Eliza 19 Feb. 1925 Aged 89 yrs.

E

Eaton Mr Thos. Murder'd in London 16 May 1793

Ellis Mr Willm. Junr. 8 August 1815

Ellis Mrs   May 1823

Eames Mrs 19 Jany. 1852 Aged 51

Eames W 6 June 1856

Elliot Mr (Stone Mason) died 31 Decr. 1856

Elliott Mrs (Stationer) died 8 April 1881

Emery Mr draper died 24 April 1888 Aged 75

Eves Mrs formerly of Melbourne died at Clifton. Bristol Tuesday 29 March 1904. Aged about 60

Edmonds Mrs Elizabeth 3 March 1914. Buried in Ashby Cemetary

F

Farnel Mrs 3 Aug. 1793 Aged

Farmer Mr Thos. Taylor 24 Sept. 1799

Farnell Mr Jos. Banker Ashby 7 Dec., 1802 Aged

Fisher Mrs Ashby 6 March 1806

Farnell Master Martin 11 Jany., 1809

Farnell Mr Thos. At Manchester 3 Novr. 1809

Forster Mr London 20 March, 1811 Aged 64

Farnell Mrs Henry Castle 28 Sept. 1818 Aged

Farnell Mr Henry Castle Inn 13 Decr. 1822

Farnell Miss Ann 12 Sep., 1832 Aged 66

Faux Mr New House 11 Sept., Buried 16 Sep. 1834 Aged 81 years

Faux Mrs Ditto 19 March, 1836

Fowler Mr S died from an accident on the railway 16 January 1838 Aged 53

Faux Mr Edward 10 Feby. 1849 Aged 19

Festin Mr 2 June at the Baths 1849

Farnell Mr Jos. March 1850

Frearson Mrs died 8 May 1853

Faux Mr Chilcote 6 September 1853 Aged 62

Fell Miss Rawdon House 10 July 1864 Aged 83

Fisher Mr Thos. (Solicitor) 5 July 1866 Aged 34

Faux Mr Charles 26 August 1866 Aged 63

Faux Mrs Elizabeth 28 May 1877 Chilcote

Fisher Mr Edwd. Solicitor died 1 Oct. 1878 Aged 80

Faux Mr Edwd. of New House died 26 May buried at Merovale 31 May (Saturday) Aged 80 1878 The last of the family at the old home

Faux Catherine widow of Robt Faux (Cliff House Twycross) died 15 Novr. (Sunday) at her residence Ashby-de-la Zouch Aged 84 1885

Fisher Mrs widow of Mr Ewd. Fisher Solicitor died at Farnboro hants at her son in law's Mr Holts 15 Feb. 1892 Aged 85

Faux Joseph Wright died at his residence Oakfield Ashby-de-la Zouch. Buried at Chilcote 7 May 1898 Aged 69

Richard Faux brother of the above died at Chilcote 5 April 1895 Aged 74

Fisher Mr Edwd. Solicitor died and was buried at Newton Abbot Devonshire 31 July 1895 Aged 64

Fisher Mrs Edwd. Widow of the above died at Newton Abbot 3 February 1897

Farmer Mr C Organist at Trinity Church died 27 Sep. 1903 aged 45

Faux Mrs Wright died at West Hampstead London 22 Nov. 1906 Aged 79

G

Gilbert Mr Wm. 11 Feby. 1796 Aged
Gibbs Mr John 4 Feby. 1797 Aged
Green Mr Atty 22 May 1798 Aged   22 Feb. 1808
Green Mr Francis 11 Sep. 1798 Aged
Green Miss Eliz. 10 March, 1803 Aged 26
Glazebrook Revd Jams 1 July, 1803 Aged 59
Gest Mr G Aged 10 Feby. 1804
Gaudin Mrs 2 May 1805 Aged
Gibbs Mrs Ed. 20 Oct. 1806
Green Mrs 22 Feb. 1808
Glazebrook Mr John 6 Dec. 1809
Gill Mrs Elizabeth nurse 18 Augt. 1815
Gaudin Mr Louis 21 Feby. 1816 Aged 22*
Gaudin Mr 1 May 1817 Aged
Garland Mr Thos. Taylor 13 March 1821
Gibbs Mr Edwd. Organist 16 June, 1822
Green Mrs Edwd. 20 March 1836 Aged 29
Grace Mr Saml. 10 July 1838 Aged
Glazebrook Mrs 22 Sept. 1834 Aged 87
Gibbs Mrs 1 Jany. 1840 Aged 75
Goadby Mr 3 Augst. Aged 67 42 yrs Baptist Minister
Glazebrook Thos. Kirkland at Southport Aged 74 Died 18 Jany. 1855
Green Mrs I S 8 August. 58 Aged 50
Goodman Mr Thos. (Tailor) 11 Dec. 1858 Aged 76
Gascoyne Mrs W 28 Nov. 1874 Aged 41
Gimson Joseph Cape 16 May 1878 Aged 28
Gate Mrs Grace Winefred (Isons) died 16 July 1905 Aged 33
German Mrs John died 14 Nov. 1906 aged 69
Gibbons Mr Thomas died 21 July 1915

---

* Letters of administration to the estate of Louis Peter Gaudin were granted out of the Archdeaconry of Leicester to Euphemia McDouall, the sister and next of kin and administratrix on 3 June 1820. John Gaudin the natural and lawful father of the said deceased survived his said son but died without having taken out any administration (Leicester country record office DE 73 PR/T/1820/60. The bondsmen were The Revd McDouall and John Eames. The estate was sworn and did 'not amount in value to the sum of twenty pounds'.

Gascoyne Mr William 26 March 1916 aged 82

H

Hachet Mrs (Waggon Horses) 1 Feby. 1794 Aged
Hachet Mr   do   23 May 1794 Aged
Hickingbottom Jno. (Red Lion) 24 Jany. 1794 Aged 56
Hogg Mr London 25 Feby. 1794
Hallum Mr Heny. 30 Nov. 1798
Holditch Mr James Mastr. of the Blue school charity 9 April '99
Hollingsworth Molly 3 April 1800
Hollingsworth Thos. 5 Ocr. 1800 Aged 78
Hollingsworth Jos. 1 Jany., 1803
Hatton Mrs Thos. Junr. 12 Decr. 1799
Hanson Mr Atherstone Wednesday 8 Aprl. 1801
Hatton Mr (Hatter) 2 Aprl. 1800
Hatton Mrs Junr. Second Wife 6 March, 1802
Hatton Mr (Glazier) Senr. 18 Jany. 1805 Aged
Handley Mr Geo. Senr. 25 Augt., 1805 Aged
Hanson Mr Willm. Atherstone Monday 9 Dec. 1805 Aged 21 8
    November ult
Handley Mrs wife of Geo. Handley 30 Decr., 1805
Hextall Mr Tho. 17 March 1806
Hartwell Mrs at Mrs Allts. 2 Jany., 1808
Hallam Mr Josh. Parish Clerk 27 Jany. 1812
Hopkins Mr Angel Inn 4 Augt. 1812
Hall Mr Anthony Bull's Head 24 January 1814
Hall Mrs   do   D 4 April 1815
Handley Mrs George 19 Nov. 1814
Hatton Mr Danl. 5 October 1818
Hood Mr Currier 24 Jany. 1820
Hastings Lady Willesley 11 February 1834
Hartwell Mrs 19 February 1839 Aged 51
Hawksworth Mrs M died 13 March 1839 Aged 31
Hastings Lady Flora at Buckingham Palace 5 July 1839
Hardy Sir Thomas Captain on board the Victory Lord Nelson's
    Flag Ship at the Battle of Trafalgar Friday 20 September, 1839
Hastings Marchioness Countess Loudon 9 January 1840 at Kilbourn
    Ayrshire Aged 59
George Agustus Francis second Marquis of Hastings died 13 Jany.
    1844 Aged 35 (Southampton)
Hartnell Mr 1 May 1850 Aged 61

Paulyn Reginald Serlo third Marquis of Hastings Earl of Rawdon Born 2 June 1832 died 17 January 1851

The Honble Paulyn Francis Cuthbert Rawdon Hastings 19 October 1907

Gilbert Theophilus Clifton Hastings 3rd Baron Donington 31 May 1927

Hood, Sir Joseph died at Wimbledon, 10 January (Great Benefactor to Ashby) 1931

The Revd Hewitt D D died 15 March 1852 Aged 81

Hawkesworth Mr H M died 9 May 1852 Aged 44

Harrison Mrs 10 May 1855 at Repton Aged 88

Hanson Miss L died 20 Jany. 1856 Aged 68

Hamp Mr Edwd. Farmer (Wine Merchant   ) died 14 Dec. 1856 aged 30

Hastings Sir Charles Abney 30 July 1858 Aged 65

Hextall Mr W 28 Dec. 1858 Aged 60

Hastings Marchioness wife of George A F second Marquis of Hastings at Bonn 18 Novr. 1858

Holland Mrs Ivanhoe Road 7 Augst. 63 Aged 84

Holdron Mrs 19 March, 1928 Aged 77

Holland Mr   September 1864 Aged 85

Hamp Mr 3 July 1865 Aged 44

Hextall Miss 18 Augst. 1868 Aged 72

Heafield Mrs (Breach Farm) 14 May 1869 Aged 63

Heafield Mr (Breach Farm)   1870

Holbrooke Mrs (sister of Mrs T B Dalby) 7 Feby. 1873 Aged 71

Hastings Edith (Abney) Maud Countess of Lowdoun etc and eldest daughter of the 2nd Marquis of Hastings 23 Jany. 1874 Aged 40

Hextall Mr John 20 March 1875 Aged 87

Hextall Miss Sarah

Hextall Miss Elizth. died 1886 23 March Aged 88

Hemsley Mr The Manor House died 22 Jany. 1899 Aged 80

Hextal Mrs William Feby. 1902 Aged 92

Hastings Lady Maud Rawdon 3 Sept. 1929 Aged 72

I

Ison Mrs Thomas 6 Decr. 1806

Ison Mr Tho. 11 July, 1807

Ingle Mr Wm. Surgeon

Ingle Mrs Wm.

Ingle Mr Mathew

Ingle Mrs Mathew 11 June 1836
Ison Mrs John 2 November, 1852 Aged 33
Ingle Mr N 8 July 1854 Aged 59
Ison Mr John Halford 26 Jany. 59 Aged 35
Ingle Miss at Ravenstone 4 April 1865 Aged 81
Ison Mr Josh (Donington) 12 June 65 Aged 66
Ingle Miss Elizth. 23 Jany. 1876 Aged 87 (Ravenstone)
Ingle Miss Eleanor died at Ravenstone Hospital 11 Novr. 1880 Aged
   86
Ison Mrs 26 Decr. 1897 Aged 80 or more
Ison Mrs Edwd. died 14 Feby. 1900 Aged 62
Ison Mr C Frederick died 11 June 1929 Aged 67
Ingle Mr Wm. Surgeon 24 Feby. 1823 Aged 63
Ingle Mr Saml.   1832

J

Joyne's Mrs King's head 13 Octr. 1798 Aged
Joyce Mr Henry 4 Feby. 1810
Joyce Mrs (late Brown) 18 Sept. 1821 Aged 82
Johnson Mr J 23 September 1853
Jarvis Mrs 17 Oct. 1870 aged 81
Jarvis Mr (Baker) died   April 1884 Aged
Jarvis Mrs Wife of above died April 1884 Aged
Johnson Mrs (Widow of Banker) died April 1888 aged 79
Joyce Mr William Surgeon died   1885 Aged
Joyce Mrs Widow of above died 6 June 6 Aged 73
Jesson Mr Thos. Solicitor died 2 Jany. 1909 aged 52
Jesson Mrs J. Fisher died 4 July 1919 Aged 39

K

Kirkland Mrs wife of Dr Kirkland (Buried 28/1/1785)
Kirkland Mrs Nottingham 6 March 1796 Aged 46
Kirkland Mrs Loughboro 31 Decr. 1796
Kirkland Doctr half past 6 morn'g Wednesday 17 Jany. 1798 Bd
   22nd Aged 75
Knight Mr Thos. Wheelright
Kimberly Mr Att'y at Mr Pestel's 29 Decr. 1798
Knight Mrs Crossyard 23 Feby. 1799
Kirkland Mr Frances Nottingham Tuesday 18 May 1802 aged
   51

Kirkland Mr John half past 11 at night 11 May 1803 Aged 42 Buried
16 May 1803

Kirby Mr Senr. Church Street 15 Octr. 180

Kiddier Mrs Junr. 11 Jany. 1809

Knight Mr Robt. 8 Jany. 1811

Kirby Mr Willm. at the Bull 13 Oct. 1812

Kirby Mrs Waggon & Horses 6 March 1819

Kirby Mrs Senr Church gates 16 June 18

Knight Mr John Comber 2 April 1814

Kirkland Mr Jas. Aged 66 15 June, 1821

Knight Miss 2 November 1831

Kirkland Mr Willm. 7 May 1833 Aged 38

Kirkland Mrs Wm. 19 Augt. 1833 Aged

Kirby Mr Thos. 16 Sept. 1836 Aged 69

Kirkland Mr Thos. John 4 Augt. 1824 Aged 64

Kirby Mrs Jas. 9 Feby. 1837 Aged 55

Kiddear Mr Joseph 7 Augst. Aged 75

Kirby Mr Jas. 22 Jany. 42

Knowles Mr Kings Head 11 Novr. 1843

Kirkland Mrs N S 12 Nov. 1843

Kirkland Mrs widow of Thos. John Kirkland at Warrington 24
March 1845 ½ past 11 Aged 86

Knowles Mrs Kings Head Inn 10 Sep. 1848

Kergrist Mrs at Brest France 15 March 1836 Aged 67

Kirkland Mr Nicholas Smith at Whitwick 16 June 1856 Aged 69

Kergrist Captain at Brest 15 Augst. 1859

Kirkland Thos. Smith MD 15 August. 1869 Aged 84

Knight Mrs Widow of S B Knight of Coleorton 14 Feby. 1870

Knight Mr Robt. died 2 Jany. 1875 Aged 74

(Kahes) Miss 1 Feb. 1876 Aged 69 (Buried at Holy Trinity 5 Feb.)

Kidger 12 May 1878 Aged 29

Knight Mr John Lawyer died 31 Dec. 1880 Aged 84

Kidger Mr Joseph died 9 April 1882 Aged 82

Kirkland Hannah Widow of Thos. Smith MD died 5 Augst.
1883 Aged 86

Kerby Mrs Joseph died 27 Augst. 1883 Aged 82

Kirkland Thomas Louis Kirkland   de

Kergrist Admiral died in Paris 9 Feby. 1895 and was buried in his
family vault at Toulon Aged 82

Kirkland Miss Catherine elder daughter of Thos. Smith Kirkland
MD of Ashby-de-la Zouch died 6 Oct. 1897 Aged 75 buried at
the Cemetery Ashby-de-la Zouch.

Kirkland Thos. Smith MD died Sunday 15 Augst. 1869 Aged 84

Kirkland William 11 April 1909 Aged 75 Buried at the Cemetary 14 April

Kidger Louisa Sarah died 24 July 1911 at Ashby-de-la Zouch (Aged 77)

Kidger Mary Edith died 25 Feb. 1927 at Ashby-de-la Zouch (Aged 83)

Kidger Emily Mary died 28 March 1927 Ashby-de-la Zouch (Aged 89)

L

Large Miss 6 March 1799

Large Mr Mercer 17 July 1799

Litherland Mr Fisher 17 Decr. 1799

Lotty Mrs Senr. 27 Jany. 1803 Aged

Lester Mrs at Mr Snelsons 29 Decr. 1804

Lee Mrs Adam 16   1809

Lakin Mr 12 Decr. 1814

Lindup Mrs Mary at Jos. Snelson's 18 Sept. 1815

Lakin Mr Charles 19 Sept. 1816 Aged

Lovett Mrs Robt. 22 December, 1817

Lakin Mrs 29 Feby., 1820

Lovell Mrs Ivanhoe Terrace April 1850

Lee Mr Charles 23 Decr. 1851

Linforth Mr School Master   Oct. 1857

Lovell Miss C 10 Jany. 1865 Aged 62

Lovell Mr (Draper) 27 July 1870 Aged 71

Lovell Miss 19 May 1871 Aged 78

Lovell Miss F 4 March 1872 Aged 75

Leedham Miss (Ivanhoe Terrace) 28 Nov 1875 Aged 69

Lovell Mrs Widow of Mr J Lovell 28 March 1876 Aged 63

Love Mr queenhead 3 Sep. 1877 Aged

Litherland Mr Thomas 30 April 1880 Aged 74

Lilley Mr Surveyor died 11 May 1901 Aged 61

Logan Miss Honor Killed by an accident 28 April 1925

M

Mee Mr Senr

Mee Mrs Senr 12 June 1795

Mee Mrs Junr 12

Mathew's Mrs (Cross) 15 July 1798 Aged
Mathews Mr Willm. 29 March 1800
Mathew's Mr John Senr 25 Febr. 1801
Mee Mrs John his second Wife 6 March 1801
Mollady Mr John Chandler 25 Oct. 1810
Mollady Mrs John's Wife 22 April 1811
Meeson Mr Supervisor 17 Augt. 1812
Meeson Mrs 26 December 1812
Mee Mr John Shoemaker 18 Augt. 1813
Moore Miss Ann Milliner 22 February 1818
Measures Mr New George Inn 1 Oct. 1818
Mathews Mr John Carpenter 6 Feby. 1822
Mammatt Mrs 9 Feby. 1832
Matthews Mr Thos. 8 Sept. 1832 Aged 30
Mammatt Mr (at O'Seal) 15 January 1835
Measures Mrs W died 7 Feb. 1839
Mathews Mrs at the Lamb 12 Feby. 1841
Moore Mr Wm. Old Parks 30 April 1841 Aged 65
The Revd William McDouall died 15 Dec. 49 Copt Hall Luton
Mammatt Mr John 12 Feby. 1851 Aged 46
Measures Mr Wm. 14 June 1856 Aged 64
Mammatt Mr Ed. 23 April 60 Aged 53
Measures Mr John 26 Sept. 1861
Measures Mr Thomas James 21 May 1863
Mills Mr (Hotel)   Decr. 1866 Aged 63
Musgrove Mrs 12 April 1868 Aged 71
Mason William (Book Maker) 10 Augst. 1868 Aged 73
Mammatt Mrs Edward 19 September 1896
Matthews Miss Jane 10 Jany. 1887 Aged
Mammatt Mr Edwd. Fredk. Lawyer 5 Feby. 1891
Matthews Miss Caroline died 5 March 1891 Aged 73
Mousley Mrs (Chilcote) 1 July 1898 Aged 77
Morris Mrs Elizth. wife of Mr Sam Morris and daughter of Francis
    Bangham Surgeon of Ashby died at Exeter 2 July 1900 Aged 38
Mammatt Revd Arthur Simmonds Vicar of Packington died 23
    Dec. Aged 53
Mammatt Mrs Edwd. (widow of Mr E F M) died 16 Feby. 1902
    Aged 58
Morris Mr Samuel Superintendant of the GWR at Exeter died 14 April
    Aged 56 buried in St Davids Churchyard in his wife's grave
Moore Rev C died 21 July Buried at Appleby Magna 24th 1924
Musson Mr William Alfred died 30 Jan 1929

N

Newton Mr Tanner 13 Novembr. 1808
Newton Mrs Do   4 September 1814 Aged 83
Newbold Mr Francis Taylor 19 Feby. 1816
Newbold Mrs wife of Mr. Jas. Newbold Taylor 2 Augt. 1816
Noon Mr Wm. Watchmaker 7 May 1821
Nicklinson Mrs December 1835
Newton Mr   13 Feby. 1844
Neale Revd Thos. Sibson Rectory 26 Jany. 59 Aged 91
Noon Mrs November 1875 Aged 83

O

Orton Mrs (Bear) 8 March 1798 Aged
Oakey Mrs Beng Taylor 23 March 1813
Oakey Mr Jas. Senr Taylor 17 July 1818
Orchard Mr Robt. Canier 12 June 1836
Oweston Mr Hiram (Snareston)
Oweston Mr George Leicester 10 Sept. 1848
Orton Mrs Confectioner 17 Sept. 1848
Owston Mr Wilborn 21 July 1849
Orchard Mrs January 1852
Orchard Mr John 19 Sep. 1862 Aged 55
Owen Mrs 3 Oct 1882
Orchard Charles died
Orchard Robert (Cabinet maker) died 13 March 1885 Aged 81
Orchard James Sept. 1887 Aged 76
Orchard Mrs George died 22 May 1901 Aged 80
Oakey Mr Thos. died 6 Novr. 1901 Aged about 70
Orchard Mrs G D 7 July 1927
Orchard Mr G D died 10 Jan. 1930 Aged 76

P

Pulling Mr Benj. 27 Jany. 1794 Aged
Piddocke Mrs Senr 28 Novr. 1795 Aged
Piddocke Mrs Junr 14 July 1798 Aged
Palmer Mr Richd. Son of Mr Walter 29 Feby. 1796 Aged
Pulling Mrs 7 May 1799
Poynton Mr Willm. 19 July 1799
Poynton Mrs Kitty 9 Octr. 1800

Prior Revd John Senr 15 Oct. 1803

Palmer Mr Walter 25 Sep. 1803. Mrs 2 Jany. 1805

Pestell Mr E S Attorney 2 April 1809 Aged

Palmer Mr Bridgefoot 30 May 1811

Piddocke Mrs Leo. 19 October 1814

Prior Mrs 20 July 1774 Aged 43*

Pilkington Miss Elisabeth 3 December 1816

Pilkington Miss 4 Feby. 1817

Pilkington Miss Mary 27 May 1817

Piddocke Mr John Junr. 20 January 1818 Aged 19

Piddocke Miss Frances 7 Feby. 1818

Pipe Mrs 5 January 1819

Pilkington Mrs 20 Oct 1820

Pilkington Mr Geo. 20 Decr. 1821

Parkinson Miss 6 July 1835

Pegg Mr   Decr. 1835

Piddocke Mr Leod. Attorney 30 July 1836 Aged

Piddocke Mr Leod. Junr 3 Sept. 1838 Aged 41

Peck Robert 26 May 1840 died suddenly

Piddocke The Revd John 31 August 1841 Aged 77

Pegg Mr K 21 July 1847 Aged 52

Paterson Mrs 31 Augst. 18 [50 ?]

Piddocke Mr Thos. Solicitor died 19 Jany. 1855 Aged

Piddock Mrs Leo. 4 June 1856

Pilkington Mr Henry   June 1858

Pimm Mr Thos. S 8 March 60 Aged 68

Power Mr Rawdon Terrace 8 Decbr. 61 Aged 85

Pegg Mrs 15 July 1861 Aged 92

Ponton Mr 26 Oct. 1868 Aged 69

Postlethwaite Mr Master of the Blue and Green School 21 Feby.
  1872 Aged 55

Pegg Miss Ann 2 April 1874 Aged 65

Pegg Mr John 23 June 1876

Pegg Miss Susan died 7 Oct. 1878 Aged 81

Price Mrs (at the old lock up) 13 April 1879 Aged 75

Price Mr   do   14 May 1879 Aged 84

Parker the Revd Mr (Worthington) 29 April 1879 Aged over
  70

Proudman George (Christmas Day 1881) Aged 85

---

* This entry is in the handwriting of Thomas Smith Kirkland and must
have been written between 1814 and 1816

Piddocke Mrs Thos. wife of the above died 11 Sep. 1882 Aged 77
Pratt the Revd Charles died 6 Novr. 1908 Aged 89
Pratt Mrs Thomas 10 May 1924
Power Mrs Emma S 2 Aug. 1926 Aged 85

R

Ridgeway Rich'd.
Richard's Thos. Esqr 6 June 1788 Aged
Ratcliff Mary 4 Octr. 1791
Roe Mr Senr. Baker
Roe Mr Wm. Baker 14 July 1796
Ragg Mr Thos. 9 Feby. 1798 Aged 97
Roe Mrs Senr. 17 May 1799
Rose Mr Carpenter 25 March 1803
Rice Mr Wm. 21 July 1804
Roe Mr E Breechesmaker 8 Feb. 1805
Ragg Mr Saml. Flaxdresser 19 Feb. 1807
Roe Mrs Widdow of Mr Edw. Roe 27 Octr. 1810
Roe Miss Milliner 31 May 1811
Richards Jas. Esqr 30 Augt. 1799. Aged 53
Rice Mr Jos. at the Queens Head 23 Apl. 1813
Ratcliff Mr Chas. Carrier 11 March 1816
Ross Mrs 5 Feby. 1818
Ragg Mrs Midwife 27 Decr. 1819
Rossell Mr School-master 25 Decr. 1821
Ratcliff Revd Mr at Leamington August 1832
Roe Mr April 1845
Rylands Mrs Peter died
Rylands Mr Jno. Warrington 23 Augst. 1848
Ragg Mr Wm. 19 March 1851 Aged 76
Rylands Jane Chapman died 23 Oct. 1856 Aged 31
Roe Mrs (Hosier) 1856
Ragg Mrs Wm. 6 Decr. 1864 at Edmonton
Redferne Mr (Druggist) 4 March 1867 Aged 52
Rylands Mrs (Warrington) 12 Feby. 1870 Aged 87
Ragg Mrs Thomas 10 Oct. 1870
Ragg Mr Sam.   Decr. 1870
Ragg Mr Thomas Butcher Decr. 1879
Ratcliffe Mr died   1889 at Highfields Ashby-de-la Zouch
Ratcliffe Mrs Widow of the above died 26 May 1898 Aged
    69

Redfern Mrs The Hollies died 25 Jany. 1898 Aged more than 70

Rylands Thos. Glazebrook died at Highfields Thelwall 14 Feb. 1900 Aged 81

Ragg Mr William (Chemist) Home is at Edmonton died 12 Oct. 1901 Buried at Edmonton Aged 83

Ratcliffe Mrs Charles of Highfield died 29 Augt. 1902 Aged 25

Ragg Mrs William died at Edmonton 17 Nov. 1903 Aged 77

Rylands Mrs J G died at Highfields Thelwall 23 June 1906 Aged*

Rostron Mrs Hubert 14 July 1917 Aged 30 yrs.

Redfern Mr Thomas 16 May 1925

S

Sailsbury Mr Tanner 23 July 1794 Aged

Sharpe Mr Edwd. (Lamb) 7 May 1794 Aged

Slaney Mr Jnr (Hatter) 9 Feby. 1797 Aged

Simpson Mrs 30 Novr. 1796 Aged

Simpson Mastr Wm. (last son) 4 July 1797

Smith Mrs Robt. 1 May 1797 Aged

Shieffield Mr John 2 Feby. 1799

Sailsbury Mrs (Sadler) 27 Feby. 1799

Sowter Mr John 27 Novr. 1799

Sharp Willm. (Black horse) 11 Dec 1799

Sabine Mrs 9 May 1800

Sutton Mrs 3 June 1800

Springthorpe Mrs Park 21 Febr. 1801

Smith Mr Thos. Turner 11 March 1801

Shaw Mrs Mr Shaw's mother 14 Mar. 1807

Shaw Mr Tho. Carpenter 20 May 1808

Slater Mr Thos. Mercer 13 Jany. 1810

Smith Mr Thos. Stamford 23 Novr. 1809

Slater Mr W Liquor Merchant 24 Febr. 1810

Shaw Mastr Saml. Common 6 Dec., 1810

Slater Mr Robt. 25 June 1812

Snelson Mr Josh. Senr 7 Dec. 1813

Savage Mrs Selbys Lane 18 Sept. 1814

Severn Mr Luke 26 April 1815

---

* Wife of J Paul Rylands FSA compiler of the Kirkland Pedigree

Slaney Mrs John 27 May 1815
Sailsbury Mrs Senr. Mill Lane 13 Novr. 1814
Sailsbury Mr Wm. Junr Saddler 26 July 1818
Selby Mr John Farrier 29 Decr. 1818
Snelson Mrs Jos. Senr 10 March 1819
Senlson Mr John 16 June 1819
Snelson Mr Jonathon 28 October 1821
Simmonds Miss Jane 8 September 1822
Simmonds Mrs 17 Decr. 1836 Minutes past   Aged
Sharpe Mrs November 1837 Aged 79
Snelson Mrs Mark 5 June 1841 Mr S first Wife
Sheppard Mr Gardener, 9 Augst. 1848
Shaw Mr S 18 Novr. 1850
Snelson Miss 1 April 1852
Spencer Mr Veterinary Surgeon, 12 July 1855
Snelson Mr James Junr. 25 July 58
Sutton Mr John (Parish Clerke) 19 October 1858, Aged 50
Salisbury Mr John, Aged 80 30 April 61
Simmonds Mr (Measham Fields) 2 Augst. 1862 Aged 63
Snelson Mr Thos. 9 July 1864
Shaw Mr Thos. (Common Farm) 31 March 1868 Aged 78
Salisbury Mr William (Jeweller) 20 Feby. 1872 Aged 38
Shaw Miss Louisa 24 June 1872 Aged 71
Staley Daniel (Blacksmith) Sep. 1872 Aged 85
Simmonds Mrs widow of Joseph Simmonds of Measham Fields died
    22 May Aged 82 1885
Sandlant Mr Butcher died March 1888 Aged
Smith Mr William Edwd. Lawyer died 1891 Aged 73
Shaw Miss Elizth. died Bowden, June, Buried at Ashby 27 June
    Aged 79
Simpkin Mr (Grocer) died 6 Sepr. 1898
Street Mrs James 18 Novr., 1898
Smith Mrs W E widow of Lawyer, 14 Decr. 1899, Aged over
    80
Smith Upholsterer 3 April 1900 Aged 83
Smith Mrs Haberdasher died 9 April 1900 Aged 70
Smith Mrs widow of Upholsterer died 18 Novr. 1901 Aged
    92
Smith Mr Tobacconist March 1904 Aged 73
Simmonds Miss Maria, died 7 Decr. 1904, Aged 70
Scott Mrs 30 Sept. 1916
Simmonds Miss Jane, 13 June 1923 Aged 82

T

Timm's Mr Jnr (Ashby Mill) 5 July 1794
Toon Mr Josh. Farm Town Coleorton 24 Feby. 1799
Timm's Mrs Senr (Ashby Mill) 22 April 1799
Thornley Mr James 26 Aprl. 1801
Thornley Mr Thos. 3 Augt. 1801
Timms Jos. Mill Lane friday 11 July 1800
Thornley Miss Eliz. 8 June 1802, Tuesday
Timms Miss Ann 17 June 1803
Turner Mrs late of the Mill, 10 Febr. 1810
Thornley Miss Susanna, died 5 Feby. 1812
Thornley Mrs 18 May 1815 Aged
Tunnaley Mr Hugh 2 August 1816
Tompson Mr Joseph Mercer 29 May 1817
Tompson Mrs Senr Mercer 26 June 1818
Tabberer Mrs 11 Octr. 1823
Thornley Mr Robert 13 October 1842
Toplis Mrs 4 May 1856 Aged 70
Tivey Wm. 20 May 1856 Aged 82
Toplis Mr 1860
Toplis Mrs James 22 Augst. 1861 Aged 45
Townsend Miss 25 Sep. 1861
Timms Mr S 5 Dec. 1863 Aged 85
Timms Mrs S 12 May 1865 Aged 94
Toplis Miss 18 April 1869 Aged 50
Thirlby Miss 24 Feby. 1871 Aged 53
Thornley Mr (Sadler) died 5 March 1888 Aged 65
Toplis Mr James (Basketmaker) 15 Feby. 1889
Toplis Mr James died 27 July Aged 66
Thompson Miss Annie died 12 May 1901 Aged
Thornley Miss Eunice died 20 Feb. 1927 Aged 80

U

Usherwood Mr (Tax collector) 18 Oct. 1872 Aged 85

V

Vinrace Mrs wife of Wm. V 10 Jany. 1805
Vinrace Mr Wm. Junr
Vinrace Miss 10 Sept. 1822

Vinrace Mrs 30 April 1855 Aged 84

Vinrace Mr Luke 24 Sept. 1880 Aged 72

Vavasour The Revd Marmaduke late Vicar of Ashby-de-la Zouch died at Clifton 6 Nov. 1879 Aged 83

Vavasour Mrs widow of the above died at Clifton 17 Jany. 1881 Aged 86

Vinrace Mrs widow of Mr Luke died   Augst. 1883 Aged

W

Wallis Mr Jno. 2 Sepr. 1795 Aged 75

Wrigglesworth Mr R at Mrs Thornley's, 12 Sepr. 1796 Buried next day

Wilds Mr Surgeon drownd 1 Aprl. 1800

Wright Miss M Daughter of Mr W Currier, 1 April 1805

Ward Mrs At the Angel, 17 March 1806

Woodward Mrs 6 May 1806

Ward Mr Thos. Cooper, 21 July 1808

Wood Mr 13 Novr. 1808, Mercer

Wayte Mr Thos. Farmer, Ashby 10 Novr. 1809

Wright Mr Benj. (9 March 1810) Blacksmith

Wright Mrs Thos. Whitesmith 3 Nov 1810

Worstall Mrs 27 May 1811

Webster Mr Attorney, 17 December 1812, Aged

Widdowson Mr Senr Carpenter 5 Augt. 1814

Willson Miss Common, 28 May, 1815

Wright Mr Currier 7 Feby. 1818

Wright Mrs 12 April 1820, Aged 70

Worstall Mr Jas. 28 June 1820, Aged 87

Wilkins Mrs 21 August, 1820

Wayte Mrs 25 May 1833

Whyman Miss S 6 Feby. 1837, Aged 19

Whitehurst Mrs at Mr Thos. Dewes 7 August 1838

Whyman Miss Eliza 3 April 1852, Aged 30

Whitehurst Miss Jane 20 Oct., 1857

Webb Mr Manager of the Bank 23 Oct. 1857 Aged 45

Whyman Mr Henry 12 July 1858 Aged 71

Wilkins Mrs 7 Feb 1864 Aged 74

Wayte Mr Post Master 29 Nov 1867 Aged 74

Woodhouse W William Henry at the Bedford Hotel London 25 June 1864 Aged 49

Webb Mrs 19 May 1862 Aged 41

Ward Mr Prior Park (formerly of the Breach Farm) 6 Nov.
 1872 Aged 70

Witt Mrs 17 Aug. 1877 Aged 73

Woodhouse Mr John Thomas of Overseal died at Scarborough 27
 Sep. 1878 Aged 70

Whyman Mrs widow of Henry Whyman died 4 Feby. 1881 Aged
 88

Wright Mr Benjamin (Saddler) died 24 Sepr. 1880 Aged

Wright Mrs B widow of above died 26 Jany. 1881 Aged 53

Wayte Mrs widow of Postmaster   1887

Mrs William Wright died 30 May 1889 Aged 84 (wife of draper)

Whyman Mr Edwin Hairdresser etc died 29 Oct. 1889 Aged 63

Wright Mr (Shoemaker) died 3 Sep. 1892 Aged

Wright Mr William draper died 5 Decr. 1898 Aged 86

Wright Mrs widow of Shoemaker died 13 April Aged 69

Wilkins Mr William Prior Park died 12 Dec. 1908

Williams Dr Charles Roberts 7 Dec. 1925 Aged 70 yrs.

Wenham Rev John 17 June Aged 55 1927 RC Priest

Y

Young Mr Francis 1 April 1799; he left Caulke the preceding
 evening his hat was found in a pool of water nr Caulke
 from which he had extricated himself and proceeded half
 a mile when being exhausted by the efforts he had made and
 chilled by his wet clothes fell a victim to the extreme
 severity of the night.

Z

Donington Lord Gilbert Theophilus Clifton Hastings died
 31 May 1927. Aged 68 yrs.

Marriages

A

Armstrong Mr Quarter Master to Miss Timm's 2 April 1795
Anstead Mr London to Miss Elizth. Prior 22 June 1796
Abney Mr and Mrs Richards Monday 8 Sept. 1800
Adams Mr Jams. to Miss Dixon 24 May, 1803
Armstrong Mr Josh. to Miss Ashbinshaw 13 Feby., 1804
Adams Miss Mary to Mr Grice 31 Decr., 1804
Adams Mr Jams. to Molly Buskill 28 Sept. 1807 his third wife
Adams Mr Thos. Butcher to Mrs Ragg 18 Aug. 1812
Adams Mr Jas. Junr to Frances Binley 11 May 1813

B

Burslem Major to Miss Brook's 4 March 1798
Beadsmoore Mr Saml. to Miss Sabine 20 Aug. 1798
Bath Miss to Mr King Leicester 22 March 1803
Beavington Miss Eliz. to Mr T Clarkston 9 Feb. 1804
Beavington Mr Benj. to Miss Sharpe 18 June 1804
Brown Mr to Miss Snelson 22 April, 1804
Bedford Mr Thos. Bolton to Miss Fowler 29 September 1805
Bedford Miss Jane to Mr Francis Robert 13 May, 1806
Brewin Mrs (widow of the late Mr T Brewin) aged 73 to Mr
    Oakey 28 Octr., 1809
Bowles Mr Chals. to Miss Shakespere of Staunton 30 May 1810
Beavington Mr Benj. to Miss Mary Mathews his second wife 6
    September, 1814
Beavington Mr W to Miss Sarah Smith 1 May 1813
Beadsmoore Mr Samuel to Miss Green 30 June 1822
Beavington Mr John to Miss Eliz. Clarkson 13 March 1823
Bobart Mr to Miss Matthews   1832
Beavington Miss Eliz. to Mr Blenkarne 16 Dec. 1834
Boyer Mr Surgeon to Miss Piddocke 2 June, 1836

Binley Miss Ellen to Mr Hill Birmingham 19 Feb. 1839
Binley Mr John to Miss Wood 21 July 1840
Brunt Mr to Mrs Salisbury 29 June 1841
Beavington Miss to Mr Grimes   Jany. 1844
Beavington Miss Grace to Mr Sturland 22 Augst. 57
Brown Miss to Mr Charles Shakespear of Langley Priory 19 July 59
Beadsmore Mr John to Miss King
Bagnall Mr William to Miss Wilkins 31 March 1862
Brown Miss to Mr Carrington 9 Sep. 1862
Brown Miss daughter of Mr G Brown (Glazier) to Mr Charles of Pelsal – Staffordshire 9 Sep. 62
Brunt Miss to Mr Savidge 3 July 1866
Brunt Miss Sarah June to Mr Cooper 24 March 1866
Brill Miss daughter of Mr D Brill to Mr Adland of Postlip Hall Gloucestershire 15 Nov. 1871
Blood Miss to Mr W O Spencer of Clavering Essex 30 April 1873
Bangham Thomas Kirkland to Maria Constance Jagger 29 Sept. 1880
Bangham Miss Elizth. to Mr Samuel Morris 12 April 1887
Bullen Mr Chemist to Mrs Cartledge 5 Oct. 1903
Bullen Miss Eva Jane Margaret to Mr George Eric Shelton 16 Oct. 1913

C

Cantrel Mr Surgeon to Miss Mary Beavington 19 Jany., 1796
Charlesworth Mr Thos. to Miss Charlesworth his second wife 1809
Carder Mrs at Mr Gaudins 27 March 1810 to
Crosley Mr Charles to Miss Charlesworth 11 Octr. 1819
Crossley Mr Senr to Miss Hannah Leitherland 8 Octr. 1820
Cantrell Mr Jos. to Miss M Whitehurst Augt. 1830
Cape Mr F to Miss Sarah Shaw 20 Oct. 1836
Chubb Mr Geo. to Miss Cathe. Dawes 3 May 1838
Cheatle Richard to May Palmer 2 Feby. 1841
Cheatle Mr John to Miss Ann Wright 8 Octr., 1850
Cantrell Miss to Mr Storer Derby 4 Sep. 1851
Cooper Miss Emma to Mr Mills Isley Walton 9 June 1854
Cantrell Miss M J to Mr Shaw (Derby) 19 Sep. 1854
Cradock Miss to Dr Fry 4 July 1867
Cradock Miss Mary C to Mr John 9 Oct 1873

Carman Mr W H to Miss Alice J Smith 31 Dec. 1913

D

Denstone Mr to Miss Sarah Mathews 21 July 1803
Dalby Mr Thos. Atty. to Miss S Springthorp 27 Aug. 1804
Dewes Miss S to Mr Sarjeant, 28 Augt. 1804
Davenport Mr to Miss Cox of Haunton 13 Feb. 1805 . . .
Davenport Mr Wm. to Miss Wright 5 July 1810
Dawes Mr to Miss Willder 5 March, 1811
Dewes Mr Josh. to Miss Brian 4 April 1814
Douall Mac Revd to Miss Gaudin 7 Feby. 1815
Dinwoodie Mrs to Mr Boultbe 20 March 1817
Dewes Mr Solicitor to Miss Saunders 1 Decr. 1819
Dewes Mr Thos. C to Miss Whitehurst of Derby 11 Jany., 1821
Dewes Mr Henry to Miss Watson 30 Decr., 1821
Duglas Mr to Miss Gibbs 10 Jany. 1831
Davys Mr Thos. to Miss Patterson 30 April 1833
Dewes Mr Henry to Miss Swinnerton 20 Augt. 1833 (2nd wife)
Dalby Miss Matilda to Mr Gascoyne 14 June 1833
Deavenport Mr Wm. Butcher to Mrs Sweet 23 August. 1836
Deavenport Mr John to Miss Stinson 5 December 1837
Dalby Miss Lucy to Mr Edwd. Dalby 28 May 1839
Dalby Mr Thos. B to Miss Elizth. Tabberer Tutbury 15 Augst. 1839
Dalby Mr Chas. A to Miss Sarah Bartlett of Lymmington 29 Octr.
   1839
Dawes Mr Wm. to Miss Haywood of Derby Decr. 1839
Deavenport Mr to Mrs Willson December 1839
Davys Mr J to Miss Swinnerton 20 Octr. 1842
Dewes Mr Henry to Mrs Choice 8 Augst. 1843
Dalby Miss
Dewes Miss to Mr Welchman of Southam 2 March 1848
Dewes Mr Willm. to Miss Munday 18 March 1848
Davenport Mr Thos. to Mrs Allen 4 Feby. 1853
Dewes Miss to Mr Taylor (Higham on the Hill) 7 Jany. 64
Dewes Mr Wm. to Mrs Lamb
Davys Miss to the Revd Case Humfrey 11 June 68
Dalby Mr Thos. B to Miss Grundy (2nd wife) at Whitwick 5
   Augst. 1875
Davenport Mr J to Miss Lowe 14 Jany. 1885
Denton Miss Alice second daughter of the Vicar of Ashby to Mr
   Hughes Hallett Lawyer of Derby 13 Sepr. 1887

Denton Miss Florence to Captn Shaw of Derby 23 Oct. 1890

Dewes Mr Hugh (Dentist) to Miss Osmund both of London 24 July 1890

Denton Miss Eldest daughter of the Vicar of Ashby to Mr Vicars of Leicester & Wigston Magna 6 Augst. 1893

1897 On 8 July at S Peter's, San Jose de Flores, Buenos Ayres (by the Rev S F Handcock), Henry Thomas Kenyon, of El Prado, Gualequaychu, youngest son of the late Rev Charles Orlando Kenyon, of Morton Shropshire, to Hilda Beatrice, youngest daughter of the late William Petit Dowes, solicitor, Ashby-de-la-Zouch. By cable. 1899 Denton-Hope On 28 June, at the Parish Church Thames Ditton, Surrey by the Rev W D Bainbridge Bell, MA vicar, John Fleming St Andrew Denton youngest son of Canon Denton, vicar of Ashby-de-la-Zouch and rural dean, to Lionie Eleonora, youngest daughter of the late Francis Hope, Esq, of Guernsey.

Dalby Miss Sarah to Mr Ronald Faulkner 28 Oct. 1914

Davenport Major Arthur to Miss Lucy Micklejohn 7 Jan. 1925

E

Mr Everett Station Master to Mrs Mullis 8 Sep. 1903

F

Farnell Miss Eliz. to Mr Checkett 13 July 1809

Fowler Miss Hannah to Mr Day 21 April, 1814

Forster Mr Edwd. to Miss Hood 6 May, 1823

Farnell Mr Jos. to Miss Hall   183

Fell Revd T to Miss Acklum   Jany. 1840

Fisher Mr Thos. to Miss Drewey of Newton Solney 28 April 1859

Fisher Miss to Mr Holt of Harrogate 6 June 60

Foster Miss D to Mr Huntress 21 June 1930

G

Gibb's Mr Edwd. to Miss Mary Newbold 31 Decr. 1798

Glazbrook Thos. to Miss E Iryambrook Saturday 23 May 1801

Do Mr John to Maria Allen Chelmsford

Do Miss Marta to Mr Rylands 13 Sept. 1808

Gibbs Mr Edwd. to Mrs Buckerfield 20 Augt. 1811

Garland Mr Taylor, to Ann Salisbury (his second wife) 4 November, 1819

Green Mr Edwd. Attorney to Miss Susanah Freer   1830
Green Mr Edwd. Attorney to Miss Craddock 30 May 1837
Goodman Mr Junr to Miss Spencer November 1861
Green Miss A Ellen to Mr L J Hart 9 Jany. 62
Green Miss to Mr Smithers 1 Nov. 1866
Goodman Miss to Mr J H Warner 13 Augst. 67
German Mr George to Miss Emmaline May Jesson 12 Sept. 1900
German Miss Margery to Major Eric Treharane 23 April 1924
German Miss Phyllis to Mr Arthur Sutton 2 June 1927

H

Hatton Mr Thos. Jun to Miss Eleanor Sutton 3 Dec. 1798
Hopkins Mr James to Miss Ward 3 Jany. 1799
Halbrook Mr and Miss Sutton 5 May 1801
Hatton Mr Thos. to Miss Ann Sheffield his second wife 11 March 1800
Hatton Mr Thos. Junr to his third wife Miss Barlow of Loughborough 8 Sept., 1804
Hatton Mrs to Mr Clarke Donisthorpe 18 March 1806
Hanson Miss Atherstone to Mr Sale 24 July 1806
Hartwell Mr Ashby to Miss Martha Moore 23 May 1814
Hood Mr Wm. to Miss   10 June 1823
Hastings Marquis of at Walston Church, by the Hon. and Revd W Eden to the Right Hon. Barbara Baronefs Grey de Ruthyn of Brandon House Monday 1 August 1831
Hawksworth Mr H M to Miss Ford 3 Sep. 1837
Husbands Mr to Miss Dawes (at Derby) 17 July, 1834
Hastings Lady Selina Constancia Rawdon Campbell to Charles Henry Esq, nephew of the Duke of Leinster. 1838
Hartnell Mr to Miss Lawson 13 October 1840
Hextall Mr W to Miss Brown 26 September 1842
Hawksworth Mr H M to Miss Briggs   1843
Hastings Lady Sophia Frederica Christina to John Crichton Stuart Marquis of Bute at Loudoun Castle 10 April 1845
Hawkesworth Mr H M to S Lewin 1847
Hastings Henry W C Plantagenet 4 Marquis to Florence Cecilia Paget youngest daughter of the Marquis of Anglesey St Georges Hanover Square London 16 July 1864
Hastings Lady Flora to the Duke of Norfolk 29 Nov. 1878
Hastings Miss Isabel Jacqueline Rawdon Hastings to Major Hubert Rostron 20 Sept. 1916 at the Parish Church Ashby-de-la-Zouch

Hastings Miss Edith Maud Rawdon Hastings to Captain Reginald
  Huddleston 12 Dec. 1916 at St Marys Cathedral Edinburgh

I

Ingle Miss to Mr Cheatle May 1811
Ingle Miss Judith to Mr Dregg 23 Augt. 1819
Ison Mr to Miss Eliza Halford 15 Augt., 1822
Ingle Mr N to Miss Shaw of Arley 27 Sept. 1838
Ison John to Miss Shaw Alton 5 Novr. 1850
Ison Mr John to his second wife Miss Johnstone 16 January
  1855 . . .
Ison Mr Josia to M⸻ Brown of Leicester
Ison Miss to Mr Parsons 27 April 58
Ison Mr Josiah to Miss Adkins⸻ October 59
Ison Mr James to Miss S Jackson of⸻ 23 Oct. 59
Ingle Miss Agnes to Mr Prince 30 April 1881

J

Joyce Mr H to Mrs Brown 17 Augt. 1801
Johnstone Mr T to Miss Ingram⸻ March 1833
Ingle Mr N to Miss Shaw of Arley 27 Sept. 1838
Johnson Revd Edward to Miss Bindley 12 Nov. 63
Jesson Mr Fisher (Solicitor) to Miss Mary Dalby 27 Sepr. 1905
Constance Charlotte Jesson to Francis C Stevenson 12 Sept. 1909
Jenkins Mr to Miss Hanson 20 Nov. 1855
Joyce Miss Annie Mabel to Mr Hall Hogg 4 Sept. 1930
Ingle Mr Mathew to Miss Carrington 4 Oct. 1855

K

Kirkland Mr Thos. Nottingham to Miss Twells 18 Decr. 1798
Kirkland Miss Mary to Mr Wm. Stain⸻ 1805
Kirby Mr Tho. to Miss Sarah Slater, 12 May, 1805
Kirby Mr Jas. to Molly Green (Second wife) 29 July 1813
Kiddear Mr Joseph to Mrs Noon 2nd wife 27 Augt. 1822
Kirby Mr Jas. to Miss Lakin (his third wife)
Kirby Mr Jas. to Mrs Day (his fourth wife) 28 May, 1839
Kirkland Miss Eliz. to Mr Foster 9 Sept. 1845
Kirkland Miss M to Revd A Creighton 27 Sep. 66 Vicar of
  Stallingborough Lincolnshire

Kirkland Miss Lucy to Francis Bangham 9 Feby. 1854

L

Lloyd the Revd Mr to Miss Bleak 10 Feb. 1812
Lee Mr Draper to Miss   Cartwell 11 May 1819
Lever Mr Mercer to Miss Lovat
Lever Mr Baker to Miss Lovat 27 Oct. 1814
Linsey Mr Attorney at Mr Piddocks 12 May 1820
Lovell Mr Draper to Miss Armstone 30 May 1837

M

Mathews Mr Wm. to Miss Caulher 28 Augt., 1804
Mathews Miss Ann to Mr Checkett 27 Novr., 1894
Moore Miss Ashby Old Parks to Mr Sanders 25 Augst. 1813
Mammatt Mr John to Miss Hall May 1832
Mathews Mr W Surgeon Atherstone to Miss Lee of Bosworth
    2 April 1835
Mammatt Miss to Mr Festir of Maden Bradley, Wilts 26 September
    1835
Mammatt Mr Edward to Miss H Buller 2 June 42
McDouall the Revd Patrick Geo. to Miss Caroline Jane Fisher June
    1851
Mathews Miss H B to Mr W Joyce Surgeon 19 Sepr. 61
Mammatt Mr Ed. to Miss Hall 11 August 1868
Matthews Miss Constance Helen to Mr Francis Ison 2 June 1880
Musson Mr Alfred William to Miss A Hamp 9 Sepr. 1880
Matthews Miss Mary to Mr West 17 Febr. 1881
Mr Edward Mammatt to Miss Jessie Green 25 April 1900
Musson Miss Mary B to Mr Robert I Williamson 29 Jan. 1907
Musson Mr William Pratt to Miss Annie Joyce 11 June 1908
Musson Edward Lional (Major) King's African Rifles to Laura
    Emily Nateci 14 Nov. 1916
Moorcroft Geoffrey Herbert married 12 Feb. 1925 to Marjorie
    Kathleen Lake of Burton-on-Trent

N

Needham Mr Thos. to Miss Toopot 16 April 1799
Newton Mr Brazier to Mrs Barker

O

Owston Mr Hiram A to Miss Spencer of Snareston 21 July 1818
Orchard Mr John to Miss Knowles
Orchard Mr Charles to Miss M A Peach 30 May 1838
Owston Mr W to Miss Redfern 14 Sepr. 1847
Owston Mrs W to Mr Hardwick 25 April 1853
Owston Miss to Mr Smith of Langley Notts 14 Sep. 1875
Orchard Mr Alfred (Surgeon) to Miss Scott 26 Oct. 1892

P

Pegg Mr Watchmaker to Miss Bott 29 Decr. 1793
Piddocke Revd Jno. to Miss Harris 6 Novr. 1794
Piddocke Mr Leo'd to Miss Sarah Beavington 23 Augt. 1796
Pilkington Mr to Miss Newton 28 May 1795
Marshall Mr to Miss Cape 23 Augt. 1835
Proudman Miss to Mr Swinnerton Jany./17
Pegg Mr John to Miss Spencer 5 September 1848
Pinn   Mr Thos. S 8 March 60
Pratt Miss Georgiana to Mr Francisco Santiago Taylor 2 July 1912
Phillimozo Capt. Paul to Miss Augusta Tredocroft 11 April 1917

R

Richard's James Esqr to Mrs Bacon 30 Novr. 1792
Rose Mrs Black Horse to Mr Ayre 14 Sept., 1804
Rice Miss Queens Head to Mr Brown 9 May 1808
Rice Miss Ann Queens Head to Mr Ward Burslem, 2 July 1810
Rice Mr Charles Queens Head to Miss   10 Feb. 1812
Rice Mr Leo Queens Head to Miss Hextall 24 Feby. 1814
Roe Mr George to Miss   20 Jany. 1815
Ragg Mr William to Miss D P Chapman 2 Feb. 1815
Ragg Mr Thos. (Butcher) to Miss Cheatle 27 Jany. 1835
Ragg Miss E C to Mr P Rylands 19 July 1844
Ragg Miss Jane to Mr G Rylands 24 May 1845
Ragg Miss Jane Chapman Edmonton to Mr Charles R Brace 26
    March 1881
Rylands John Paul to Isabel Mary Glazebrook 30 March 1883
Ratcliffe Mr Charles to Miss Hilda Stevenson of near Dover
    4 Dec. 1895

S

Smith Mr Robt. to Miss Mary Shieffield 21 Sep. 1794
Simpson Mr to his second wife Miss Foster 8 Novr. 1798
Sutton Mr to Miss Eleanor Sheffield 23 Janr. 1800
Shaw Mr Thos. Harley to Miss Ann Ingle 17 Nov. 1802
Sheffield Mr Wm. to Miss Worthington 13 Sepr. 1803
Springthorpe Miss to Mr Ingram 25 April 1805
Slater Miss Lucy to Mr Greasley 2 Decr. 1805
Slater Miss Ann to Mr Mathew   25 March, 1806
Shaw Mr Thos. Common to Miss Ayre Coleorton 19 Novr., 1816
Shaw Mr Willm. to Miss Grimbley 26 May 1818
Simmonds Miss Harriot to Mr Nedlum of Leicester 17 Augt.
   1819
Shaw Mr Thos. (Butcher) to Miss Sarah Clarke 18 April 1822
Snelson Mr Thos. to Miss   Crossley 19 May 1822
Snelson Mr to Miss Mary Halford 15 Augt. 1822
Sweet Mrs to Mr Deavenport Butcher 23 Augt. 1836
Sutton Mr to Miss Mathew, Lamb Inn   August 1841
Shirwin Mr W to Miss Pratt 30 March 1843
Smith Mr Solicitor to Miss Elizabeth Buller 19 July 1855
Shaw Miss M Altons to Mr A Rollason 24 Augst. 54
Swinnerton Miss to Mr Barnwell (Bilton) 3 Sepr. 57
Snelson Miss Caroline to Mr Thos. Grimes (Coventry) 2 June
   1856
Simmonds Mr John to Miss Barnes Chelsea 18 Feb. 62
Spencer Mr Henry to Miss Knowles 29 Sept. 1863
Simmonds Miss to Mr G Sale Donisthorpe 4 Jany. 1865
Samson Mr to Mrs Dailey 8 Oct.
Simmonds Mr John to Miss A Witt 6 Oct. 1875

T

Timms Mr and Miss Clark 16 June 1801
Timms Mr T and Mrs Fowler 11 March 1804
Timms Miss Sarah to Mr Clark 29 Jany. 1809
Tabberer Mr Benj. to Miss Dancer of Burton 16 May 1810
Tompson Mr Mercer to Miss Ann Tompson 30 July 1816
Timms Miss Ann to Mr S Clark Packington 26 Feb. 1839
Thornley Miss to Mr Walkden Grocer
Thornley Miss Ada to Mr George Farmer 24 May 1881

174

U

Usherwood Mr John to Miss Mary Cheatle 15 Sept. 1836
Usherwood Miss Mary to Mr Whittaker of Handley /84
Usherwood Miss Catharine to Mr Doodey of Handley Staffordshire
   30 September 1851

V

Miss Vavasour to Mr Gresley 25 Jany. 1849
Miss F B Vavasour to the Rev Montague Webster 11 Jany. 1853
Vavasour Miss Elizth. to the Revd J Denton 2 June 57
Vinrace Miss to Dr Hachett (Ravenstone) 6 Nov. 62
Vavasour Miss Augusta, to Mr E C Middleton of Loughborough
   on Tuesday 7 June 1864
Vavasour Miss Louisa to Jos. Taylor Esq 8 August 67
Vavasour Revd John to Miss Brooks 21 April 1868

W

Wellings Mr to Miss Ann Green 15 March 1804
Wood W Mercer to Dalby   21 Feb. 1809
Whyman Mr Henry to Miss Palmer 6 March 1815
Wilkins Mr Wm. to Miss Walton (his second wife) 10 Jany. 1822
Welch Mr to Miss Spencer Ashby 18 Feb. 1839
Wright Mr to Miss E Shaw 27 Decr. 1842
Webb Mr to Miss Hicken 24 September 1844
Whyman Miss Ann to Mr Gadby 25 Oct. 53
Witt Miss to Mr Barber of Eastwood Notts 3 Oct. 1854
Willson W Brien to Miss Mary Ponton 5 Feby. 1855
Wagstaff Miss to Mr Smith 29 Oct. 59
Wright Miss (Rawdon House) to Mr N Joyce 18 June 73
Witt Miss Amelia to Mr John Simmonds at Southport 6 Oct. 1875
Whyman Mr Edwin to Miss Leake/2nd wife/ 14 Sep. 1875
Wilkins Miss to Dr Highet 16 June 1906

References

Chapter 1

1. Thomas Kirkland, MD *An enquiry into the present state of Medical Surgery*, vol. ii (1786), p.365

2. Thomas Lawrence (1711–1783) was anatomical reader to Oxford University but resided in London where he delivered anatomical lectures from 1740 becoming a Fellow of the London College of Physicians (1744) and President (1767–1774). After 1750 he ceased to lecture, because Hunter had become so popular, and devoted himself to medical practice. He was a friend of Dr Samuel Johnson who was one of his patients. All his works were written in elegant Latin. (*Dictionary of National Biography*).

3. John Throsby. *The supplementary volume to the Leicestershire Views containing a series of excursions in the year 1790.* (J Nicholls, London 1790).

4. George Rude, *Europe in the 18th Century* (Weidenfeld & Nicolson 1972), p.97

5. Elizabeth Lane, Lecture

6. Letter from Lady Hertford quoted by W Scott. *Story of Ashby-de-la Zouch* (1907), p.123

7. *The Hastings' manuscript* Vol.i. Historical Manuscripts' Commission Vol i, p.417

8. *Ibid*, p.322

9. J G Noverre, *Letters on Dancing* (Beaumont, 1931), p.67

10. Wilson, *A Dictionary of Ballet*, p.297

11. C W Beaumont, *A Miscellany for Dancers* (1954) pp.46 and 47

12. *Ibid*, p.46

13. *The Hastings' Manuscript*. op.cit., p.80

14. *Ibid*, p.78

15. M M Reece *The Royal Office of Master of the Horse* (Theobald Books Ltd 1976)

16. Later General Sir Henry Clinton (1738–1795). Succeeded General Howe as Commander-in-Chief of British Military Forces in North America in the War of American Independence 1778. He resigned in 1781 following a disagreement with Lord Cornwallis.

17. *Leicestershire in 1777*. An Edition of 'John Prior's Map of Leicestershire' with an introduction and commentary by members of the Leicestershire Industrial History Society. Edited by J D Welding, Leicestershire Libraries and Information Services.

18. W Scott, op.cit., p.334

19. *The Diary of Fanny Burney* (J M Dent), p.48

20. *Gentlemen's Magazine* (1789), pp.959 and 960

21. M M Reece, op.cit. p

22. *The Complete Peerage of England, Scotland, Ireland, Great Britain and the United Kingdom*. New Edition by the Hon. Vicary Gibbs and N A Doubleday (St Catherine's Press, 1926.)

23. Breedon-on-the-Hill Parish Registers. Leicestershire County Records' Office.

24. Ferrers' MSS. William Salt Library, Stafford. *The Weekly Telegraph*, 21 May 1898.

25. This account of the murder is based on *Mr Kirkland's Narrative of the murder of Mr Johnson and the facts previous and subsequent to it* (1760), Public Record Office Treasury Solicitor's Records TS 11/442

26. House of Lords Record Office: Trial of Lord Ferrers MSS 1760. Inquest of John Johnson Deposition of Margaret Clifford.

27. W Scott, op.cit. p.283. Will of John Mynors 3 June 1749.

28. *Gentlemen's Magazine* Vol XXX (1760), p.234

29. Holograph autopsy report written by Thomas Kirkland on the fly-sheet of his copy of the *Trial of Earl Ferrers for the murder of John Johnson* published by the Order of the House of Peers 1760 on which this account of the trial is based.

30. John Throsby, op.cit. quoted by James Thompson, *The History of Leicester* F Hewitt, (Leicester 1879) pp.173–174

31. *Gentlemen's Magazine*, op.cit.

32. Leicestershire County Records Office. Ferrers MS 2638/2639

33. Public Record Office. Calendar of Home Office Papers 1760–1765.

34. *Dictionary of National Biography* op.cit.

35. *Blackstone's Commentaries* (Chitty) 1826. Vol iv pp.355 and 359

36. Nigel Walker. *Crime and Insanity in England* (Edinburgh University Press, 1968), vol i p.58

37. *Ibid* p.62

38. *Gentlemen's Magazine* vol xxx, 9 May, 1760, p.236

39. Newspaper Report. *The Weekly Telegraph*, 21 May, 1898

40. Ferrers' MSS. William Salt Library, op.cit.

41. *Dictionary of National Biography*, 1909, vol 18, p.135

42. R Chambers. *The Book of Days* (W R Chambers 1881), vol i, p.41

43. Ferrers' MSS, The William Salt Library, op.cit.

44. *Gentlemen's Magazine* (1760), op.cit. p.236

45. Ferrers MSS, The William Salt Library, op.cit.

46. Leicestershire County Records office Ferrers MSS op.cit.

47. *Walpole Letters* (1857–59) vol iii 304, 310

48. *Dictionary of National Biography*, op.cit. vol 18 p.135

49. Horace Walpole, letter to George Montague, 6 May 1760.

50. Harriet Bridgeman and Elizabeth Drury *Society Scandals* (David & Charles, 1977), p.35

51. Ferrers MSS Leicestershire County Records Office op.cit.

52. Greater London Record Office and Library. St Pancras Church Burial Register, (1760), p.91

53. In the Register of Burials at Staunton Harold Church is this entry: '8 June 1782. The Rt. Hon. Laurence Earl Ferrers (*qui ab hac Luce migravit* 5 Maii 1760) was brought to Staunton Harold and interred in the vault there recording the promise of the Rt. Hon. Robert Earl Ferrers (his brother) made to him in his lifetime.' (*Stimmate Shirliiana* p.197, William Salt Library, Stafford)

54. *Dictionary of National Biography*, op.cit. vol 18, p.135

55. *Diary of Mary Grose, Daily Telegraph* 12 Feb. 1988, quoting Mrs Sheila White, St Helens, Isle of Wight

56. *Dictionary of National Biography*, op.cit.

57. *Concise Dictionary of National Biography* Part I (Oxford University Press 1983), p.955

58. Miss E McNeill, Librarian and Keeper of the Records, the Hon. Society of the Middle Temple, London EC4

59. W Scott, *Story of Ashby-de-la Zouch*, op.cit.

60. *The Gentlemen's Magazine*, op.cit. (1798) p.245

61. Leicestershire County Records Office, Ferrers MSS, op.cit.

62. *The Complete Peerage of England*, op.cit. vol i p.337

63. *Dictionary of National Biography*, op.cit. vol 18 p.135

64. Public Record Office. Calendar of Home Office papers 1760–1765
65. Leicestershire County Records office, Ferrers MSS, op.cit.
66. Derbyshire County Records Office, Melbourne Parish Registers.
67. Dictionary of National Biography, op.cit. vol 18 p.135
68. H J Wain. *The Story of Staunton Harold.* (Parker & Son, 1965)

Chapter 2

1. Charles Seager & E Ashworth, *A Short History of Medicine,* (Clarendon Press 1962), p.484
2. John Pringle, *Diseases of the Army in camp and garrison,* 1780.
3. *A short History of Medicine,* op.cit.
4. T Kirkland *An Inquiry into the present state of Medical Surgery,* op.cit., vol i p.12
5. University of St Andrews, University Muniments, University Library, St Andrews, Scotland.
6. Mr R T Austin FRCSED, 'Interesting GPs of the Past,' *British Medical Journal,* Vol 293, (25 October 1986), p.1075
7. William Gardiner, 'Music and Friends', vol i, p.95
8. Alec Macdonald, *A Short History of Repton* (Ernest Benn Ltd, London 1929), p.134
9. *Ibid* p.130
10. *The Journal of Rev William Bagshaw Stevens,* edited by Georgina Galbraith (Clarendon Press, 1965)
11. Dr Edward Jenner (1749–1823) had turned his attention to cowpox in about 1776. He steadily pursued his investigation, and despite opposition succeeded in introducing vaccination at the London Hospitals, the Army, and the Navy by 1796. He was also the author of a paper entitled 'The Natural History of the Cuckoo'.
12. The Accounts of the Overseers of the Poor for the Parish of Nailstone, Leics. Kindly supplied by Dr E C Cawte of Ibstock, Leics.
13. *A Short History of Medicine,* op.cit. p.391
14. Thomas Kirkland 'Dedication' op.cit. vol i
15. Thomas Kirkland. An Account of the Distemper among the Horned Cattle at Caulk in Derbyshire.

16. James Thompson, *The History of Leicester* (F Hewitt 1879)
17. Local Newspaper Report – August 1869
18. J Nicholls quoted by W Scott *The Story of Ashby-de-la Zouch* op.cit. p.420
19. Birmingham Weekly, *Mercury* (1897)
20. John Raphael Smith (1752–1812) the son of Thomas Smith (Smith of Derby) possessed great artistic talent combined with an humorous and convivial temperament which led him much into society and often into dissipation. His later works were very slight and sometimes finished in an hour. He was engraver to George Prince of Wales. (*Dictionary of National Biography*, op.cit.)
21. *Gentlemen's Magazine* (1798) op.cit. p.89
22. *Ibid*, p.62

Chapter 3

1. Leicestershire County Records Office, op.cit. *John Simmonds' Diary*
2. *Sale Particulars* – unpublished
3. *Dictionary of National Biography*, op.cit.
4. Public Record Office. MSS Kew, Richmond, Army List Ref: Q1191
5. *Leicester Journal* – 10 December 1813
6. *E M Green's Letter Book 1831* – unpublished.
7. Leicestershire County Records Office, St Helen's Church, Ashby-de-la Zouch, Parish Records
8. Francis Abell, Humphrey Milford, *Prisoners of War in Britain 1756–1815* (Oxford University Press 1914), p.291
9. Public Record Office MSS ADM 98/195-203
10. Roy Bennett *French Prisoners of War on Parole in Britain 1803–1814*. (University of London 1964), p.312
11. F C Hipkin, *Repton and Neighbourhood*, p.97.
12. Baron Louis Francois Le Jeune. *Memoirs*, Germain Bapst, 'En prison et en guerre' (London 1897)
13. Leicestershire County Records Office, Earl of Moira's Survey (1802)
14. Baron Louis Francois Le Jeune, op.cit.
15. John T Thorp *History of Freemasonry in Ashby-de-la Zouch 1809–1909*
16. Service Historique de la Marine, Ministère de la Défence (Marine), Château de Vincennes, Paris.

17. National Maritime Museum, Greenwich. M/S
18. *Ibid*, Miss B J Fletcher Library
19. Service Historique de la Marine M/S
20. Leicestershire County Records Office. Parish Records
21. John T Thorp, op.cit.
22. Dr Marilyn Palmer *Francis Rawdon-Hastings, 1st Marquess of Hastings and the Development of the Leicestershire Estates (1780–1830)*
23. *The British Martial Register*, Roger Macdonald 1806
24. J M Hammel BA *Consolidation and Change, The Union of 1813* The Lodge of Research No 2429, Transactions 1977
25. *Leicester Journal* 1823
26. *The Centenary Celebrations of the Tyrian Lodge No 253.* (1885) W Bacon Becket Mill Works, Derby
27. *The Text Book of Freemasonry*, (Reeves and Turner, 1874), second edition, p.100
28. Biblical Reference to Hiram Abif can be found in the Revised Standard Bible (1952) II Chronicles 2 v. 13. Hiram was the heroic martyr for Freemasons in the course of duty.
29. *John Simmonds' Diary*, Leicestershire County Records Office
30. *History of St John's Lodge No 279.* Leicester Masonic Library, Freemasons' Hall, Leicester
31. *John Simmonds' Diary*, op.cit
32. W Chambers, *The Book of Days*, op.cit. Vol i, p.198
33. Earl of Moira's Survey (1802) Leicestershire County Records Office
34. *Leicester Journal*, 2 February, 1798
35. Hon Sir J Fortescue, *History of the British Army*, Vol iv Part i p.28
36. *Short History of Medicine*, op.cit. p.200
37. *Leicester Journal* 16 December, 1808
38. *Ibid*, 1 May and 22 May, 1812
39. *Ibid*, November 1793
40. *White's Nottinghamshire* (1832)
41. *Leicester Journal*, 27 March, 1801
42. *The Story of Ashby-de-la Zouch* op.cit., p.450
43. W and J Hextall, *History and Description of Ashby-de-la Zouch* op.cit. p.101
44. *Kelly's Directory of Leicestershire and Rutland* (1895), p.22
45. David Howarth, *The Greek Adventure*, Collins
46. Public Record Office, M/S WO 25/746.

47. *The Hastings MSS, 4 Vols 1928–1947* now in the Huntingdon Library, San Marino, California
48. *The Hastings MSS*, op.cit.
49. *History and description of Ashby-de-la Zouch*, op.cit., p.57
50. Monument in Willesley Church
51. Derbyshire County Records Office MSS.
52. *The Story of Ashby-de-la Zouch*, op.cit., p.148
53. *The Gentlemens' Magazine*, vol 94 part ii p.190, (1824)
54. Leicestershire County Records Office MSS

Chapter 4

1. Levi Fox, *A Country Grammar School*, University Press, Oxford (1967), p.64
2. *Repton School Register*, Repton School Library, Repton, Derby
3. Plan of Ashby-de-la Zouch, John Wood (1837)
4. Unpublished Race Cards
5. Local Newspaper Report (1869)
6. *The Ferrers and Ivanhoe Lodge no 779, 1859–1959* J W Jackson, Hughes and Harper Ltd. – Longton
7. Kenneth Hillier, *Ashby-de-la Zouch, the Spa Town.* (1983)
8. T Wayte, *Guide to Ashby-de-la Zouch*, op.cit., p.119
9. The author. E M Green's Letter Book.
10. Ashby-de-la Zouch Museum, Beaumont Papers.
11. *Piggot and Co's Commercial Directory*, (1828/29), p.473
12. E M Green's Cash Book, Leicestershire County Records Office.
13. *Dictionary of Daily Wants* (Snowfield and Jones, 1858)
14. *A Short History of Medicine*, op.cit., p.391
15. *Ibid* pp.214, 215
16. Leicestershire County Record Office. Report of the General Board of Health for the Parish of Ashby-de-la Zouch (1850)
17. Malcolm Elliott, *Victorian Leicester* (Phillimore and Co, 1979)
18. BBC Home Service 21 January 1970
19. T Wayte, *Guide to Ashby-de-la Zouch*, op.cit., p.139
20. *Blackstone's Commentaries*, op.cit., vol iv p.432
21. Barnwell and Alderson Law Report (1817) p.
22. *White's Leicestershire and Rutland*, op.cit., 1879
23. Unpublished correspondence
24. 'Marquess of Hastings' Estate Book', (1837)
25. *White's Leicestershire and Rutland*, op.cit.

26. *Ibid*
27. Local Newspaper
28. D A Lake *History of Golf in Ashby-de-la Zouch* (Willesley Park Golf Club Limited 1988)
29. Local Newspaper Report, 12 Feb., 1879

Kirkland Notes

1. W Gardiner Leicestershire Records Office, Earl of Huntingdon's Estate Map (1735)
2. The Road from Oxford to Coventry continued to Darby, J Ogilby
3. Earl of Huntingdon's Estate Map, op.cit.
4. Levi Fox (1967) *A Country Grammar School*, op.cit.
5. Chitty *Blackstone's Commentaries* (1826) Book IV p.82
6. Earl of Huntingdon's Estate Map, op.cit.
7. Ordnance Survey Sheet 43 (David and Charles)
8. T Wayte *Guide to Ashby-de-la Zouch and the Neighbourhood* (1831), p.69
9. Eilert Ekwall *The Concise Oxford Dictionary of English Place Names* (Clarendon Press 1960)
10. T Wayte, op.cit., p.48
11. Earl of Huntingdon's Estate Map, op.cit. and Ashby-de-la Zouch Enclosure Award, 1768 op.cit.
12. *Ibid*
13. Leicestershire County Records Office, St Helen's Church Parish Records.
14. T Wayte, op.cit., p.99, Blackstone, op.cit., Book IV p.273
15. T Wayte, *ibid* p.100
16. W and J Hextall *The History and Description of Ashby-de-la Zouch* (1852) p.52
17. Georgina Galbraith, op.cit.
18. Kelly, *Directory of Leicestershire and Rutland* (1895)
19. T Wayte, op.cit., pp.99, 100
20. W Scott, op.cit.
21. T Wayte, op.cit., p.141
22. Whites Nottinghamshire, op.cit.
23. Transactions of 8th Congress on large dams, Edinburgh 4–8 May, 1964
24. David Smith *Industrial Archeology of the East Midlands* (David and Charles 1965)

25. Leicestershire County Records Office, Earl of Huntingdon's Survey (1802)

26. *Ibid*

27. Georgina Galbraith op.cit.

28. Levi Fox *A Country Grammar School*, op.cit., pp.114, 115

29. Earl of Huntingdon's survey (1802)

30. *Ibid*

31. Leicester Journal

32. *Ibid*

33. Earl of Huntingdon's Survey (1802)

34. W Kelly *History of Freemasonry in Leicestershire* (1870) p.26.

35. Georgina Galbraith op.cit., p.18

36. *A Country Grammar School*, op.cit.

37. Arthur Bryant's *Years of Endurance*, Collins, p.273

38. Hextall, op.cit., pp.82, 83

39. Wayte, op.cit., p.117

40. Wellington wrote to Lord Liverpool on 15 September, 1813 'It gives me great satisfaction to report . . . behaved remarkably well as well as the second Battalion 27th Regiment.' General Lord W Bentinck reported, 'I am sorry to say that Colonel Adam has been severely wounded as well as Lieutenant Colonel Reeves and several other valuable officers of the Second Battalion 27th Regiment.' *Wellington's despatches volume xi* p.149, Gurwood. Nicholas Kirkland's battalion had been engaged in an action against the French under Marshal Suchet at the pass of Ordal on 12 and 13 September 1813.

41. Hextall, op.cit., pp.86–88

42. White, op.cit.

43. *Ibid*

44. Michaela Reid *Ask Sir James*, (Hodder & Stoughton 1987) p.224

Appendix I

Mr Kirkland's narrative of the murder of Mr Johnson and of the facts previous and subsequent to it.

In order that this affair may be understood in its true light it seems necessary to observe that, notwithstanding when Lady Ferrers was separated from Lord Ferrers and his Lordship's estate put into the hands of Trustees by Act of Parliament, Mr Johnson accepted the Receivership, by Lord Ferrers's particular desire; Yet the Connection which necessarily followed betwixt Mr Johnson and the Trustees soon made his Lordship jealous that Mr Johnson was more in the Interest of the Trustees than his Lordship; he declared to Mrs Clifford that he would make Mr Johnson repent having anything to do with them, threatening he would shoot him: and soon after my Lord granted a Lease of it to Mr Clifford and he came with Clifford and served him with a notice to quit his farm: but not being able to Accomplish this Point, the Trustees having granted Mr Johnson a new Lease, his Lordship apparently became better Tempered and behaved with civility to Mr Johnson for some time: but a Transaction which will be mentioned in the course of this Narrative put an end to this calm, and determined his Lordship to commit the horrid Act.

That his Lordship might the better accomplish his intention he came to Mr Johnson on Sunday 13 January 1760 in every good Humour – stayd with Mr Johnson an hour & half, gave him some Franks – and asked him to come and settle him some Accounts on Thursday for that he was going to London in a few days. Mr Johnson desired it might be Friday he having some business to do on Thursday with which my Lord was satisfied and desired he would be there at 3 o'clock in the afternoon, unless Mr Johnson received a Letter from Mr Shirley on Monday, which he was to carry to Staunton as soon as it came.

The Horses were shod ready for the Journey two or three days before the murther proved by the lad and Mr Dobson the Blacksmith. No letter came on Monday. Mr Johnson therefore stayed 'til Friday (the 18th) when he walked to Staunton and got thither at the time fixt – Lord Ferrers had told Mrs Clifford of the appointment and on the Friday morning she told the maid Mr Johnson was to be there at three. Lord Ferrers, before Johnson came, had sent Mrs Clifford and her children to Mr Clifford's her fathers, with orders to come again at half an hour past five – he also sent his lad and the other man out of the way on some errand or other – though three maid servants only were left in the house.

As soon as Mr Johnson arrived he knocks at the door where my Lord sat, which was at the upper end of the long passage, his Lordship bid him go into the Still room, and he would call when he wanted him – and accordingly after some time he called him in and the door was locked – they were together near an hour and part of the time they were cheerful and laughing – after this two of the servant girls in the kitchen heard his Lordship speak very loud. Upon which they went towards the room where my Lord and Mr Johnson was, and heard his Lordship say – 'Sir down on your other knee and declare what you know against Earl Ferrers'. And they instantly heard a pistol go off.

Mr Johnson immediately got up and told his Lordship he was shot – he asked him where – Mr Johnson sayd 'he could not tell but he believed in his hip' My Lord sayd 'That cannot be I know better you are only frightened' – Mr Johnson then placed himself in a chair and my Lord called one of the girls who was run into the back kitchen upon hearing the report of the pistol – his Lordship ordered her to take Johnson to the next bed – he followed and while the girl was pulling off Mr Johnson's stockings as he sat on the bedside his Lordship pulled him by the wig and sayd 'I will send a bullet through your head' – Mr Johnson replyd 'No matter how soon' –

Mr Johnson desired a Surgeon might be sent for – my Lord asked him who he would have – he says Mr Kirkland – upon which his Lordship sent the lad for me upon his little Stone horse called Cupid – he also sent for Mr Johnson's children and one of the Girls run for Mrs Clifford – when she came my Lord told her he had shot Johnson and that he intended doing it – However seeing no blood and Mr Johnson Walk upstairs he was not yet thoroughly satisfied he had hit him; but upon her examining and showing his Lordship

186

the wound he was convinced and ordered Mrs Clifford to wash it with Arquebusade –

Miss Johnson now arrived and after she had seen her Father, his Lordship sent for her downstairs and told her if her father died he would take care of the Family if they did not prosecute him – He then went with her upstairs to Mr Johnson and abused him very much, and seemed very anxious about my coming, – imagining I had heard of what had happened and would not be found –

I was not at home when the Messenger came, who sayd Mr Johnson was taken Ill and would soon be dead, and that my Lord was with him. My Horses being all engaged my servant immediately mounted the horse the lad came on and brought me the message, to Coleorton to which Place I was gone to set a childs arm – we made Lount in our way where I was first informed at Mr Johnson's house what accident had happened –

Thinking it not safe to get to Staunton without seizing my Lord I took along with me several Colliers for this purpose; but before I got to the house I was met by Saxon one of the Servant Girls, who sayd that His Lordship had been Charging Guns and pistols and that he would shoot anybody that offered to seize him – upon which by her persuasion I ordered the men to stay behind, and went with the girl for I walked from the Lount (my man riding my mare) thinking it cruel to let Mr Johnson lie without Assistance though going to him might be attended with very bad Consequences –

We met his Lordship with Mrs Clifford in the yard – he immediately called out, 'who's there', imagining somebody was come to seize him, but upon my speaking to him he said, Come along – I directly went to him, and finding him in liquor, for he began to drink very freely as soon as he had shot Mr Johnson. We went Arm in Arm into the house – as we went along his Lordship told me he had shot Johnson and that he did it on purpose but he desired as Johnson was not dead I would not suffer his being seized for (says he) 'If he dies I will go and surrender myself to the House of Lords and if anybody attempts to seize me I will shoot them' – I assured his Lordship nobody should meddle with him –

We then went upstairs to Mr Johnson, whom I found complaining of great pain in his bowel with a wound made in his left side by a bullet in the Illiac Region – immediately under the lowest Rib – it was large enough to admit to the end of my little Finger: and I therefore took out my detector to examine in what direction the ball passed when my Lord upon seeing what I was going to do said 'pass your instrument downwards and rather slaunting for I held the pistol in this manner' (showing me with his hand which I did and found that the wound penetrated into the cavity of the abdomen and as it did not appear outwardly I thought all further search for it unnecessary; the chief intention seems to be to keep the inflamation within proper bounds, for which purpose, as he had not lost much blood I bled him and dressed the wound superficially – the muscles of the abdomen were become very sore and I therefore ordered a Formentation to be got ready – whilst this was doing his Lordship standing by the fireside, asked me whether I could not extract the ball, for sayd he, if the ball can be Extracted he may recover –

'I told his Lordship that as the Ball was lost in the Cavity of the Abdomen, the Extraction was impracticable, and that any attempt would not only prove fruitless but that by irratating the wound in searching, the Inflamation would be increased and air might get into the Abdomen which by bringing on a Putrid faction of the Extravasated blood would do great harm – and further that Balls often lay in the body several years without giving any trouble' –

His Lordship sayd he knew they would and desired I would persue what method I thought proper – said he 'I wonder the ball did not go through him for the pistol carried a ball thro a board and broke the brick or wall on the other side' – his Lordship then went out of the room and Mr Johnson hearing what he said said 'What a villain he is'. The fermentation came and being applied gave some ease. But he had a constant inclination to make water without being able for some time to pass any away: and he had also frequent inclination to vomit – his pulse was very weak and hands cold –

Mr Lord now came into the room again and hearing me ask for a flannel ordered Mrs Clifford to fetch one of his flannel waistcoats. Seeing Mr Johnson could not make water he imagined the bladder was wounded and asked me what would be the consequence if the kidneys or bladder were hurt – I told him I had lately cured a person who received a wound in the kidney and said that wounds in the bladder they were frequently cured and mentioned some instances of recoveries after being made with a ball – but that we could not conclude from the strangury that the bladder was wounded as that symptom might be owing to the nerve which served this part of being injured for seeing from his Lordship's behaviour that he began to reflect upon what he had done and that he wanted to have Mr Johnson recover I thought it prudent to make believe that there was great hopes for his getting well fearing that he would become desperate or make his escape notwithstanding his case appeared desperate – soon after this he went and called his lad out of the Kitchen into the passage and ordered in a good humour 'to have the horses ready for he would go in the morning' –

His Lordship desired I would stay with Johnson all night and whatever was wanting his servants shall go for to Ashby – I then waited on him in the still room, where being sat down he said 'Kirkland I believe Johnson is more frightned than hurt my intent was to have shot him dead, and finding he did not fall at the first shot I intended to have shot him again but his complaining of Pain made me forbear these I confess nature did take place in the opposition to the resolution I had formed, and as I have spared his life I desire you will take care of him for it would be cruel not to have him relieved of his pain; if he dies I shall be glad and therefore, Kirkland, when you speak of this affair do not say that I repent; I'm not sorry for it It was not done without Consideration; I own it was premeditated – I had, some time before, Charged a pistol for the purpose, being determined to kill him, for he is a Villain, and deserves death, but as he is not dead I, desire I may not be seized, for I will not run away. I will stay here until he is either better or dead: if he dies I will go and surrender myself to the House of Lords. I have enough to justify the Action, may be they will not excuse me but it will satisfy myself (laying his hand upon his breast). Do not you go in the morning without letting me see you, that I may know whether he is likely to recover or not. I will at dawn, or at any time you call, and you will let me know if you think him in any danger'.

I told his Lordship I was not an early riser and that as I should sit up with Mr Johnson his Lordship was most likely to be up first but if that did not happen I would come to his Lordship's Chamber and inform him what I thought about the matter, and when I went home would effectually prevent anybody from attempting to meddle with his Lordship. He asked me what I would say; I told him that I should report what appeared to me to be true that tho' Mr Johnson was shot and there was the greatest probability of his recovery; & therefore seizing his Lordship seemed unnecessary, that he then askd me whether I would swear that before a Justice of the Peace if called upon – I answered him in the affirmative.

Mrs Clifford now came into the still room and said Mr Johnson had made Water, which she brought, and having no blood in it we concluded the Ball had not touched the Bladder – I then wrote a Prescription and sent it away by my servant whom my Lord called into the room for this purpose –

Supper was now ready in the room where Mr Johnson was shot – we went to it and I made a very bad Supper, out of a very fine cold Turkey & Brawn. His Lordship also eat very little but drank a great deal and, from having kept almost constantly drinking since Mr Johnson was shot, he was now very much in liquor – there lay several pistols upon a table in the room and amongst them a horse pistol discharged, the pan being down which I suppose was that my Lord had used.

His Lordship then told me that Mr Curzon had wrote to him that he would indite him in the Court of Kings Bench.

His Lordship then again repeated that Johnson had been a villain to him and said he had assisted in procuring an Act of Parliament to take away his estate – that he had assisted and been in the Interest of his Enemies and particularly mentioned Mr Burslam and Mr Curzon – that he insisted upon Mr Johnson drawing up and signing a paper confessing the Circumstances and whatever else he knew, transacted against him, which Mr Johnson refused, declaring he never did anything contrary to his Lordship's Interest in his Life. Upon which (my Lord told me) he ordered him to kneel down and ask his pardon and then said 'Johnson if you have anything to say speak quickly, for you must die, and immediately fired (says he) I know he did not think I would have shot him I was determined and I made sure of hitting him, for I took aim, I always aim in this manner (pointing with his hand) when I shoot with a Pistol and I was quite cool when I did it –

He several times said, 'I wonder the ball did not go through him, for he was not above three Yards from me, and at last had it, for this Pistol carrying a Ball thro an inch and half Board at a considerable distance – I have long wanted to drive him out of the farm and I fancy, Kirkland, if he recovers he will go into Cheshire from whence he came and give me no further trouble.' I replyed 'it will certainly drive him off the premises' –

He then expressed great resentment at his having £100 a year for the receivership and mentioned Mr Johnson being under great obligation to the Shirley family as having all he possessed from them –

Having drank a glass or two after supper we went upstairs again, found Mr Johnson something easier though his strangury and reaching to Vomit still continued, at which my Lord seemed disturbed, but I told him these symptoms were to be expected, and that they would probably go off after a while as the inflamation abated –

190

We did not stay long in the chamber at this time: all that past was my Lord's several times enquiring what I thought of Johnson, and what would be the consequence if the bowels were wounded – I told him that as Mr Johnson was freer from pain I thought there was great reason to expect his recovery and that People frequently got well after having the bowel shot thro' (relating to him some instances) by which I brought his Lordship to think there was not much Danger, and he then went down into the Still Room in very good humour. He called for a Bottle of Port which Mrs Clifford brought but before we sat down he again repeated 'I own I did not shoot Johnson hastily, the shooting of him was premature – he added premeditated – he deserved death. I can justify the action in my own conscience.' We then sat down and began the bottle of port and his Lordship presently sayd 'I have long intended to shoot the villain but I will tell you, Kirkland, the reason I did it this time was Curzon and Bursalem's affair, for he assisted and advised them about the coal and slack. As you say, Kirkland, this I imagine will proove a slight affair – however if he recovers I will make him confess his being a rogue to me or I will shoot him through the head or heart. Be sure, Kirkland, you don't tell me any lyes for, by God, I shall break your head if you do.'

Mrs Clifford came into the room alone: she came and sat down with us and asked me if Mr Johnson could not be taken home. My Lord sayd 'No he shall not be removed until he is out of danger' and soon after he sayd 'I am glad I have him under these circumstances, in my own House, for I can plague the rascal.' 'You shall see, Kirkland, in the morning I shall make him confess his being a villain or I will whip him to death.'

Our conversation turned again to different things and being very drunk he repeated a part of Shakespeare's plays and said in a joking manner 'If Johnson died and they take off my head I will turn up this Lock of Hair: it's only one Chop and there is an end – will you be present Kirkland?' – I replyed 'We are now upon a very disagreeable Subject. I hope Johnson will recover and nothing of that kind happens' – 'but if my head is cut off', sayd he, 'I insist on your being present.' I promised I would, he again repeated his reasons for shooting Mr Johnson and added that he began his villainy in 1753 – Dont you think sayd he he deserved shooting, I answered 'your Lordship had high provocation indeed' –

My Lord now talkt of his Exploits and Amours with Women upon which subject we were very merry and the bottle being finished about 12 o'clock, he sayd 'Come Kirkland pull off your

Boots we will go and see Johnson and then to bed, but be sure you do not go in the morning before I see you – I owe you a bill and if you will sett this affair in a favourable light so that I may not be seized or if Johnson dyes – that I may go and surrender myself to the House of Lords without being molested, you may have some money now and the remainder when you want it' –

He sayd 'I assure you I will not leave this house 'til Johnson is either better or dead: you know I might easily have gone if I wanted but I will not attempt going' –

I told his Lordship I hoped there was no danger, but Mr Johnson would recover and thereby prevent any attempt to seize him, and as to the Bill I did not desire it but when it was most convenient for his Lordship –

We then went to Mr Johnson and my Lordship going to the bed's feet sayd 'You know you have been a villain to me (with a deal more the same strain) have you not?' Mr Johnson did not answer him but wished his Lordship would let him alone at this time. Miss Johnson and Mrs Clifford desired the same, but he still insisted upon Mr Johnson's confessing his being a Rogue and mocked him when he complained of pain in his bowels – his passion rose and he began to pull the bedclothes off the bed, which we prevented, when Mr Johnson sayd 'I believe I have done wrong as well as other people' – My Lord seemed to understand he meant him and and directly came up to the bedside as if he would have struck him – (Miss Johnson lay over her father to defend him) and asked 'What did you say?' 'Have not you been a villain to me?' I went up to the bedside and winked at Mr Johnson who then sayd 'I may have been a villain to your Lordship' – upon which he immediately sayd 'I beg your Lordship will come away, this Treatment will do him harm and I have heard him confess he's a villain' – upon which he went to the fireside –

Notwithstanding his behaviour to Mr Johnson he behaved very well to his daughter and upon seeing her cry he sayd 'Miss Johnson I am sorry for you but you know your father always talked and acted against me', she replyed 'he never did'. 'But do not you (continued he) make yourself uneasy for if your father dies and you do not prosecute I again promise you before Kirkland, whom I desire will be witness, that I will take care of your family, you shall never want' –

Soon after his Lordship left the room and I wish't him a good night – The Medicades being come I gave these – my Lord sent for me downstairs again. When I came to him he sayd 'I am afraid I have made Miss Johnson uneasy by talking to her father, but tell

192

her I will certainly be a Friend to her'. We then came to the landing place upon the stairs together and though his Lordship was so full of liquor that he could hardly stand he sayd 'Do you think, Kirkland, Johnson will recover and I may go lye with P-Y tonight in safety?' I replyed 'Yes, and again wisht his Lordship a good night and we Parted. I directly went to Mr Johnson and told him my Lord was gone to bed. He sayd 'Pray cannot I be removed from this place for God knows what my Lord may do in the morning: nobody is safe'. I told him I shod be glad to have him removed, for I was in the same opinion with himself of having great reason to think that if my Lord did not shoot him again, which was not unlikely, he would at least continue to harass and plague him. I also consider that if Mr Johnson should feel to require my assistance anytime I could not have free access to him and if he died there was great reason to expect my Lord's resentment for having deceived him or was it unlikely that his Lordship would shoot me in order that he might safely make his escape and prevent my repeating the conversation that has passed that evening.

While we were talking my Lord opened his bed chamber door at which Mr Johnson seemed much alarmed expecting his Lordship of coming into the room again but were soon relieved from this anxiety by hearing his Lordship call up the Pointer bitch to be in his room, as we imagined to give his Lordship notice if anybody came to seize him while in bed.

Mr Johnson again desired if he possibly could be removed. I saw he was under great apprehensions of danger and I therefore told him I would go and bring a posse of men from the Lount and carry him away upon a couch. He desired I wod and added 'Pray get about it immediately for no time should be lost for it is now 2 o'clock and morning will be coming on apace', we then fixed what signals Miss Johnson should give by placing a candle in the window, that our design was not discovered, and it was agreed if my Lord came before I returned that he shod be told I was call'd away upon emergent Business and wod be there again early in the morning. Mr Johnson sayd 'I think you better bring arms with you I have a gun and you may borrow another and if my Lord shod get up while you are gone, and your scheme be defeated bring a proper number of armed men to take me away by force' which I promised him.

My servant went with me to the Lount where we soon swaded seven or eight colliers beside Mr Johnson's farmyard and Mr Berridge who lay there that night, I told Mr Berridge I apprehended the wound would prove mortal.

After charging two guns we went back to Staunton without the least distrubance and effected our scheme. Mr Johnson being ready and having with his daughter's assistance got on his clothes he walked to the bottom of the back stairs, leaning upon my man's shoulder, where he was received into a great Chaise lined with pillows, blankets and the like. When he came into the Great Flats I asked him how he did: he sayd 'I am faint but I feel easier. Thank God I am got out of my Lord's reach'. We marched very slowly and being carried upon poles he bore going home very well the blankets kept him very warm though it was a frosty night.

Being got home he walked into the Parlour room how he usually lay and almost immediately to bed.

I then asked Mr Johnson whether my Lord was in liquor when he shot him: he sayd 'No I think he wasn't. I believe he got his liquor after. I did not think he would have shot me; I thought he only wanted to frighten me and make me sign a paper'. I then sayd 'Pray were you down on your knees when my Lord shot you?' He sayd 'My Lord bid me kneel down but I think (though I cannot be sure being hurried) that he fired at me just as I was rising.' Says he 'I shall die he has killed me and it will rid the country of a villain' He sayd he found he was shot, but as it did not affect my rising I thought it, for he only felt a soreness in his thigh and knee. I now asked him whether he had settled his affairs. He sayd 'No' and desired I would make him a Will which I complied with finding his hands cold and without any feeling and concluding there would best to have to get a proper person to do it Berridge asked me whether it would not be proper to seize his Lordship. Mr Johnson immediately sayd 'I think he should be seized,' and I was of the same opinion but told him Mr Berridge should walk home with me and we would ask proper advice. Mr Johnson then sayd he would be moved upstairs lest my Lord should come and shoot him through the window which faced the bed. I told him he might make himself perfectly easy in this respect for I would place sentries at the kitchen door with proper directions how to act if his Lordship came. We left him about 7 o'clock and soon afterwards, when we were gone, he attempted to walk up the stairs but found himself incapable before he got out of the Parlour, and therefore returned to his bed and desired a feather bed might put against the window to prevent a ball coming through but, poor man, his sore became rather easier and died about 9 o'clock.

In the meantime Mr Berridge and myself called on Mr Piddock and Mr Pestell to consult with them what shold be done. We agreed upon seizing his Lordship for which propose Mr Berridge immediately went back but Mr Johnson was just dead when he arrived at the Lount. His death was immediately known to the neighbourhood who soon assembled & went armd to my Lord's house. Mrs Clifford and the rest of the family had notice to leave the house and upon my Lord coming down the stairs and finding everybody gone he immediately came toward the stables with his garters in his hand and seeing a great number of men he sayd to Mr Springthorpe who had a pistol in his hand 'What do you want?' He told him they wanted his Lordship 'That he was their prisoner and demanded his Lordship himself upon which he was going to pull out a pistol but seeing they were armed he turned about and went towards the house. Several persons shot at him run along but happily missed him others also fired at him when he was just got within the house and had shut the door in order to intimidate him and that they might drive him out of the house they several times fired at the windows. After some time his Lordship appeared at the Garrett window and asked Mr Springthorpe how Mr Johnson did. Being answered he was dead my Lord sayd 'I am glad of it but it is a lie; he is not dead, nor I will not believe he is dead 'till Kirkland tells me so. I will not surrender myself.' Upon which several people stopped firing at the house. After six or seven hours seige his Lordship was taken making his escape over the lawn by Henry Cutler, a collier, when Springthorpe who had been at the other side of the house immediately came up. My Lord had with him a double barrelled gun besides several pistols loaded and a dagger, but upon his seeing the collier armed he surrendered and though the fellows gun went off by accident his Lordship did not attempt to make the least resistence – that Mr Springthorpe assisted in taking him into the house, where they found several guns and pistols loaded, that Mr Springthorpe heard him say that he had killed the villain and he gloried in his death. From thence they brought him upon a horse to the White Hart at Ashby where his Lordship again insisted on his having done right in shooting Johnson, saying he was a villain and had assisted in taking his wife from him.

The Coroner was immediately sent for upon Mr Johnson's death, and came the same day. He summoned a jury to meet the next day at Mr Johnson's house (being Sunday 20 January), when I opened the body and found the ball after entering in his left side just under the lowest rib, had passed obliquely downwards, thro the colon, under the psoas muscle, thro the oss innominatum at its junction with the spine and rested in the oss sacrum, from which place I extracted it.

Appendix II

20 January 1760

Inquisition taken in the liberty of Staunton Harold in the County of Leicester upon the view of the body of John Johnson there lying dead

County of Leicester To wit, The Information and Examination of Witnesses taken on oath before me William Tilly one of his Majestys Coroners for the said County the Twentieth day of January in the year of our Lord One thousand seven hundred and sixty at the house of the late Mr John Johnson situate in a place called the Lount in the Liberty of Staunton Harold in the said County how when and in what manner the said John Johnson there lying dead came to his death.

Elizabeth Burgoland of Staunton Hall in the Liberty of Staunton Harold aforesaid spinster (servant to the Right Honourable Lawrence Shirley Earl Ferrers of Staunton Hall aforesaid) being sworn and examined on her oath says That on Friday last about three of the clock in the afternoon, the said John Johnson came to the Earl Ferrers' house at Staunton Hall aforesaid and enquired if his Lordship was within That she this Informant told him he was and showed him to a Parlour in which his Lordship was. That Mr Johnson rapp'd at the door and his Lordship opened it and desired he would walk into another Room into which he went And soon after his Lordship called him into his own Room and then locked the Door. That about an hour after she this Informant and another Maid Servant being in the kitchen heard a pistol go off which she apprehended was in my Lords

Room. That being affrighted she immediately ran into the yard and afterwards went into the wash house That his Lordship soon after came there and asked her this Informant where she had been and desired she would follow him to his Room which she did and as soon as she entered ordered her to go out again That presently after he called her in again and desired she would take Johnson to the first bedd she came to. That his Lordship asked Johnson if he was badly wounded And he said Yes he was a dying Man. That she this Informant then took Johnson by the hand and led him up stairs to bed where he layed himself down which is all she knows

Signed with the mark of
Elizabeth X Burgoland

Elizabeth Saxon of Staunton Hall aforesaid spinster (servant to the Right honourable Laurence Shirley Earl Ferrers above named) being Sworn and Examined on her oath Says That on Friday last about four o clock as she was in the kitchen at Staunton Hall aforesaid with the above named Elizabeth Burgoland she heard his Lordship her Master who was in the parlour with Mr Johnson say 'Sir down upon your knee and declare that whatever you acted against Earl Ferrers' And then heard a pistoll go off upon which being surprised she ran with the said Elizabeth Burgoland into the yard which is all she knows

The mark of Elizabeth X Saxon

Elizabeth Doleman of Staunton Hall aforesaid spinster (servant to the Right Honourable Laurence Shirley Earl Ferrers above named) being Sworn and Examined on her oath Says That on Friday night last soon after it was dark his Lordship came into the kitchen to her at Staunton Hall aforesaid and desired she would go up stairs and take care of Johnson which she Accordingly did by fetching a bed out of the Garrett into the Room where Mr Johnson was and he layed himself thereon. This his Lordship came into the room and Taking Johnson by the wig said I'll send a Bullett through your head upon which Mr Johnson replyed no matter how soon

The mark of Elizabeth X Dolman
Examined with the original by me
Wm Tilly Jun, Coroner

Margaret Clifford of the Parish of Staunton aforesaid spinster being sworn and Examined on her oath says that about three of the Clock in the Afternoon of Friday last she was at Staunton Hall at the Earl Ferrers' and his Lordship came into the Still Room where she this Informant was and called out, where are you all upon which she said here my Lord All but the two youngest (Meaning the children) who were up stairs. That he Desired they would take a walk and she this Informant how long they might stay he said till five o clock or half an hour after by your Watch upon which she and the children went to this Informant's Father's House about a mile from Staunton Hall That she had not been gone about two hours before the above named Elizabeth Burgoland came in and Desired she would go down to the Hall as fast as she could for Mr Johnson was shott upon which this Informant asked where he was and she said upon the Bedd in the Striped Room That she immediately went to the Hall and when she came there the First person she met was the Earl Ferrers who told her Johnson was shott upon which she replyed I am sorry for that. That his Lordship desired she would go and give him what assistance she could, that she immediately went, Says That she heard his Lordship say as Mr Johnson would not confess to what he thought he was Guilty off he thought to do what he Did

Margaret Clifford

Sarah Johnson of the Lount in the Parish of Staunton aforesaid Spinster (daughter of the Deced) being sworn and Examined on her Oath Says, That on Friday last betwixt four and five of the Clock in the afternoon the Earl Ferrers sent a Man from Staunton Hall aforesaid to this Informant's Father's House and Desired his children would come to the Hall for Mr Johnson their Father was very ill. Upon which she this Informant immediately went to Staunton Hall aforesaid and Going into the Kitchen she saw Lord Ferrers standing by the Fire that she asked him for what he had sent for her That his Lordship then Asked her name she told him and he Desired her to go op stairs to her Father and Ordered a Maid to go with her. That she this Informant went up stairs to her Father who was in Bedd and he told her That my Lord (meaning the Earl Ferrers above named) had shott him and believed he should Die. That the Earl Ferrers afterwards came up stairs and this Informant heard him say he had shott him and it was what he designed to do.

Sarah Johnson

Thomas Kirkland of Ashby-de-la-Zouch in the said County Surgeon being Sworn and Examined on his Oath says That being called to Lord Ferrers at Staunton Hall aforesaid on Friday last the Eighteenth of this Instant January about five or six of the Clock in the Evening to dress Mr Johnson who had received a wound in his left side the Earl Ferrers repeatedly told him That he had shot Johnson into the side with a Pistol loaded with a Ball That Mr Johnson by his Lordships Orders was upon his Knee when he fired at him about the Distance of Three yards and that he took aim that he might be the surer of hitting him That his Lordship further told this Informant that his shotting him was Premeditated. That he was quite Cool when he did it and that he had some time before charged the Pistol for that purpose being Determined to kill him for that he Deserved Death That and the reason of his Shooting was because Mr Johnson helped to procure an Act of Parliament for taking away his Estate and that he held Correspondence against him (meaning his Lordship) with Mr Burslem and Mr Curzon with regard to some Coal Slack and would not sign a paper confessing these Circumstances and if Johnson recovered and did not acknowledge his being a rogue he would still kill him and this Informant says that he heard Mr Johnson say when he was in bedd on Fryday night 'what a villain this is he has killed me' or words to the like effect and this Informant further says that he has this day examined the body of the deceased John Johnson and found a wound made by a Leaden Bullett imediately under the lowest rib on this left side which Bullet passing obliquely downward had made another wound through the Gut called Colon and going under the Psoas Muscle through the Os Inominatum at its junction with the spine rested in the os sacrum from which place this Informant says he Extracted it. And further says That there was a considerable quantity of Extravasated Blood in the Abdomen The Viscera in consequence of the Violent Injury done to the parts were greatly inflamed and that he this Informant therefore is of Opinion that the wound above described was the Cause of his Death.

Tho. Kirkland

William Tomlinson of Newbold in the said County Ironmonger being Sworn and Examined on his Oath Say That on Saturday Morning last about Eight o'Clock he came over to Mr Johnsons house at the Lount in the parish of Staunton aforesaid and there found the said John Johnson who had been removed from Staunton aforesaid to his own House That he Attended him till he Died which was about nine of the Clock on Saturday Morning last the Nineteenth Day of this instant January

Willm. Tomlinson
This is a true copy taken from the)
Original Depositions and Examined)
therewith this Nineth Day of February)
1760 – Before me
Wm Tilley Jun,
Coroner

County of Leicester to wit, An inquisition taken at the House of the late Mr John Johnson situate in a place called the Lount in the liberty of Staunton Harold in the said County the Twentieth day of January in the year of our Lord one thousand seven hundred and sixty before me William Tilly one of his Majestys Coroners for the said County upon the View of the body of the said John Johnson now lying Dead by the Oaths of John Almey John Hood Thomas Flavel Joseph Toone Henry Whirledge Thomas King John Clarkson John Avarnes Edward Bodell Samuel Harris John Armson and Francis Harley good and lawful men of Ashby-de-la-Zouch Coleorton Breedon and Worthington in the said County the four villages next adjoining to the Liberty of Staunton Harold aforesaid Sworn to enquire on the part of our Sovereign Lord the King how when and in what manner the said John Johnson came to his Death who say on their Oaths That the Right Honourable Lawrence Shirley Earl Ferrers now or late of Staunton Hall in the parish of Staunton Harold in the said County is Guilty of the Wilfull murder of the said John Johnson for that he the said Right Honourable Laurence Shirley Earl Ferrers on Friday last the Eighteenth Day of this Instant January about four or five of the Clock in the afternoon of the same Day at Staunton Hall aforesaid in the parish of Staunton Harold aforesaid in the said County did foloniously and wilfully fire a Pistol loaded with a Leadon Ball which Ball entered under the lowest rib on the left side of the Body of the said John Johnson which gave him a mortal wound off which wound the said Johnson Languished until Saturday Morning last the Nineteenth day of this Instant January till about Nine of the Clock in the Morning of the same Day and then Died in the parish of Staunton Harold aforesaid in the County aforesaid And the Jurors upon their Oaths further Say That the said John Johnson came to his Death in manner as aforesaid and not otherwise and that the said Pistol is a Deodand and forfeited In Witness whereof as well as the aforesaid Coroner as the aforesaid Jurors have hereunto Set their hands and seals the Day Year and place first above mentioned

John (ls) Almey
John (ls) Hood
Thos (ls) Flavel
Jos (ls) Toone
Henry (ls) Whirledge
Thos (ls) King

John (ls) Clarkson
John (ls) Avarne
Edward (ls) Bodell
Sam (ls) Harris
John (ls) Armson
Francis (ls) Harley

This is a true copy taken from the)
Origl Inquisition and Examined)
therewith this ninth day of)
February 1760 By me)
Wm Tilley Jun
Coroner

County of Leicester)   To the Constables of Staunton and
To Wit)   Ashby-de-la-Zouch in the said County of
                                    Leicester and to the Keeper of his Majestys
                                    Gaol for the said County

Whereas by an Inquisition taken in the Liberty of Staunton aforesaid upon the View of the Body of John Johnson there lying dead before Me William Tilley one of his Majestys Coroners for the said County by a Jury of good and lawfull men there sworn by and before Me to enquire on the part of our sovereign Lord the King how the said John Johnson came to his Death The said Jury have found That the Right Honourable Laurence Shirley Earl Ferrers late of Staunton Hall in the Parish of Staunton aforesaid in the said County is Guilty of the Murder of the said John Johnson; These are therefore in his Majestys name to require and command You the said Constables and Each of You to convey the said Right Honourable Laurence Shirley Earl Ferrers to his majesty's Gaol for the said County of Leicester and to deliver him to the Keeper thereof together with this precept Requiring and Commanding also You the Keeper of the Said Gaol to receive the said Right Honourable Laurence Shirley Earl Ferrers into your custody and gaol and him there safely keep until he shall be from thence discharged by due course of Law And hereof fail not Given under my Hand and Seale the Twentyeth day of January in the Year of our Lord 1760

Wm Tilly Junr
Coroner   (ls)

Friday next after fifteen days from the Day of

202

Saint Hilary in the thirty third year of King
George the Second
England It is Ordered That a Writ of *Habeas Corpus* issue directed
to the Keeper of his Majesty's Gaol in and for the County of
Leicester to bring into this Court the Body of the Right Honourable
Laurence Shirley Earl Ferrers to undergo etc.
On the Motion of Mr Crofts
By the Court

Appendix III

The Fight between *Le Bélier* and *H.M.S. Fox*

The fight between the French brig *Le Bélier* and the English frigate *HMS Fox* recalled by the drawing lent by M. A. Deschard to the Exhibition of Naval Heroism has no official existence. Neither English nor French historians mention it. The Navy seems only to have heard of it indirectly several years later from statements made by officers wishing to have record of this action entered in their service records. What exactly were the circumstances of the battle? Should, one following the story of the picture, attribute the credit to the Second in Command of *Le Bélier*, Lieut. Le Normant de Kergrist, who claimed to have locked up his Commanding Officer and to have usurped his authority because he refused to engage the enemy.

We had searched in vain through the Log Books of *Le Bélier* in Naval Archives. We believed these to be lost or destroyed until we heard of their existence among General Decaen's papers kept at Caen City Library. M. Y. Bequignon, Lecturer at the Faculty of Arts and Naval Reserve Interpreter Officer was happy to look through the papers and send us some extracts. These documents, in addition to the information extracted from the Muster Roll of the brig and from the service records of the officers, have enabled us to reconstruct the history of an almost unknown episode of the naval war in the Indian Ocean, under the Consulate. The social rank of the people involved lend it an unusual interest.

Le Bélier, a twenty gun brig, was fitted out in September 1801 under command of Lieut. De Vaisseau Hulot (Victor, Andrée,

Gury). As this individual was destined to play the principal role in the story we will set out some details of his career.

Born at Port-Louis Ile de France [now Mauritius] on 5 April 1775, Hulot was the son of the chief treasurer to the Navy of the Mascareignes. His mother, whose maiden name was Jeanne Perine Lory, was descended from Breton ancestry and was a member of the high society of the colony. Victor Andrée joined the Navy in 1790. For ten years he served in the waters round the Ile de France sometimes in merchant ships, and sometimes in men of war as an acting midshipman. He reached France in January 1800 soon after the *Coup d'Etat* of *18th Brumaire*.

His mother and his sister[1] were then living in Paris. They belonged to a select Creole circle which Josephine Bonaparte gathered around her and whose influence continued to increase with the advent of the new regime. Both were very scheming – they knew how to exploit their friendship with Josephine. Hulot took advantage of all this to solicit his entry into the regular navy. On 19 April 1800, he was commissioned as Lieut. de Vaisseau and almost immediately was given command of a brig being fitted at Lorient – *L'Enfant Prodigue*. He was the First Consul's choice at the end of November to go to St Domingo to find out what he could about the situation in the colony.

The Hulot family had come into the centre of public life. On 9 November Alexandrine, sister to the new Lieutenant, had entered into a whirlwind marriage with General Moreau, who had come to Paris and left almost immediately for Germany; three weeks later he would open up to his troops the road to Vienna by the victory of Hohenlinden. His marriage was Josephine's work: she it was who counted on Madame Hulot and her daughter to bring permanently to the side of the First Consul that General who had rendered such good service on *18th Brumaire*, but whose popularity and military success had already caused offence. In fact, the influence that 'his Corporal of a mother-in-law and his nutcracker of a wife' exercised on Moreau did not work out in practice as Josephine would have wished. One knew that he had come to it several years too late. For the moment confidence was supreme and one understands the reasons which went to the choice of Hulot to reconnoitre the ground where Bonaparte's brother-in-law should operate the following year.

---

[1] Alexandrine Louise Eugenia Hulot, born at Post-Louis in L'Ile de France 5 July 1781.

Returning to France in June 1801, Hulot gave an account of his mission to the First Consul, who expressed complete satisfaction with the report and caused the young officer to be given command of another brig – *Le Bélier* – being fitted out at Le Havre. The second in command of *L'Enfant Prodigue*, Sub-Lieutenant Le Normant de Kergrist, followed his commander to the new ship.

Kergrist was then twenty-two years of age. Promoted to sub-Lieutenant in April 1799 for his good conduct during the action of the *Cornelie* at Belle-Isle, he had just received a wound at St Domingo, which resulted in the loss of the use of his right hand; the event occurred on land, without doubt, because *L'Enfant Prodigue* was never involved in an engagement. Hulot and Kergrist made up a good team because they did not try to work independently.

Le Bélier was ordered in October 1801, to L'Ile de France, to the Seychelles and to Anjouan to take news that preliminaries of peace had been signed. The ship returned to Lorient on 26 October 1802.

The peace of Amiens did not last. Right from the beginning of 1803 England's attitude portended a breach; but the first Consul still counted on a respite of one or two years. He hastened the fitting out of the expedition which he was preparing to re-occupy French trading posts in India and reinforce the positions so as to be ready in good time for the renewal of hostilities. General Decaen appointed Commissioner General for French possessions in the Indian Ocean, left on 9 March 1803 with Linoir's squadron taking with them the first contingent of troops destined for Pondicherry.

Le Bélier, two months after being fitted out, waited at Brest for the departure of the second echelon. She would be able to serve as an escort for the troop ships and afterwards to remain at the disposition of the Commissioner General. This choice, it seemed, was not only the result of Hulot's experience of the Indian Ocean; Decaen was one of Moreau's most loyal friends; he had ensured his success at Hohenlinden by bringing up his division on the night before the battle. Among the sailors, who Decaen really did not like and with whom his relationship became more and more sour, the brother-in-law of his former Commander in Chief would be a man with confidence in him. Linoir and Decaen had only just sailed when disturbing news came from London. Hostilities were starting almost at once. Time was being lost: Bonaparte decided to pull back the expedition from the L'Ile de France and to keep it there awaiting developments. *Le Bélier* was ordered to carry these new directions. She left Brest on 25 March and on 12 July rejoined

Linoir's squadron at Pondicherry. The latter had only arrived the night before. He hastened to get under way to reach L'Ile de France with all his ships. The *Berceau* brought news to him on 25 September of the declaration of war. It was no longer a question of Pondicherry. Linoir left on 9 October to lie in wait for the English convoys at the entrance to the China seas. *Le Bélier* stayed at Port Louis at Decaen's disposal who sent her on 18 October to carry orders to the Governor of the Seychelles, Queauquincy, and to the new French Resident at Muscat, the former member of the convention, Cavaignac, who had already left a month before on board the *Atalante* to take up his post.

After a short call at Mahe, Hulot set sail for Muscat where he arrived on 10 December. Cavaignac had not been able to land and had left. His mission being to no purpose *Le Bélier* got underway on the evening of 13th for the Malabar coast where his orders were to harass English merchant ships. On 22 December at 6 a.m. when about to land at Cap Jacquette to the north of the Gujarat coast, Hulot saw a ship coming from the Persian Gulf and proceeding towards Bombay.

In his report he said 'I gave orders to my Second in Command that in the event of her only being a merchant ship necessary steps should be taken to board her. At 10 a.m. finding myself within range, I gave the order to open fire on the ship with all guns that could be uncovered approaching all the time without being able to establish the strength of the enemy and this forced me to be very wary – but she would without doubt have taken flight if she had been a merchant ship.' The repost was not delayed. Hulot recognized 'by the intensity of her fire and from the number of cannon balls of 12 and 6 calibre received on board, that he had to deal with a frigate.' It became known later that she was the *Fox* (32 guns) under Captain Washon. He decided 'to disengage from the unequal struggle' and to speed his flight he manned his oars while continuing to fire on the enemy.

'During the following seventeen hours the crew did not cease rowing. Despite the great fatigue that they had suffered there was no complaint. I cannot pay sufficient tribute to the conduct of my Officers who themselves set an example and themselves worked with our brave sailors and soldiers. It will be difficult to describe the courage and composure that was shown by my staff in such a perilous crisis. Monsieur Kergrist, my second in command, deserves commendation for the care he took in making the necessary dispositions which the action demanded. Everything had been forseen and provided for with the greatest accuracy'. This action cost the life of Sub Lieutenant P. Desportes who was the only individual killed on that day. *Le Bélier* eventually managed to escape successfully from her adversary.

On 26 December in sight of Diu at 1½ leagues from land a new action took place with a Company coast guard armed with 14 cannonades of 32. 'After the first broadsides' said Hulot, 'I judged it more expedient to keep within two thirds of the range to the windward of it. Then his cannonballs were out of range and mine caused him considerable damage. The ship owed her salvation to being so close to land and to the night which was to her advantage because I was keeping her so very close to the coast that she had no option but to beach herself or surrender. Finding myself in shallow water, I was forced to take to the open sea at 6 p.m.' There were no deaths or casualties on board *Le Bélier*. Hulot gave 'full praise' to his officers, soldiers and sailors who all conducted themselves in exemplary fashion.

The next day at 2 p.m. *Le Bélier* chased a brig which was sailing towards Bombay: he took it over and manned it at 6 p.m. It was the French Corsair *L'Espiegle* (Captain Dubois) captured by the English frigate *La Dedaigneuse* off Cochin. A prize crew consisted of two midshipmen and six English ratings and were taken prisoner and the ship *L'Espiegle* sent on to L'Ile de France under the command of Sub Lieutenant J. Malvery.

Hulot cruised for two more days off Bombay, then he made for Ceylon and finally to L'Ile de France where he docked on 3 February 1804. Good news awaited him of his promotion to the rank of Capitain de Frégate substantive from 24 September 1803. Kergrist had been promoted Lieutenant de Vaisseau on 5 March 1803 shortly before his departure from Brest.

As soon as he had berthed, Hulot submitted reports to Decean of the voyages and from which we have just read some extracts. The events that he disclosed cannot possibly be doubted because they agree exactly with the details of the Officers' service records and the ship's muster roll. However, in this last document the spaces for action and prize have been left blank. Sub Lieutenant Desportes is recorded as having died during the night of 29/30 frimaire (22/23 December) but not as killed in action. It is difficult to explain these omissions because the rest of the document is very well completed. Decaen has been guilty of another more serious omission in failing to send Hulot's reports to Paris. The Admiralty and the port of registration of merchant vessels thus ignored the two actions fought by *Le Bélier* in December 1803. Hulot himself neglected to give an account of it in a new report on his return to France; his records contain no mention of it. To bring these wartime engagements to their credit the officers should some years later have established the truth by affidavits or evidence. Kergrist in particular applied on 8 March 1815 for affidavits from five of his old shipmates to support his nomination for a decoration. These officers declared 'Commanding Officer being now dead' that during the action with the *Fox* Kergrist 'distinguished himself particularly and that his courage his steadfastness and his perseverance contributed greatly to the safety of the brig and the 160 worthy men who formed his crew.' It is a simple confirmation of what one reads in Hulot's report; nothing gives any indication so far as Kergrist is concerned of a different attitude to that which corresponded to his position as second in command.

One is therefore very surprised to read what follows:
In a letter written by Kergrist to the Admiralty on 30 July 1833 – thirty years after the event – 'to be sure the dogged resistance of *Le Bélier* against the English Frigate *Fox* and the very special circumstances of this action should have earned a place in the records of the Navy if family considerations affecting the Captain of the brig had not been strongly conflicting. Therefore, complete silence was kept on this affair.'

'However, the Minister appreciating my action immediately on my arrival in Spain promoted me to Second in Command on the Frigate *Guerrière* – I served on the Frigate in 1806 during the Spitzberg Campaign under Captain Hubert (not the gallant Hubert). We were attacked by the English frigate *Blanche* and during the action I had the misfortune to find myself in the same position as when on board *Le Bélier*. In this unhappy situation, I once again did everything that a man of honour could but I did not dare this time to take over command because I had reason to believe my previous conduct on board *Le Bélier* had in some way been criticised because I had never been rewarded although I had saved the brig. *The Guerrière* was taken and I spent eight years a prisoner.'

The tradition retained in the Kergrist family adds some details to this version of the affair. In recognizing a Frigate where he expected to see a merchant man Hulot would have lost his head and ordered the ship to strike its colours. Kergrist would have prevented this by force and would have shut him up in his cabin and made the crew think he was either ill or mad; he would then have taken over command of the ship and directed the battle.

If one can admit on the strength of this tradition that Hulot panicked at the start of the battle and could not bring himself to fight under pressure from Kergrist the hypothesis of a bid for power or of usurping command on the part of the latter is altogether unlikely. The compliments paid to his second in command in his report of the voyage show that a complete harmony still prevailed between the two men. After the battle, their relationship remained as cordial as before. When *Le Bélier* arrived at Galic the following summer, Hulot being ill asked leave to disembark and recommended Kergrist to succeed him to whom he again paid a very generous tribute. Would he have considered such a course of action if his second in command had made him suffer publicly on the day of the battle so serious an insult? To believe that seems to vest in Hulot an excessive propensity to forget the injury done to him. If Kergrist had confined his commanding officer it was only to bring him to his senses and it was only for a short time in order to give him time to regain his self control. One can very easily understand in this case, that the Officers of *Le Bélier* have said nothing about it on returning from the voyage. They knew of their Commanding Officer's influence with the Tuileries and with Decean as well as his family ties with the important families on the island. It was better to keep quiet than provoke a scandal as a result of which Kergrist would have suffered as much as Hulot. But these considerations were no longer applicable in 1815; the officers' silence would be explained even less at this time as their old Commander had been dead for almost six years. It was easier for them by an illusion more or less transparent to show the true role played by Kergrist during the battle: one sees nothing of this in their affidavits.

Should one think that Kergrist's memory has failed him thirty years after the event? Should one not admit rather that he gave in to the temptation to exaggerate his merits? One is driven to the conclusion on seeing him in the action with the *Guerrière* as the only officer capable of saving his ship and declaring with absolute confidence that he could not resist the temptation to use that command again for fear of being known as an inveterate rebel.

The engagement between *Le Bélier* and the *Fox* resolved itself into an honourable fight and without any mystery like many such under the Consulate and the Empire. The memory of it is lost from the French side because of administrative negligence; on the English side because the engagement was of little importance. Chance has

210

brought it to light again; one regrets a little to note that reality is again this time very different from legend.

It remains to tell, by way of epilogue, what happened to the heroes of this story. Decean sent back *Le Bélier* to France in March 1804 giving her the task of sending home again the unfortunate Cavaignac who had not been able to take over his functions as Resident at Muscat. He reported in a letter to Decrès that 'very distinguished conduct' and the qualities of Hulot in announcing that he would himself report directly to the Admiralty on his mission on the Malabar coast. We know that Hulot did nothing about it, perhaps because he fell ill on arriving at his destination. He did not try to make port at Brest or Lorient which were being blockaded by the English fleet: he sailed towards the Bay of Muros in Galicia where he arrived without incident on 30 June 1804 and placed himself under command of Capitain de Vaisseau Gourdon, commander of the naval division of Ferrol.

Le Bélier was laid up on 5 September and was put up for sale during the winter. Kergrist, as we have seen, continued on *La Guerrière* which fell into the hands of the English two years later.

Hulot returned to Paris. The conviction and exile of Moreau does not seem to have diminished his favour which he enjoyed at the Tuileries. Decrès sent him on another mission to the Antilles at the beginning of 1805 and designated him on his return a Chevalier of the *Légion d'honneur*. In January 1807 he gave him the command of the vessel *Commerce de Lyon* at Antwerp. The following year serious illness forced Hulot to take sick leave. He returned to Tours where he died on 14 November 1809 leaving a widow and two children. He had been Capitain de Vaisseau for eight months.

Kergrist remained a prisoner in England until June 1814. His career afterwards continued fairly slowly in spite of his very brilliant service record. He alone of all the old ship's company of *Le Bélier* reached the Rank of Capitain de Vaisseau, even so, he had to wait until 1823. He never became a staff officer and went into retirement in 1842. His descendants treasured the memory of the exploits of his campaigns that he told his children in his old age. The episode of *Le Bélier* takes on the appearance of a legend. Kergrist loved recalling this adventure of his youth. He made between 1830 or 1840 a drawing and a painting that his great grandsons still have and which has prevented the battle of *Le Bélier* and the *Fox* from passing into oblivion.

Appendix IV

*To the Funeral of the Right Honble Laurence Earl Ferrers
by George Cole*

1760 May 5th	£.	s.	d.
To 255¾ yds of Black baize to hang the scaffold @ 20d	21.	6.	3.
To 5 yds of black cloth to cover 4 cushions	3.	0.	0.
To ticking to line and feathers to fill the cushions	2.	0.	0.
To tacks and hanging the scaffold	2.	0.	0.
To an elm case covered with black lined and quilted with white crape and a squab	1.	15.	0.
To ostrich feathers and velvet for the hearse and six horses	3.	10.	0.
To 2 men in black to attend from the Tower and back to Surgeons Hall as by order	0.	10.	0.
To 4 Bearers in black to putt the body into the hearse and take it out at the hall	0.	10.	0.
To 2 men to attend the hall from monday to thursday, night and day	1.	15.	0.
To a strong elm coffin lined with very fine crape quilted with 2 squabs the one under the other over my Lords body	3.	0.	0.
To a suit of super fine crape and sheet	2.	5.	0.
To a strong leaden coffin	5.	10.	0.
To a plate with Inscription	0.	18.	0.

To 6 men in black to carry the coffin to
the hall   0. 15. 0.
To a strong elm case covered with fine
black cloth richly ornamented with brass
nails and 4 pair of rich handles   7. 10. 0.
To 6 men in black to carry in   -do-   0. 15. 0.
To 6 men going again to putt the body in in
order for soldering butt was prevented by the
surgeons till the next day   0. 15. 0.
To 6 men putting in the body and bringing it
into the Library for soldering   0. 15. 0.
To a hearse and pair and 2 coaches and pairs from
the hall to Pancras church   1. 16. 0.
To 8 men to putt the body into the hearse
and take it out at the church   1. 8. 0.
To going the second time to pancras and
putting the body into the grave and a coach
for Mr.Ford   1. 5. 0.
To 6 men going 2 different times to pancras
to remove the body   1. 4. 0.
Paid a mason for a large stone and making
good the pavement   4. 8. 0.
Paid the dues   12. 12. 0.
                                                   _____
                                               £ 81. 2. 3.

Appendix V

Kirkland of Ashby-de-la Zouch, co. Leicester

Compiled from Entries in Old Bibles, Parish Registers, Monuments, etc.

BY J. PAUL RYLANDS, F.S.A.

Elizabeth, daur. of Thomas Baguley of Ashbourne, merchant, marr. at Ashbourne 10 Dec. 1708. Died 2 Jan. 1717-18. (Monument in Ashbourne Church.)

= Thomas Kirkland, of Ashbourne, co. Derby, solicitor. Buried at Ashby 27 March, 1751. The family of Kirkland has been settled in Derbyshire for many centuries. Mr. Walter Kirkland, in an article contributed to the 'Reliquary,' vol. xiii., pp. 219–223, gives many notices of the family, and deduces their descent from Gamel, lord of Kirkeland, co. Lancaster, temp. William the Conquerer. A and **B**

= Mary, daur. of Colonel ... Allsop of Ashbourne, marr. at Brailsford 11 Jan. 1721, by licence: Bur. at Ashbourne as 'Mrs. Kirkland of A.' 10 Aug. 1753.

ARMS.— *Sable, three doves rising argent, legged and beaked gules.*
CREST.—*A dove rising.* (Old Seal.)

Michael Kirkland, bapt. at Ashbourne 7 June, 1710. Died young. (Monument.)

1. Thomas Kirkland of Ashby-de-la Zouch, co. Leicester, M.D. Bapt. at Ashbourne 14 Oct. 1722. Died at Ashby 17 Jan., and buried in the chancel of the Church near Mr. Bate, 22 Jan. 1798. See memoir in Nichols' 'Leicestershire', vol. iii. pp. 632 and 774, 'Gent.'s Mag,' vol. 58, part i. p. 267; vol. 68, part i. pp. 62, 88, and 254. 'Annual Register,' 1760. 'Life and Times of Lady Huntingdon,' vol. i. p. 401. 'Trial of Lawrence, Earl Ferrers, for the Murder of John Johnson. London folio, 1760.' Biographical Dictionaries, etc.
C D

= Dorothy Palmer, daur. and coh. of ... Palmer, Esq. Barrister-at-Law (See 'Bate Pedigree.') Married at Packington 3 Aug. 1747. Bur. at Ashby 28 Jan. 1785. C. [Middx. Johes. Palmer, generous, admissus est in Societatem hujus hospicii 13 April. 2 Annoe, 1703. Henry Martyn, E. Henry Martyn, jun. Norman, jun. (Sureties). Records at Lincoln's Inn. T. Helsby, Esq.]

John Kirkland of Loughborough, co. Leicester, Solicitor, Bapt. at Ashbourne 16 Oct., 1726. Bailiff of Loughborough and Keeper of the Gaol from 12 Jan. 1767, until his death 1776. Bur. at Ashby 4 March 1776. His predecessor in the office of Bailiff, etc., was Thomas Herrick, Esquire, and his successor, Samuel Topp, Esquire. (Nichols' Leicestershire.)

= ... dau'r of ... Browne, gent. Died 31 Dec. 1796. See 'Gent.'s Mag.' vol. 67, p. 80

Anne Kirkland, died about 1818. Mar. to Thomas Dalby of Castle Donnington, co. Leicester, Solicitor. C

ARMS.— *Barry wavy of six argent and gules.* CREST.—*A demi griffin sergeant.* (Old Seal.)

Mary, bapt. at Ashbourne 23 Sept. 1724. Died young. Buried in Ashby Church.

Elizabeth, daur. of Mr. Thomas Kirkland,' bapt. 17 Jan. 1728-9. (Ashbourne Par. Reg.)

? S.P.

1. Dorothy Kirkland, born 1 May, 1748. Marr. at Coventry 8 Aug. 1779. Died at Warrington 22 Sept. 1834. Buried in Old St. James's Ch.-yard.

= The Rev. James Glazebrook (son of William Glasebrooke of Madeley, co. Salop, gent.) Vicar of Belton, co. Leicester, and first Incumbent of St. James's Church, Warrington, co. Lanc. Born at Madeley 11 Oct. 1744. Died at Belton, 1 July 1803. (Monument in Belton Church.) Will dat. 21 Oct. 1802; pr. at Leic. 16 Sep. 1803. See 'Gent.'s Mag.,' vol. 73, part ii. Nichols' 'Leicestershire,' iii. p. 647. 'Ormerod's' Cheshire,' 2 edit, vol. ii., p. 603. 'Life and Times of Selina, Countess of Huntingdon,' etc. **F**

2. Mary Kirkland, born 2 Dec. 1750; bapt. at Ashby 2 Jan. 1751. Died before 1767.

3. Elizabeth, born 5 June, 1750; bapt. at Ashby 24 June, 1754. Bur. there 18 Oct. 1754

4. Jane Kirkland, born 8 Aug., bapt. at Ashby 5 Sept. 1755. Died 10 Oct. 1835. Marr. at Ashby 25 Jan. 1776, to Thomas Fowler Chapman of Ashby, gent. (son of Thomas Chapman of Whitrington, parish of Whitwick, co. Leic. gent.) **G** ARMS.— *Per chevron arg. and gu. a crescent counterch'd, a canton of the second.*

5. Elizabeth Kirkland, born 30 Aug. 1763. Dead in 1767.

---

1. Thomas Kirkland Glazebrook, F.L.S., etc., Captain and Adjutant Warrington Militia. Born 1780. Died 1855. Of Orford Lodge, Warrington, afterwards of Southport Marr. Elizabeth, dau. of Thomas Twanbrook of Appleton, co. Chester, gent. See Fishwick's 'Lancashire Library'; Kendrick's 'Warrington Worthies,' etc. **H**

2. John Kirkland Glazebrook, bapt. at St. James's Warrington, 5 Sept. 1784. Died unmarried 6 Dec. 1807.

1. Jane Glazebrook bapt. at Grappenhall, co. Chester, 1 Nov. 1781. (Also ent. in St. James's Ch. Reg.) Died unmarried.

2. Martha Glazebrook, born 9 Oct. 1782. Died 12 Feb. 1870. Mar. to John Rylands of Bewsey House, Warrington, merchant.

3. Elizabeth Glazebrook, bapt. at St. James's 12 March, 1786. Bur. there 24 May, 1788.

---

1. Francis Bate Kirkland, Surgeon, born 7 Nov., bapt. at Ashby 18 Dec. 1749. Died at Nottingham 18 May, 1802. See 'Gent.'s Mag.,' vol. 72, part i., p.586. **I.**

= Sara, dau'r of Bucker-field, marr. at Ashby 29 Jan. 1770. Died at Nottingham 6 Mar. 1796. aet. 46.

2. Thomas, b. 17 May, bapt. at Ashby 1 June, 1752. Bur. there 10 April, 1753.

3. James Kirkland Bate of Ashby-de-la Zouch, Surgeon Apothecary to the Tower, born 5 June, 1753. Died unmar. 15 June, 1821. **R**

4. Thomas, b. 28 Nov. 1756. Bapt. at Ashby 11 Jan. 1757. Bur. there 6 Feb. 1757.

5. Thomas John of Kirkland of Ashby-de-la Zouch, Surgeon, born 25 June, bapt. at Ashby 28 July, 1760. Died 4 Aug. 1824. See 'Gent.'s Mag.,' vol. 94, part ii, p. 190.

= Mary dau'r of Nicholas Smith of Atherstone, Surgeon. Died at Warrington, co. Lancaster, 24 March, 1845. (Monument at Ashby). **M** (Monument with arms in Ashby Church). **L**

6. John Kirkland, b. 16 June, bapt. at Ashby Aug. 1761. Died there, 18 May, 1803, unmarried. See 'Gent's Mag.', vol. 73, parti., p. 598.

7. Michael, born 18 Aug., bapt. at Ashby 9 Oct. 1764. Bur. there 7 April, 1765.

---

1. Thomas Booth by Kirkland of Nottingham, Surgeon, bap. at Ashby 11 Jan. 1774. Mar. 18 Dec. 1798, Miss Twells of Nottingham. See 'Gent.'s Mag.,' vol. 68, pt. ii., p. 1151

2. John, bapt. at Ashby 10 Jan. 1776.

2. Mary, bapt. at Ashby 14 May, 1770. Mar. to Mr. John Stain.

2. Elizabeth, bapt. at Ashby 6. Feb. 1772.

3. Jane, bapt. at Ashby, 3 April, 1777.

Mary, dau'r of ... Harrison, of Packington, gent. Died 28 April, 1820, aet. 22. First wife. (Monument). = 1. Thomas Smith Kirkland, of Ashby-de-la Zouch, M.D. Born 14 May, bapt. at Ashby 6 Sept. 1785. Died there 15 Aug. 1869. Bur. in the Cemetery. (Monument in Ashby Church).

2. Nicholas Smith Kirkland, Esq., Captain in H.M.27th Enniskillens. Born 11 May, bapt. at Ashby 9 Aug. 1787. Died at Whitwick 16 June, 1856. Marr. secondly Mrs. Sarah Reynolds, but had no issue by her. = Hannah, dau'r of Richard Faux, of New House Grange, Merivale parish, co. Leic. gent. Died at Ashby 5 Aug., 1883. Second wife.

2. William Henry Kirkland, of Warrington, Surgeon. Born 1795. Died 7 May, 1833, S.P., having married Miss Elizabeth Bratt, who died 19 Aug. 1833, æt. 34. (Tomb at Warrington.) = Grace, dau'r of William Beavington, of Ashby. Died 12 Nov., 1843, aet. 55.

Mary Anne Kirkland. Bapt. at Ashby 5 May, 1789. Married there. Died 14 Mar, 1856, at Brest France. = Louis François le Normant de Kergrist, of Kergrist, near Brest in Brittany. Captain in the French Navy. Commander of the Legion of Honour, etc., etc., Died at Brest 15 Aug, 1859.

S.P.

1. Nicholas Smith Kirkland. Born 24 May, 1815. Died at Demecara, 16 July, 1837, unmarried.

2. James Kirkland, born 17 March, 1819. Is married.

3. Thomas Bate Kirkland. Marr. to Margaret Woolley.

4. William Kirkland, born 14 Mar. 1834. Marr. Miss Poyser. Died 11 April, 1909.

1. Mary Anne Kirkland. Marr. at St. James's Church, Great Grimsby, 27 Sept. 1866, to the Rev. Archibald Creighton, M.A., Vicar of Stallingborough, co. Lincoln. Died 4 Feb. 1909.

2. Elizabeth, born 31 Aug. 1817. Marr. to Mr. Wm. Foster, R.N., 9 Sep. 1845.

3. Grace, marr. to Mr. Joseph Dixon of Castle Donnington.

4. Sarah, marr. firstly to Mr. Thomas Haskard and secondly to Mr. Harrison.

5. Frances, marr. to Mr. John Humphreys. — 6. Jane, marr. to Mr. Mere.

7. Isabella Bate, marr. to Mr. William Woolley. Died at Tunbridge Wells 16 Dec. 1864, æt. 36.

Catharine Kirkland, d. and coh. at Ashby. Died 6 Oct. 1897

Lucy Kirkland, d. and co. heiress. Marr. at Ashby 9 Feb. 1854. Now living. = Francis Bangham, formerly of Bridgnorth, Salop, Ashby-de-la Zouch, Surgeon. Died 14 Feb. 1882.

Thomas Louis Kirkland le Normant de Kergrist, bapt. at Ashby, 17 June 1813. Admiral in the French Navy, Commander of the Legion of Honour, Governor of Martinique, etc., etc. Died at Paris, 9 Feb. 1895. Leaving issue.

Marie Thérèse Rose. Bapt. at Ashby, 16 Feb. 1817.

Louis François Joseph, born 8 Jan. 1824. Ensign in the French Navy. Died 23 Oct. 1849.

Maria Constance Jagger = Thomas Kirkland Bangham, of Jesus College, Cambridge. Born at Ashby, 19 Feb. 1855. Died 10 June 1891.	1. Alethea Bangham. Buried at Ashby Cemetery, 12 May 1950, æt 94.	2. Mary Ellen Bangham. Unmarried, living in 1909.	3. Lucy Catharine Bangham. Died 18 June, 1885. æt 26.	4. Edith Bangham. Buried at Ashby Cemetery, 13 July 1835, æt 75.	5. Elizabeth Bangham. Married Samuel Morris, 12 April 1877. Died at Exeter, 2 July, 1900, æt 38.	6. Florence Jane Bangham. Unmarried. Living in 1909.

NOTES TO KIRKLAND PEDIGREE

A *John Kirkland* was Churchwarden of Ashbourne 1698.

B *Paul Kirkland* by will (1714) gave all his lands in Wyaston (subject to the yearly payment of 20s. and 5s. to the Minister and Parish Clerk of Edlaston upon trust, as to one moiety of the rents and profits for the poor of Edlaston and Wyaston, and the other moiety thereof to be distributed half yearly, or otherwise, to the poor of Yieldersley and Painter's Lane, in the parish of Ashbourne, at the discretion of the Trustees, etc. (Mosse's 'Hist. of Ashbourne Church.')

C 'August y⁵ 3ᵈ 1747. Mr Thomas Kirkland and Mrs Dorothy Palmer both of Ashby-de-la Zouch were married with Licence by Mr Peter Cowper, Vicar of Ashby.' (Packington Par. Reg.)

D Dr. Kirkland was a very voluminous writer. Among his works are the following:— 'Treatise on Gangrenes,' 1754; 'Essay on the Methods of suppressing Haemorrage,' 1763; 'Essay on the Cure of Diseases caused by Fevers,' 1767; 'A Reply to Mr Maxwell's Answer to Mr. Kirkland's Essay on Fevers,' 1769; 'Observations upon Mr. Pott's Remarks on Fractures,' 1770; 'Appendix to the Preceding,' 1771; 'Treatise on Childbed Fevers,' 1774; 'Animadversions on a Late Treatise on the Kink-Cough,' 1774; 'Thoughts on Amputation,' 1780; 'Enquiry into the Present State of Medical Surgery,' 2 vols.— Vol. I., 1783; Vol. II. (dedicated to Francis, Earl of Huntingdon), 1786; 'Commentary on Apoplectic and Paralytic Affections,' 1794; 'Observations on the Use of the Sponge after Amputation' ('Medical Observations and Enquiries,' vol. ii.); 'Observations on the Use and Abuse of Mercury in the Case of Syphilis' ('London Medical Journal,' vol. vii.); 'An Essay on the Inseparability of the Different Branches of Medcine, etc.' (dedicated to Francis, Earl of Huntingdon); 'An Account of a Distemper among Horned Cattle at Caulk in Derbyshire in 1783.'

Dr. Kirkland is one of the principal characters in a novel entitled 'Ferrers, A Romance of the Reign of George the Second,' by Mr Charles Ollier. (Three volumes, 8vo, London, Richard Bentley; no date.) This romance is founded upon the unfortunate murder of John Johnson by Lawrence, Earl Ferrers. A full account of the trial was printed in 1760.

E For notices of the *Dalby* family, see Nichols' 'Hist. Leicest.', iii., pp. 774, 782, 854, 1089, and iv., part 2, 453.

F Author of 'A Defence of Infant Baptism, etc.,' in reply to the Rev. Mr. Wakefield, 1781, printed at Warrington by William Eyres; 'The Practice of Extempore Preaching recommended, etc., '1794, printed at Warrington by Wm. Eyres; 'The Minister's Enquiry into the State of His People, etc.,' 1798, printed by W. Eyres; and a Volume of Sermons published after his death, 1805, printed at Warrington by J. Haddock.

G Authoress of 'Miscellaneous Poems,' dedicated to Lady Charlotte Rawdon, 1802, printed at Derby; 'Elegies on the Deaths of Several of Her Valuable Friends, etc.,' 1805, printed at Burton upon Trent.

H Author of 'A History of Southport,' 'A Chronological List of Trades,' 'Report upon Cholera,' 'Lissa,' 'Translations from Virgil,' 'Poems,' etc.

I Our uncle Frank Kirkland sold Kirkland House (not far from Sudbury Park, Staffordshire), and an estate at Deveridge, during the lifetime of his father; this took place within my recollection. The Kirklands I believe lived at Kirkland House before they removed to Ashbourne; it was standing thirty years ago, now probably vanished (1868). (Information of the late Miss Jane Chapman, daughter of T. Fowler Chapman and his wife, Jane Kirkland.)

K Author of 'An Appendix to an Inquiry into the Present State of Medical Surgery by the late Thomas Kirkland, M.D.' Dedicated to Francis, Earl of Moira. 1813. London, pp. 144.

L Sold his estate in Peckleton, 53 acres 2 roods, to Mr. Boultby of Tooley in 1808.

M The Smith arms, impaling *Arg. a balista or catapult azure, thereon a stone or*, are upon old plate now in possession of Mrs. Kirkland, Ashby.

Appendix VI
Shirley Family Tree

1066 Henry de Ferrers comes to England with William the
Conquerer and is given land near Chartley in Staffordshire.

1615 A female descendent of the Ferrers family married Sir Henry Shirley

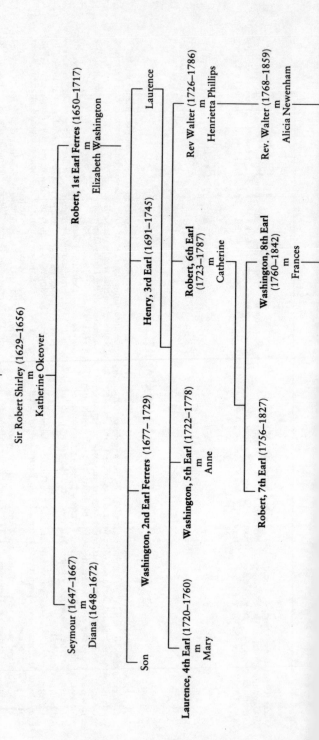

Sir Robert Shirley (1629–1656)
m
Katherine Okeover

Seymour (1647–1667)
m
Diana (1648–1672)

Robert, 1st Earl Ferres (1650–1717)
m
Elizabeth Washington

Laurence

Washington, 2nd Earl Ferrers (1677–1729)

Henry, 3rd Earl (1691–1745)

Son

Laurence, 4th Earl (1720–1760)
m
Mary

Washington, 5th Earl (1722–1778)
m
Anne

Robert, 6th Earl (1723–1787)
m
Catherine

Rev Walter (1726–1786)
m
Henrietta Phillips

Robert, 7th Earl (1756–1827)

Washington, 8th Earl (1760–1842)
m
Frances

Rev. Walter (1768–1859)
m
Alicia Newenham

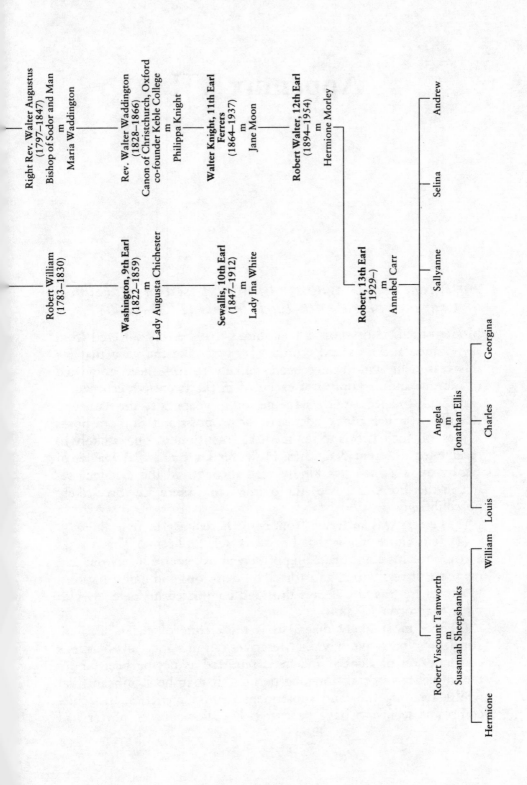

Right Rev. Walter Augustus
(1797–1847)
Bishop of Sodor and Man
m
Maria Waddington

Robert William
(1783–1830)

Rev. Walter Waddington
(1828–1866)
Canon of Christchurch, Oxford
co-founder Keble College
m
Philippa Knight

Washington, 9th Earl
(1822–1859)
m
Lady Augusta Chichester

Walter Knight, 11th Earl
Ferrers
(1864–1937)
m
Jane Moon

Sewallis, 10th Earl
(1847–1912)
m
Lady Ina White

Robert Walter, 12th Earl
(1894–1954)
m
Hermione Morley

Robert, 13th Earl
1929–
m
Annabel Carr

Andrew

Selina

Sallyanne

Angela
m
Jonathan Ellis

Georgina

Charles

Louis

Robert Viscount Tamworth
m
Susannah Sheepshanks

William

Hermione

Appendix VII

An Attempted Diagnosis of the supposed mental illness of Laurence Shirley 4th Earl Ferrers (1720–1760)

Modern medical opinion is unanimous that Ferrers suffered from severe mental illness and criminal lawyers take the view that for this reason he would have been unlikely to have been convicted of murder and certainly not executed in the twentieth century. It is difficult to speculate over the period of years as to the nature of that illness, which adds credence to the proposition that if one poses a question such as this to ten medical practitioners, one is likely to receive ten different diagnoses. However Dr Richard A Davies of Ashby-de-la Zouch has kindly read through all the evidence set out in this book and is of the opinion that there are three likely possibilities:

(1) Ferrers was suffering from some hereditary mental illness.

(2) It is more likely that he was a schizophrenic. This would account for his emotions being displayed by bizarre behaviour and his sense of reality being distorted by delusions and hallucinations. However he was not always thus and conducted his defence with more than ordinary skill.

(3) The most likely diagnosis is the effects of excess alcohol. Kirkland's narrative vividly describes an instance of Ferrers's consumption of alcohol and he is reported as having been under the influence of drink for long periods. It may be significant that whilst awaiting trial and subsequent to his conviction, his chief complaint seems to have been that his allowance of porter had

been reduced. Excess alcohol could produce changes in behaviour of the type seen in Ferrers. In particular (a) Alcoholism can cause impairment of memory and judgment and in severe cases of memory loss; the sufferer may confabulate – make up fanciful experiences – to fill in the gaps. (b) Alcoholism can produce pathological jealousy; partly because of the sufferer's own sexual difficulties and partly because of the revulsion of his partner or wife, who may seek to avoid sexual contact with a drunkard. An alcoholic may hold a delusional conviction that the spouse is unfaithful and may repeatedly cross-question and suspect all actions. 'Doctors should be aware of this condition as it can be dangerous and may lead to murder' [D M Gath, *Oxford Textbook of Medicine*, vol ii, 25.23] Cf. R V Dingwall (1867) where the defendant was tried for the murder of his wife, who said before she died, 'Drink threw him into a sad state of excitement so that he did not know what he was saying or doing' – [Nigel Walker, *Crime and Insanity in England*, Vol. i, Chapter 8, p.143]

Medical Glossary

Apoplectic Seemingly about to have apoplexy or sudden paralysis with some loss of consciousness and feeling caused when a blood vessel in the brain breaks or becomes clogged.

Asiatic Cholera An acute infectious disease characterized by severe diarrhoea and loss of water from the body.

Bladder The urinary bladder in the pelvic cavity, which holds urine flowing from the kidneys.

Bolus A large pill.

Caecum The pouch that is the beginning of the large intestine.

Child Bed Fever See Puerperal Fever.

Cinchona A tropical South American tree named after the Countess Del Chinchon, wife of the seventeenth century Peruvian Viceroy who was treated with the bark of the tree. Quinine is obtained from the bark formerly called 'Jesuits Bark.' The Indians used the bark in the treatment of Malaria.

Cineritius The grey substance of the brain.

Cicatrix The contracted fibrous tissue at the place where a wound has healed. A scar.

222

Cocaine An alcoloid (a nitrogen-containing substance produced by a plant) derived from the leaves of the cocoa plant, *Erythroxylon coca* or prepared synthetically, sometimes used as a local anaesthetic in eye, ear, nose and throat surgery. Causes feelings of exhilaration which may lead to dependence.

Colon That part of the large intestine extending from the caecum to the rectum.

Compound facture A bone fracture in which broken ends of bone have pierced the skin.

Compressing Fevers A compress is a pad of folded cloth often medicated or wet for applying pressure, heat or cold to a part of the body.

Contagious Bovine pleuropneumonia An acute contagious disease of horned cattle involving the combined disorders of pleurisy and pneumonia.

Corrosive Drugs Drugs administered in Kirkland's time and made up from substances such as Mercury, Antimony and Nitric acid.

Cowpox A contagious disease of cows that causes pustules on the udders; smallpox vaccine is made from the virus.

Cupping The use of a glass cup from which the air has been exhausted to draw blood to the surface of the skin.

Diphtheria An acute infectious disease caused by a bacterium and characterized by weakness, high fever, and the formation in the air passages of a membrane-like obstruction of the breathing.

Dissection To separate a corpse into parts for the purpose of study. By statute 25, George II c37 the Judge before whom any person was found guilty of wilful murder should direct that the body of the executed murderer be delivered to the surgeons to be dissected and anatomized.

Distemper (i) a mental or physical disorder, disease.
(ii) an infectious virus disease of young dogs.

Dura Mater   The outermost and toughest of the three membranes covering the brain and spinal cord.

Extravasated Blood   Blood that has escaped or been forced to follow into surrounding tissue.

Flaccid   Soft and limp. Flabby.

Gangrene   Death and decay of part of the body due to deficiency or cessation of blood supply. Dry gangrene is death and withering of tissues caused simply by cessation of local blood circulation. Moist gangrene is death and putrefactive decay of tissue caused by bacterial infection.

Gout   A disease marked by deposits of uric acid salts in tissues and joints especially of the feet and hands with swelling and great pain.

Hemiphegia   Paralysis of one side of the body.

Humerus   The bone of the upper arm extending from the shoulder.

Ilium   The flat uppermost section of the *Os inominatum*

Kink Cough   Whooping Cough.

Leech   (i) formerly a physician.
(ii) a blood-sucking species of annelid worm up to eight cm long formerly used to bleed patients.

Malaria   Known in Thomas John Kirkland's time as Walcharen Fever. Also known as ague, Paludism, Jungle Fever, Marsh Fever, and Periodic Fever. Malaria is a disease caused by the presence of certain parasites in the blood. It is transmitted by the Anophiles Mosquito and is confined mainly to tropical and sub tropical areas. Bouts of fever occur periodically varying from mild to very severe, amounting to fatal. A dreaded complication is black water fever associated with malignant tertian Malaria, and occurs in Central Africa, India, and the Far East.

Medicinal Rhubarb   (*Rheum Officinale*) Dried Rhubarb in powder form when mixed with magnesia and water was used as a mild purgative. The vegetable was first cultivated at Banbury, Oxon, in 1777. English Rhubarb was kiln dried as opposed to Turk rhubarb which was sun-dried.

Miasma   A vapour arising as from marshes or decomposing organic matter, formerly supposed to poison the air.

Mortification   Old term for gangrene.

Os Inominatum   Either of two large, irregular bones of the pelvis, each formed of the illium, ischium and pupis. Hip bone.

Os Sacrum   A thick triangular bone forming the illia at the lower end of the spinal column.

Parietal Bone   Either of the two bones forming part of the top and sides of the skull.

Persecution Complex   An acute irrational fear that other people are plotting ones downfall.

Placebo   A medicine that is ineffective but may help to relieve a condition because the patient has faith in its powers.

Placenta   A vascular organ developed within the uterus, connected by the umbilical cord to the foetus and supplying it with nourishment.

Plaster   A pasty preparation spread on cloth and applied to the body as a medicine.

Porphyria   Now thought to have been the malady afflicting George III in 1789 and subsequently. It is a very rare hereditary disease. It is not a mental illness but results in the brain being affected by toxins in the system.

Pott's Disease   A disease of the spine, usually caused by tubercular infection and characterized by weakening and gradual disintegration of the vertibrae and the intervertebral discs.

Pott's Fracture   A fracture – dislocation of both leg-bones at the ankle.

Psoas Muscle   A muscle of the loins and pelvis.

Puerperal Fever   Septic poisoning occurring during childbirth.

Purging   To empty the bowels by means of a laxative.

Radius   The shorter and thicker of the two bones of the forearm on the same side as the thumb.

Reaching to vomit   To undergo the straining action of vomiting especially without bringing anything up.

Sagittal Suture   The line of junction of two bones especially in the skull.

Schizophrenia   A major mental disorder of unknown cause in which, typically, a person's emotions are displayed by bizarre behaviour, his sense of reality is distorted by delusions and hallucinations, etc.

Scurvy   A disease resulting from a deficiency of vitamin C in the body and causing weakness, anaemia, spongy gums, the bleeding from the mucous membranes etc.

Scrofula   Tuberculosis of the lymphatic glands especially of the neck in which the glands become enlarged.

Smallpox   An acute, highly contagious virus disease causing fever, vomiting, and pustular eruptions that often leave pitted scars, or pockmarks.

Strangury   To cause an intestine or other tube to be squeezed so that a flow, as of urine, is cut off. Painful excretion of urine, drop by drop, caused by muscular spasms of the urinary tract.

Trephine   A type of small circular saw used in surgery to remove discs of bone from the skull.

Typhoid Fever   An infectious disease caused by a *bacillus* and acquired by eating food or drinking water contaminated by excreta, it causes fever, intestinal disorders etc.

Typhus Fever An acute infectious disease caused by a rickettsia transmitted to man by fleas, lice, etc and causing fever, red spots on the skin etc.

Ulna The larger of the two bones of the forearm on the side opposite the thumb.

Uterus Womb.

Viscera The internal organs of the body, especially the intestines.

Select Bibliography

Thomas Kirkland MD, *An Enquiry into the present state of Medical Surgery* Vol. I and II (1786)
The Dictionary of National Biography
John Throsby, *The Supplementary Volume to the Leicestershire Views* containing a series of excursions in the year 1790 (J Nicholls, London, 1790)
George Rude, *Europe in the 18th Century* (Weidenfeld and Nicholson, 1972)
W Scott, *Story of Ashby-de-la-Zouch* (1907)
Historical Manuscripts Commission. *Hastings Manuscript*, Vol. I
J G Noverre, *Letters on Dancing* (Beaumont, 1931)
Wilson, *A Dictionary of Ballet*
C W Beaumont, *A Miscellany for Dancers* (1954)
M M Reece, *The Royal Office of Master of the Horse* (Theobald Books, 1976)
Leicestershire Industrial History Society. *Leicestershire in 1777*. An Edition of John Prior's Map of Leicestershire. Edited by J D Welding. Leicestershire Libraries and Information Services.
The Diary of Fanny Burney (J M Dent)
William Gardiner, *Music and Friends*
Alec MacDonald, *A Short History of Repton* (Ernest Benn, 1929)
Georgina Galbraith, *The Journal of Rev William Bagshaw Stevens* (Clarendon Press, 1965)
Francis Abell & Humphrey Milford, *Prisoners of War in Britain 1756–1815* (Oxford University Press, 1914)
Roy Bennett, *French Prisoners of War on Parole in Britain 1803–1814* (University of London, 1964)

Nigel Walker, *Guise and Insanity in England*. Edinburgh University Preess 1968. 2 Volumes.

F C Hipkin, *Repton and its Neighbourhood (A J Lawrence, Repton, second edition, 1899)*

Baron Louis Francois Le Jeune. *Memoirs*. Germain Bapst. 'En Prison et en guerre' London 1897

John T Thorpe, *History of Freemasonry in Ashby-de-la-Zouch 1809–1909.*

Dr Marilyn Palmer, *Francis Rawdon – Hastings 1st Marquess of Hastings and the Development of the Leicestershire Estates 1780–1830*

Roger Macdonald, *The British Martial Register 1806.*

J M Hammel, *Consolidation and Change. The Union of 1813.* The Lodge of Research No 2429 Transactions 1977.

The Gentlemen's Magazine.

The Complete Peerage of England and Scotland Ireland Great Britain and the United Kingdom. New Edition edited by the Hon. Vicary Gibbs and H A Doubleday, Vol. IV (St Catherine's Press, 1926)

Trial of Earl Ferrers for the Murder of John Johnson published by the order of the House of Peers 1760.

James Thompson, *The History of Leicester* (F Hewitt, Leicester, 1879)

The Public Record Office Calendar of Home Office Papers 1760–1765.

W R Chambers, *The Book of Days 1881*. Vol.I

Walpole Letters

Harriet Bridgeman and Elizabeth Drury, *Society Scandals* (David and Charles, Newton Abbott, 1977)

H J Wain, *The Story of Staunton Harold* (Parker & Son, Burton upon Trent, 1965)

Charles Singer & E Ashworth Underwood, *A Short History of Medicine* (Clarendon Press, 1962)

John Pringle, *Diseases of the Army in camp and garrison* (1780)

R T Austin, 'Interesting G.P.s of the Past.' *British Medical Journal* Vol.293, 25 October 1986

W Bacon Becket, *The Centenary Celebrations of the Tyrian Lodge No 253* (Mill Works, Derby 1885)

The Text Book of Freemasonry (Reeves and Turner, London, second edition, (1874)

History of St John's Lodge No 279, Leicester Masonic Library.

Hon. Sir John Fortescue, *History of the British Army*. Vol.IV.

White's Nottinghamshire 1832

W & J Hextall, *History and Description of Ashby-de-la-Zouch* (1852)

Kelly's Directory of Leicestershire and Rutland 1895

David Howarth, *The Greek Adventure* (Collins)

The Hastings MSS. Huntingdon Library, San Marino, California, USA

Levi Fox, *A Country Grammar School* (Oxford University Press, 1967)

J W Jackson, *The Ferrers and Ivanhoe Lodge No 779. 1859–1959* (Hughes and Harbur, Longton)

Kenneth Hillier, *Ashby-de-la-Zouch – The Spa Town* (1983)

T Wayte, *Guide to Ashby-de-la-Zouch and the Neighbourhood* (1831)

Blackston's Commentaries. Chitty (1826) Book IV

Eilert Ekwall, *The Concise Oxford Dictionary of English Place Names* (Clarendon Press, 1960)

Repton School Register. Repton School Library, Repton, Derby.

Piggot & Co's Commercial Directory 1828/29

William White, *History of Leicestershire* (1846)

Snowfield & Jones, *Dictionary of Daily Wants* (London, 1858)

Leicestershire County Record Office. *Report of the General Board of Health for the Parish of Ashby-de-la-Zouch* (1850)

Malcolm Elliott, *Victorian Leicester* (Phillimore, London & Chichester, 1979)

Barnewall & Alderson. *Law Report 1817*

D A Lake, *History of Golf in Ashby-de-la-Zouch* (Willesley Park Golf Club, 1988)

Transactions of 8th Congress on large dams. Edinburgh 4 – 8 May 1964

David Smith, *Industrial Archiology of the East Midlands* (MacDonald, 1965)

W Kelly, *History of Freemasonry in Leicestershire* (1870)

Arthur Bryant, *Years of Endurance* (Collins)

Michaela Reid, *Ask Sir James* (Hodder & Stoughton, 1987)

Index

232

234

236